IRAN'S rivalry with SAUDI ARABIA between the GULF WARS

IRAN'S rivalry with SAUDI ARABIA between the GULF WARS

HENNER FÜRTIG

WITH A FOREWORD BY
ANOUSHIRAVAN EHTESHAMI

Durham Middle East Monographs Series

ITHACA PRESS

IRAN'S RIVALRY WITH SAUDI ARABIA
BETWEEN THE GULF WARS

Ithaca Press is an imprint of Garnet Publishing Limited

Published by
Garnet Publishing Limited
8 Southern Court
South Street
Reading
RG1 4QS
UK

First Edition

ISBN 0 86372 287 3

British Library Cataloguing-in-Publication Data
A catalogue record for this book is available from the British Library

Jacket design by Garnet Publishing
Typeset by Samantha Barden

Printed in Lebanon

Contents

Foreword

For a long while now the Persian Gulf has been regarded as an area of inter-state tensions and sub-regional instabilities. Two major wars in ten years together with several other insurgencies over a thirty year period do point to some sort of a problem, perhaps encouraging one to conclude that the sub-region was always riddled with tensions. Yet it is hard to argue that either of the two inter-state wars late last century were inevitable, or that inter-state tensions are a direct function of the politics of the Persian Gulf. Indeed, as Fürtig's excellent research demonstrates, even sworn enemies across the Gulf's divide can, for a variety of reasons, find it prudent not only to shelve their differences but even to develop quite close bilateral ties. Partnerships have been formed which have been put to good use. Whether such a pattern of 'pragmatic' alliance-building is a symptom or a cause of regional instabilities is not the issue here. The fact is that at least one of the three main actors, namely Saudi Arabia, which has for too long been regarded as passive, has been able to weather the two serious storms blown its way by its two northern neighbours, and has managed to take advantage of the opportunities presented to it by building relations with one neighbour at the expense of the other.

In the main, experts hold the view that at least since the late 1960s and early 1970s, with the announcement of Britain's withdrawal from territories 'east of Suez' and steep oil price rises, the sub-region has been victim to regional rivalries and outside intervention. These are correct observations and do partly provide the backdrop to today's tense political environment in the sub-region. In terms of the regional balance of power and the role of local actors in the political life of the Persian Gulf, however, it is an indisputable fact that three countries – Iran, Iraq and Saudi Arabia – have played an instrumental role in the drawing of its current political and strategic map, with the United States acting very much as the principal intrusive 'over-the-horizon' power. These three countries have been the Gulf's main movers and shakers, and the three combined have, in pursuit of their respective national interests, made their mark on the sub-region; sometimes with vigour and commitment, sometimes with dangerous overzealousness.

Henner Fürtig's study is the first systematic book-length survey of relations between two of the three dominant Gulf actors, Iran and Saudi Arabia, and their respective policies towards each other over the critical years following the Iranian revolution. Although Iraq has been in the Gulf limelight at least since 1980, the actors which have made a more lasting impression on the dynamics of the Middle East in general and the Persian Gulf sub-region in particular are certainly Iran and Saudi Arabia. The record throughout the 1990s testifies to this – as Saddam Hussein pressed Iraq's self-destruct button in August 1990, Tehran and Riyadh began the long process of consolidation and expansion in the region. During Iraq's absence from the scene, Tehran and Riyadh took significant steps towards each other, at the same time pursuing unilateral efforts to impose their own agendas on the post-crisis sub-region. This is the picture today, a far cry from the tensions of the early 1980s and the deep crisis in Iranian–Saudi relations.

1979 was a watershed year for the Gulf, and Fürtig's research picks up the thread from this tumultuous year and explores the impact that the change of regime in Tehran had on the sub-region. Both Iraq and Saudi Arabia were deeply affected by the revolution in Shia Iran, and Saudi Arabia was shocked by the ease with which Iranians were able to overthrow their powerful monarchy. Under the leadership of its new president Saddam Hussein, Iraq's reaction was to prepare for the 'containment' and eventual 'roll-back' of the Iranian revolutionaries, while Riyadh seemed content to follow its traditional low-key wait-and-see policy. It was accused of appeasement at the time, but its posture was more defensive than anything. Riyadh accepted the Iranian revolution, tried to absorb the ideological and political blows from Tehran now showering on the Saudi body-politic, and set about changing its own image to that of being the legitimate and only true custodian of Islam's most precious holy sites. Behind the scenes, however, it adopted a very active posture, drawing closer to the United States, aiding Iraq, reinforcing its Islamic and Arab channels of communication, and accelerating the process of building up its small armed forces.

Ten years after the Iranian revolution, however, it was not Iran which had managed to 'export' its brand of revolution to the rest of the region; nor was it Iraq which had emerged victorious from its war with

Iran. Although both claimed major moral and practical victory, it was plain to all that they were exhausted from a pointless war. With its northern Gulf rivals on the ropes, it was Saudi Arabia which perhaps had gained most in those dangerous times. Its position in the region was intact, stronger than ever; its alliances strong and secure; its unruly northern neighbours tamed; and its premier position within OPEC unassailable. Yet, for all the signs of a brighter future evident in early 1989, the crisis which would shape the destiny of Iranian–Saudi relations was barely a few months away.

It would again be Saddam Husain who would hastily begin penning the next chapter in the Persian Gulf's modern history. Alas, as we have seen in the years since 1991, it would not be Baghdad who would end up finishing the new chapter it had started, but its two Gulf rivals, who set about the task not so much in open competition with each other, but, certainly since 1996, in apparent harmony and orchestrated cooperation. Gloomy projections of Iraq's political and economic situation in the twenty-first century merely reinforce the core assumption in Fürtig's study: only two countries – Iran and Saudi Arabia – will be the Gulf's twenty-first century powerhouses. These will be the actors who will shape the future of this and neighbouring regions, and for this reason they must be studied and their bilateral relations watched very closely. What Fürtig has accomplished is not only to unravel the intricate details of the relationship between revolutionary Iran and an increasingly assertive Saudi Arabia, but also to lay bare, within an analytical context, the dynamics of that relationship. To understand the future we must understand the past; in Fürtig's book we have a seasoned chronicler's account of what happened between Iran and Saudi Arabia during some of the sub-region's most troubled times.

Anoushiravan Ehteshami
Durham, 2002

Preface

The worldwide fascination with the Iranian Islamic revolution is still alive. Since 1978/9, it has resulted in dozens of academic and journalistic publications about its course, and its various political, strategic, economic, cultural and religious impacts. The revolution in itself might have attracted many politicians and scholars but in addition it also occurred in one of the politically most sensitive areas of the world.

As is commonly known, the Middle East is one of the cradles of mankind. It has been a source of many civilizational impulses throughout history and is the home of three monotheistic world religions. As the border area of the three continents of Europe, Asia and Africa it is also a traditional cultural bridge.

However, it was the establishment of a new global political order after the Second World War and the simultaneously emerging dominance of liquid and gaseous hydrocarbon as the most important source of energy and raw material for the industries of the developed countries which enabled the Middle East, possessing more than 60 per cent of this vital raw product, to start playing a key role in global politics. In the emerging East–West conflict, political, economic and military control of the Middle East, as well as securing the grip on its most important raw products, promised decisive advantages for both East and West. External factors such as the massive interference of both global camps and their attempts to recruit respective clients among the local elite thus acquired great significance for the evolution and the nature of the sovereignty of the regional states after 1945. In general, their development was decisively impaired and influenced by this foreign interference.

Considering primarily these economic aspects of East–West competition for influence in the Middle East, the Persian Gulf region gains special importance because the lion's share of Middle East oil is to be found in that area. Iran, Iraq and Saudi Arabia are not only geographically the biggest countries of that region but are also its main oil producers. Therefore, to influence the production and marketing of the region's oil, or at least to secure free access to it, the main global competitors had to concentrate their efforts to control and to lobby either Iraq, Iran or Saudi Arabia. These efforts coincided with those countries' own endeavours to gain a dominant position in the Persian Gulf.

This is particularly true for Iran under the rule of the Pahlavi dynasty. The hegemonic ambitions of Mohammad Reza Pahlavi were symbiotically connected to an American strategy of supporting Iran as a cornerstone for securing its own interests in the Gulf area. The Islamic revolution of 1978/9 had an important immediate foreign policy impact since it meant a tremendous strategic defeat for the United States. For the next ten years at least, American Middle East policy was designed to compensate for the losses inflicted on it by the Iranian revolution. Not only did Iran, with its enormous geographic area, its large population, its material resources and its military strength, have to be written off by Washington and the West in a general sense, but the emerging Islamic Republic of Iran also evaded the East–West scenario by not leaning towards the Soviet Union and the Warsaw Pact.

Instead it followed a specific foreign policy of its own, fighting 'Western imperialism' as well as 'Eastern communism' while simultaneously propagating an independent 'Islamic' foreign policy. Due to the long-standing symbiosis between the Shah and the United States the latter were classified as the 'Great Satan' whereas the Soviet Union was called the 'Small Satan'. Any country with significance for the Islamic Republic that might challenge the specific Islamic approach of the new republic's leadership – either on its own behalf or that of one of the superpowers – also risked being labelled as a 'Satan'.

In the Persian Gulf area, Saudi Arabia had a good chance of becoming a 'regional Satan'. This was due to the strong bonds of the Al Saud with America as well as their pretension to global Islamic leadership, to mention just two principal reasons. There is also a long tradition of competition between Iran and Saudi Arabia for leadership in the Gulf. There were many ups and downs in the intensity of that competition. It should be noted that for most of the 1960s and especially the 1970s both Iran and Saudi Arabia were partners of the American 'twin pillar' strategy. Against that background, the fundamental changes resulting from the revolution in Iran were especially graphic. As Saudi Arabia felt endangered by the Iranian efforts to export her version of an Islamic revolution, the Al Saud intensified its alliance with the US. Washington, for its part, supported and encouraged Saudi Arabia to resist and stand up to the Islamic Republic of Iran.

As mentioned above, the picture of the balance of power in the Gulf region is incomplete without considering Iraq. Indeed after the Second World War the balance of power in the Gulf area was upheld by a triangle of states, i.e. Iran, Iraq and Saudi Arabia. If one of them gained too much weight, the other two had to try to compensate. This fundamental framework of the region's balance of power has not basically changed despite the meddling of foreign powers.

For example, during the 1960s and the 1970s, when Imperial Iran and Saudi Arabia were both allied to the West, they commonly provided a bulwark against radical Iraqi nationalism and proto-socialism supported by the Warsaw Pact. With the Iranian revolution, on the other hand, Iraq started playing a decisive role in the early attempts to liquidate that revolution – or to at least contain it – by invading Iran and thus initiating the First Gulf War. For the next decade Iraq without a doubt became the main enemy of Iran within the region, closely followed by Saudi Arabia who was the single most important supporter of Iraq, financing its war machine. Just to complete the description of the fragile, triangular balance of power within the Gulf region, it should be added that with the beginning of the 1990s, Iraq challenged the Western world by occupying oil-rich Kuwait. This U-turn in Iraq's position towards the West did not lead to a significant improvement in the relationship between Iran and the West, but Iraq's rising power promptly resulted in a détente – although temporary – between Saudi Arabia and Iran.

The collapse of Iraq after the UN operation 'Desert Storm' weakened it to such a degree that it was for the time being virtually expelled from the race for hegemony in the Gulf region. Therefore, the regional competition for dominance was not only reduced to Iran and Saudi Arabia, but their long traditional feud became more visible and decisive than it appeared during the 1980s when most observers concentrated their analyses on the relationship between Iran and Iraq.

The book takes up at this point. With the growing international dependence on the Persian Gulf region for oil supplies, the need for information, predictions and prospects about the roots, the main events and the probable outcome of the bitter rivalry between Iran and Saudi Arabia has attained more than academic significance. To provide an adequate picture of that tense relationship, it is not enough to refer only to the immediate present. The leitmotiv of the book is the Islamic Republic of Iran's attitude towards Saudi Arabia from the early days of the revolution until the aftermath of the Second Gulf War.

After the revolution, Iran's strong Islamic-universalist approach and her demands for a leading position within the umma as well as its assumed role as a model for the world's Muslims challenged the very roots of the identity of the Saudi Arabian state and its ruling family as the heart of the Islamic world. By doubting the sincerity of Saudi Islamic credibility because of their dependence on the US, the Islamic Republic of Iran challenged the legitimacy of the Al Saud by declaring that the continued guardianship of Islam's holiest places by the Al Saud was unacceptable for every true Muslim. Iran also angered the Saudis by stating that a monarchy was a non-Islamic government and by threatening to export its revolution.

The course and the specific nature of the Iranian revolution thus became the turning point in the relationship between Iran and Saudi Arabia. As already mentioned, the situation was worsened by the war between Iran and Iraq, starting in 1980, when Saudi Arabia took the opportunity to fight the Islamic revolution in Iran indirectly but efficiently, not only by supporting Iraq financially but by founding the Gulf Cooperation Council (GCC), consisting of all the littoral Arab Gulf states except Iraq, thus creating an Arab alliance against Iran. The experience of being besieged and isolated by the Arab camp, decisively influenced by Saudi Arabia, has affected the Iranian leadership to the present day.

When a new and more pragmatic leadership took power in Iran after the demise of the revolution's leader, Ayatollah Khomeini, and Iraq almost coincidentally turned out to be a more dangerous enemy of Saudi Arabia when it occupied neighbouring Kuwait and threatened the Saudi Kingdom, some prospects for détente emerged between Tehran and Riyadh. Although diplomatic relations, severed in 1987, were restored in 1991 and some negotiations took place between both governments ranging from political and economic to security matters, the détente remained fragile because the main causes of enmity between the two countries were still intact.

When the socialist world imploded at the end of the 1980s, ending the Cold War, both rivals were not only liberated from the pressures of the East–West conflict but were now able to expand the geographic area of their rivalry. The remnants of the Soviet Empire in Central Asia were now available in a contest to create a new balance of power and to secure a victory in a new 'Great Game'. Iran had shared a common border of some 2,500 km with the former Soviet Union and was now extremely interested in having a say in the further development of the emerging independent Caucasian and Central Asian Republics (CCARs). Due to its own multi-ethnicity, the Islamic Republic felt increasingly vulnerable to developments next to its border, especially with regard to transborder ethnicities. Saudi Arabia began to make use of these Iranian vulnerabilities and to challenge Iranian interests in Central Asia. Both countries now emulated each other in political, economic, cultural and religious areas to gain the upper hand in this region of immense strategic importance. Up to now, Iran seems to have scored more 'political points' in Central Asia by exploiting, with great ability, its own geographic position to the full as an ideal transition route between Central Asia and the outside world, thus helping the CCARs to overcome their geographic isolation.

Because both Iran and Saudi Arabia remain intensely dependent on oil production and export, which provides about 90 per cent of their foreign exchange income, the Gulf area has retained great importance for them. Dominating the Persian Gulf has not only become a matter of economic well-being and regional prestige but an issue of global weight. The strategic objective of Iran concerning the Persian Gulf has never changed fundamentally; to establish itself as a Gulf super-power and a major regional force. It equally seeks to ensure local and international recognition of its pre-eminence in the area, and to contain any development that it perceives as contrary to its interests and political outlook. Saudi Arabia was primarily interested in dominating the Arabian Peninsula and the oil-rich shelf. Given its small and heterogeneous population and its long-standing abstinence from using military force, Saudi Arabia is not perceived as a military challenge to the Islamic Republic's own ambitions to dominate the Gulf and its contiguous areas, despite the former's rapid rearmament efforts.

Iran was even partly successful in using the numerous differences within the GCC for its own ends. Both the Council and its member Saudi Arabia are mutually dependent on each other, especially where military and security matters are concerned. This dependence is a strong bond, but it was never sufficient to eradicate differing interests among the member states and their respective ruling families. Despite repeated efforts to establish a reliable common defence force, the Rapid Deployment Force of the GCC is still in its infant phase. In security matters, it is only America that counts.

Spreading the ideals of its Islamic revolution became one of the tenets of the Islamic Republic's foreign policy. Seeing themselves as the guardians of Islam's holiest places and thus as the guarantors of purist traditional Islam, the Al Saud could not avoid entanglement with Iran in a race to represent the ideal of Islam even in the remotest areas of the world. But as far as security is directly affected, the competition is more or less limited – leaving out Central Asia and the Gulf region – to the immediate neighbourhood, i.e. Afghanistan, Pakistan, Lebanon, Egypt and especially Sudan.

These religious aspects began playing a decisive role in the competition between Iran and Saudi Arabia after Shia clerical rule was established in Iran. There are many sects in Islam, but there is hardly any gap as deep as the one between Iranian Twelver Shiism and Saudi Arabian orthodox Sunni Wahhabism. In the early days of the Iranian revolution the Al Saud became increasingly fearful of its Shia aspects in the light of its own Shia population in the vital al-Hasa province where the majority of the country's oil installations are situated. But in more general terms, Riyadh recognized that it was exactly these Shia aspects of the Iranian revolution that could best be used as a tool against the Iranian challenge. First of all, Iran's attempt to present itself as the centre of a worldwide Muslim awakening, despite denominational differences, and as the front-runner of Islamic grandeur, had to be challenged. Therefore, Saudi propaganda started to castigate the Iranian revolution as an exclusively Shia one, underlining that Shiism was always antithetical not only to Wahhabism but to Sunnism in general, and that for these reasons Khomeini's Islam must be considered blasphemous. But anti-Shia propaganda had its pros and cons. Whereas the Iranian influence among the predominantly Sunni Muslims on the Arabian Peninsula remained weak, the Saudi government risked alienating Shiites not only in its own al-Hasa province but also abroad.

Summarizing these aspects, it has to be stated that despite the more pragmatic – or rather, national – Iranian foreign policy since the beginning of the 1990s, religion will nevertheless retain its importance for the bilateral relationship as long as the Iranian Republic and its leadership identify Islam as the precondition and the essence of its statehood.

But the rivalry between Iran and Saudi Arabia also has some significant economic aspects. Considering the predominant role of oil in the economies of both countries, it seems natural that the contest is primarily focused on production capabilities, market quotas and – last but not least – the price of oil. Saudi Arabia's proven oil reserves amount to approximately 20 per cent of the world's total, larger both in quantity and percentage than any other country. Saudi oil reserves are expected to last more than 100 years. Principally, this advantage provided Saudi Arabia with sufficient manoeuvring room to dictate its terms to OPEC and to harm Iran, even if such a policy did not prove to be economically profitable from time to time. Taking into account the vast destruction of Iran's oil industry during the revolution and the war with Iraq, it comes as no surprise that the Islamic Republic has finished the race in second place behind Saudi Arabia. But mounting economic problems in both Iran and Saudi Arabia, coupled with a stagnant global oil market, continue to provide incentives for the two countries to compete within OPEC. Geological and demographic asymmetries have perpetuated both the differences between Iran and Saudi Arabia and the leverage over Iran the Kingdom has enjoyed regarding OPEC policy.

Periods of more or less 'normal' relations between Iran and Saudi Arabia prove that enmity between both countries is not mandatory – despite continuing differences – but due to specific circumstances. It is easy to conclude from Iran's common partnership with the West in pre-revolutionary times that a normalization of ties between the Islamic Republic of Iran and the West will pave the way for an improvement of the relationship between Iran and Saudi Arabia as well. The strong Saudi Arabian reliance on American security guarantees has much to do with the fact that it feels threatened by Iran and its Islamic revolution, whereas Iran is certain that the US presence is a threat. Thus, returning to normal terms with Saudi Arabia would mean that Iran would also have to normalize relations with the United States and to accept the role of the Americans in the Gulf region. This is still not very likely, given the strategic objectives of the Iranian leadership that came to power with the revolution of 1978/9.

Both history and the present intermingle in the relationship between Iran and Saudi Arabia. The following chapters may provide a deeper insight into the details of the ongoing competition between the two Persian Gulf giants.

Henner Fürtig
2002

Introduction

Imperial Iran and Saudi Arabia, 1970–1978

The American 'twin pillars' strategy

The triumph of oil as the most important energy source for the Western economies after the Second World War led to a significant and consistent increase in the strategic weight of the world's principal oil producing area – the Persian Gulf region. Control of these vast and easily extracted resources of liquid and gaseous hydrocarbon not only meant securing a vital raw material for the Western economies but also gaining decisive advantages in the global rivalry between East and West – the Cold War.

The conditions for the development of independent or independence-seeking states in the Persian Gulf were decisively influenced by the Cold War, despite the increasing importance of internal factors. The struggle between East and West, as well as between growing Gulf Arab nationalism and the ambitions of the Shah, determined policy in the Gulf for several decades.

In 1958 a situation arose for the first time which caused the monarchs in the Persian Gulf to put aside their differences and focus on their common interests. Creating a precedent, nationalist forces of the Iraqi army overthrew King Faisal II. Furthermore the pan-Arab policy of the Egyptian President, Gamal Abdel Nasser, who leaned increasingly towards the Soviet Bloc, added to the Gulf monarchs' sense of being besieged and under serious threat. In this situation the two biggest states in the region, Iran and Saudi Arabia, sought to create a rapprochement with each other. King Faisal of Saudi Arabia visited Iran in December 1965, and afterwards diplomats of both countries continued to look for common interests. Nevertheless, the Shah's repeated proclamations that Iran would become the leading power in the Gulf region irritated Faisal.

In addition, the vehement rejection by both Egypt and Syria, supported by the Soviet Union, of this combined Iranian–Saudi Arabian approach, prevented a strengthening of the initiative. But a step had at least been taken. Despite this counter-offensive the Iranian Shah, Mohammad Reza Pahlavi, was still of the opinion that of the Arab heads of state only King Faisal was able to challenge Nasser's power. He offered Saudi Arabia every possible help, including military assistance, when the Egyptians invaded Yemen in 1962. Faisal praised the Shah for his generous offer but nevertheless rejected any Iranian involvement in Arab affairs.[1]

Egypt's disastrous defeat in the Six Day War in June 1967 diminished the attraction of pan-Arabism throughout the Middle East and as a result the ability of Egypt to pursue an active pan-Arab foreign policy was curtailed. The feeling of being endangered decreased in the Arabian Peninsula for a short time. But this stabilization did not last long.

In January 1968, after nearly two decades of costly, fruitless efforts to keep its colonial empire and constantly losing ground to American global ambitions, the British government declared its intention of withdrawing completely from the Gulf region by 1971. The Minister of State for the Foreign Office, Goronwy Roberts, travelled to the area in the same month to brief the Gulf monarchs on the details of this decision. Their reactions were very ambivalent. On one hand, the rulers of Bahrain, Qatar and Trucial Oman welcomed the possibility of gaining full sovereignty within a short period of time, but on the other hand they would have to share the burden of security in the region with Iran and Saudi Arabia. On 27 February 1968, Great Britain proposed the foundation of a federation comprising Bahrain, Qatar and the seven sheikhdoms of Trucial Oman. It was to come into effect that March and take over responsibility for guaranteeing security as soon as possible. However, the proposal failed due to irreconcilable differences between the parties. Long-standing border disputes could not be resolved within a matter of weeks, and the smaller sheikhdoms were, in addition, fearful of being dominated by Bahrain with its more developed economy and infrastructure and its greater population.[2]

However Bahrain was not only a target for grievances from its Arab neighbours but was also of great interest to Iran. The Shah saw Britain's proclamation of withdrawal as a chance to renew claims to Bahrain which originated in the eighteenth century and to assume the function of providing security in the Gulf area. As early as 7 January 1968, the Iranian government declared its readiness to 'take part in any kind of cooperation for the defence and security of the region.'[3] But in the meantime the rulers of Saudi Arabia, Kuwait and Bahrain had agreed to a joint programme for security in the Gulf region, precluding individual states signing treaties with Iran. As mentioned, there were enough reasons not to welcome Bahrain into a future Gulf federation, and Bahrain therefore had only a minimal chance of getting access to the Gulf federation, but the annexation of Bahrain by Iran would definitely have worried the Arab monarchs a great deal more.

In January of the same year, the Shah eventually retreated from his position and declared 'if the people of Bahrain do not want to join my country, Iran will withdraw its territorial claim,'[4] but he could barely hide his disappointment and on 8 July 1968, he refused to recognize the establishment of a federation of Gulf Arab states and questioned their pretensions to sovereignty. In particular he referred to the territorial affiliation of the islands of Tumb and Abu Musa, situated at the entrance to the Straits of Hormuz.[5] At the same time, the Shah reproached Saudi Arabia and Kuwait for obstructing his policy. Iran would be able and ready to look after the security of the region on its own without the approval of the Arab littoral states. The overall cooperative relationship between Iran and Saudi Arabia was thus undermined.

King Faisal reacted calmly. He reiterated Saudi support for the creation of a Gulf federation and spoke in favour of Bahrain's independence; whilst disapproving of the extension of Iranian influence to within a few miles of Saudi Arabia's coastline, including areas with considerable oil and gas resources, he had no desire to damage relations with the Shah irreversibly.

For his part, Mohammad Reza signalled his readiness to compromise that summer. If the creation of a formal security pact including all countries of the Gulf region was rejected by the Arabs, a network of bilateral agreements could be established instead. But even this proposal was not wholeheartedly welcomed by the Gulf Arabs. There were still enough reminders of the Iranian attitude towards the federation to generate mistrust and fear of Iranian domination in any kind of security network. The sheer size of Iran, its large population, and its economic and military superiority deterred the Gulf Arab rulers from signing pacts with the Shah on the sensitive issue of security.[6]

It was only radical political change in the immediate neighbourhood which brought an end to this policy of half measures and delays. On 17 July 1968, the Baath party took power for the second time in Iraq, probably for a significant duration after having learnt its lessons from the first attempt in 1963, thus creating a new danger for the Gulf states just when the radical politics of Nasser had been discredited. Although the Baath had governed Syria since 1963, Iraq was a direct neighbour with proven economic power, an educated population and huge resources of oil and other raw materials. The slogans of the new strong men in Baghdad, 'Unity', 'Freedom' and 'Socialism', were a direct challenge to the policies of the conservative Gulf monarchies. 'Unity' had clear pan-Arab implications replacing the danger of an enforced Nasserite drive for unity with a Baathist one. 'Freedom' meant the rejection of any foreign domination of the Middle East and was aimed at the close relationship between the Gulf monarchs and the West. 'Socialism', although not interpreted in a Marxist sense by the leaders of the Baath party, was the most hated word of all. It meant republicanism, the undermining of an Islamic basis for claims to legitimacy and, at the least, the liquidation of privileges for present and previous rulers.

With the containment of the civil war in Yemen, and coinciding with the British withdrawal from the Gulf, a new regime with socialist ambitions assumed power in South Yemen on 30 November 1967. It saw itself as the nucleus and starting point for the liberation of the entire Arabian Peninsula from foreign domination and autocratic monarchy. Spurred on by South Yemen, civil war erupted in the Omani province of Dhofar between 1968 and 1975. As if to confirm the apprehensions of the Gulf rulers, the insurgents called themselves the People's Front for the Liberation of Oman and the Arab Gulf (PFLOAG). At about the same time as the British were withdrawing from the Gulf, the Soviet Union was steadily increasing its naval presence in the Indian Ocean.

The coincidence of these events boosted the importance of the Gulf region in the Cold War and restored the conditions in which Iran and the Gulf Arab states had established common ground.[7] The common need to fight socialist and radical nationalist influences in the Gulf region, to ensure a stable flow of oil and gas and to increase wealth through exports, united Iran and the Gulf monarchs, despite their differences, until the end of the 1970s. As David Long states: 'prior to the revolution, the primary political confrontation in the Gulf was neither Sunni–Shii nor Arab–Persian but conservative–radical.'[8]

The Shah and King Faisal, in particular, felt under pressure to renew contacts. On 24 October 1968, both governments signed a new border agreement which modified the principle of equidistance established in December 1965 in favour of Iran. The treaty gave both Iran and Saudi Arabia equal and just access to the off-shore oilfields in the Persian Gulf. It also settled the dispute over the islands of Farsi and al-Arabiya which were put under the control of Iran and Saudi Arabia respectively.[9] The process of reconciliation culminated in the Shah's visit to Saudi Arabia between 9 and 14 November 1968. Both rulers assured each other of their common interests, and the Shah was polite enough to call King Faisal Amir al-mu'minin. This summit initiated a process of regular meetings between their respective foreign ministers, lasting till the end of 1969. Even the influential director of the National Iranian Oil Company (NIOC), Manuchehr Eqbal, visited Saudi Arabia during this period.[10]

Improved relations between Iran and Saudi Arabia facilitated the increased influence of another external power in the Gulf region – the United States of America. The American government took a markedly ambivalent position on the British proclamation of withdrawal. On the one hand it welcomed the weakening of a competitor in the global struggle for influence and markets, on the other hand it had to ensure that the resultant power vacuum in the Gulf, a region important both in terms of economy and strategy, would not be filled by the Eastern bloc and its allies. In January 1968, immediately after the British declaration of withdrawal, the Undersecretary of State, Eugene Rostow, declared that the US was expecting regional powers such as Iran, Saudi Arabia, Pakistan and Turkey to fill the gap left by Great Britain.[11]

These expectations were determined by US foreign policy. For several years now the USA had been waging a war against Vietnam, a war requiring enormous military, economic and diplomatic effort. Contrary to all Western strategic prognoses, the overwhelming American superiority in troops, military technology, and firepower had not led to a quick decision on the battlefields of South-East Asia. This, combined with the multifaceted demands of being the leading Western power, stretched the capabilities of the United States to the utmost. This situation induced President Nixon to declare on 23 July 1969 in a speech on the Pacific island of Guam that in future the USA would look for suitable states to assume regional leadership responsibilities in close cooperation with Washington.

The so-called Nixon Doctrine meant nothing more than the appointment of deputies for certain strategic areas of the world. The situation in the Gulf region seemed to provide a convenient opportunity to test out the new doctrine. James Noyes later explained this policy during a hearing of the Committee of Foreign Affairs:

> In the spirit of the Nixon Doctrine, we are willing to assist the Gulf states but we look to them to bear the main responsibility for their own defence and to cooperate among themselves to insure regional peace and stability. We especially look to the leading states of the area, Iran and Saudi Arabia, to cooperate for this purpose.[12]

It was obvious that the two biggest and most influential countries of the region would be selected to assume this new role as designed by the US.

Both Iran and Saudi Arabia were suitable for American purposes. Both had – although in different ways – the potential to assume leadership functions within the region. Both were conservative and anti-communist and would resist any changes to the *status quo* in the Gulf.

Fortunately for Washington, both Mohammad Reza Pahlavi and Faisal agreed to the American initiative. Since regaining the Peacock throne in 1953 with the decisive support of the US, the Shah had been an eager partner in what was an almost symbiotic relationship with the US, promoting the 'American way of life' in his country. In 1959, he had signed a military treaty with the US, binding the two states even closer together.

On the other side of the Gulf, King Faisal was striving hard to strengthen Saudi Arabia's and his dynasty's legitimacy by emphasizing the importance of Islam in all aspects of life. However, although he wanted to give Islam a renewed global role, he avoided any sense of a confrontational dualism embodied in the concepts of Dar al-Islam and Dar al-Harb. Neither he nor his father, Abd al-Aziz ibn Saud, the founder of modern Saudi Arabia, had ever experienced the West in its full colonial guise. As a result they saw it primarily as the defender of all the free world, including the umma, against the evils of socialism and communism.[13]

Together Iran and Saudi Arabia were to form two solid pillars supporting the building of a conservative and pro-Western policy in the region. Nowhere in the world during the early 1970s was the Nixon Doctrine more evident than in the Gulf. Both 'pillars' enjoyed Washington's constant political, economic and diplomatic support. High ranking delegations regularly travelled to both countries, and mutual consultation became a matter of course.[14] But to enable Iran and Saudi Arabia to take over the responsibility of maintaining law and order in the region within the framework of the Nixon Doctrine, it was necessary to rearm them.

The American export of military goods to Iran and Saudi Arabia between 1970 and 1975 increased from US$ 1 billion to US$ 10 billion per annum.[15] Other statistical data confirm these figures, giving specific details for each country in the whole decade between 1968/9 and 1978/9. According to these statistics, Iran bought arms worth US$ 500 million in 1968–9, US$ 2.1 billion in 1973 and US$ 10 billion in 1978–9. Saudi Arabia was a competitive runner-up, importing arms to the value of US$ 380 million in 1970–1, almost US$ 7 billion in 1976–7 and likewise US$ 10 billion in 1978–9.[16]

But during the 1970s it also became evident that the 'twin pillar' policy was being interpreted and pursued in different ways by its regional protagonists. The Shah, for example, emphasized that, although of all the Gulf Arab states, only Saudi Arabia was of any significance in military, political and economic terms, he was nevertheless sure that the Kingdom would need several years to reach a status comparable to that of Iran.[17] At the same time he concealed his lack of interest in any Saudi efforts to catch up. His main concern was to use American support to become the undisputed, dominant power in the Gulf, in particular in the military, political and economic spheres, and to extend his influence into the Gulf of Oman and the Indian Ocean. The Shah intended to become nothing less than the 'gendarme of the Gulf'.

His intentions were soon translated into actions. Unofficially, both Iran and Saudi Arabia mutually conceded a number of zones of influence in the region. Iran respected a certain amount of Saudi Arabian control over the smaller emirates and sheikhdoms, whilst King Faisal in turn had to accept the undisputed Iranian naval dominance in the Gulf. The unequal balance of power first became visible on 30 November 1971 when Iranian forces occupied the islands of Tumb and Abu Musa. These islands belonged to Ras al-Khaimah and Sharjah respectively, and were supposed to come under their control immediately after British withdrawal on 1 December 1971. Using the pretext of securing the permanent flow of oil via the Straits of Hormuz, the Shah disregarded this arrangement.

By occupying the islands on 30 November, he formally removed them from British domination rather than the sovereignty of Sharjah and Ras al-Khaimah. He thus also saved Saudi Arabia from having to support her clients on 1 December. Subsequent half-hearted protests from Riyadh proved to the Shah that he did not need to fear a Saudi Arabian denouncement of the 'twin pillar' policy. King Faisal knew only too well that Imperial Iran was superior to Saudi Arabia in almost all areas of importance.[18] This state of affairs caused Fred Halliday to comment, very dryly, that:

> these common interests [between Iran and Saudi Arabia] led many to expect that a system of Arab–Iranian Gulf security could emerge in the 1970s, under US direction and as a concrete implementation of the 'Twin Pillar' policy proclaimed by Washington. No such Gulf security system came about; rather, there was a unilateral *de facto* Gulf security system, one of Iranian hegemony.[19]

Similar opinions were also voiced by other experts. According to them it would be unrealistic to expect a permanent, close cooperation between Iran and Saudi Arabia, considering the number of historical, cultural, political, religious and other differences between them. It was more likely that Western, and especially American, arms sales would contribute to a situation in which both countries would be able to direct their growing arsenals against each other. Iran and Saudi Arabia were by far the largest countries in the region, but Iran's population outnumbered Saudi Arabia's fourfold. The Kingdom emphasized its Arab and Sunni nature whereas Iran was proud of its Persian and Shia character.[20] According to M.A. Hameed:

> the twin-pillar policy had several faults. First, it naively assumed that Iran and Saudi Arabia would cooperate on the basis of common interests rather than coming into conflict as a result of divergent interests. Second, the policy overlooked the disparity between Iran and Saudi Arabia. Third, Washington underestimated and misread Iraq. Fourth, the nature of and limits on the power of the 'pillars' were never understood.[21]

All these arguments carry weight. Indeed, the number of differences between Iran and Saudi Arabia remained consistent even after their involvement in the 'twin pillar' policy. From time to time one could even assume a growing potential for conflict. This impression arose particularly from the price policy of the Organization of Petroleum

Exporting Countries (OPEC) after 1973 when the price of oil increased within a few months from US$ 1.84 per barrel to US$ 11.67. All major oil exporters, including Iran and Saudi Arabia, gained a huge surplus income. In the case of Iran it increased from US$ 4.1 billion in 1973 to US$ 17.4 billion in 1974.[22]

Export of oil was vital to the economies of both Iran and Saudi Arabia. Nevertheless, the differing concerns of their export strategies had serious results for the politics of Iran and Saudi Arabia. The Shah was one of the driving forces behind the dramatic price increase. Given the rate of extraction in the 1970s, the deposits of oil and gas in Iran were not large enough to satisfy demand much beyond the turn of the century. The Shah's economic and political ambitions therefore compelled him to demand the highest possible price for his diminishing reserves. At the same time he was sure that Iran's growing population and expanding economy would be able to usefully absorb the giant influx of petrodollars.[23]

Iran's price policy was opposed by Western consumer countries, including the United States. Washington tried – eventually calling on the help of Saudi Arabia – to convince Tehran to cancel the price increase or at least to agree to freeze the prices. The American government argued that the involvement of Saudi Arabia was beneficial because the Kingdom's much larger oil resources encouraged a more relaxed attitude towards pricing. Furthermore, the economy of Saudi Arabia was at first unable to effectively absorb the growing profits from oil exports. But the Saudi Arabian government was able to adapt its oil export figures and its price expectations to fit its foreign policy and trade at the time. Between 1972 and 1977 Saudi Arabian oil production increased by 9.8 per cent each year, whereas Iranian production only increased by 2.4 per cent annually.[24] In this instance, Riyadh seemed to have the upper hand.

Nevertheless, events did not proceed according to this scenario. The reasons can be found primarily in the international political behaviour of both countries. Whilst maintaining good relations with the West and especially with the US, Saudi Arabia also saw itself as the heartland of the Arab world. King Faisal and his oil minister, Sheikh Ahmad Zaki Yamani, demonstrated their readiness to use oil as a political weapon in the Arab–Israeli conflict, which escalated after the Israeli occupation of Arab territory in the Six-Day War of 1967. It was only the authoritative engagement of Saudi Arabia that made the oil embargo by the Organization of Arab Petroleum Exporting Countries (OAPEC) effective in 1973–4. Because of the enormous financial reserves and the huge resources Saudi Arabia could draw on, the King and his Minister were certain that the Kingdom could tolerate – at least for a certain period of time – a reduction of income in exchange for increased political profit.

On the other hand the Shah could not afford to take such a position. He boycotted the embargo and declared oil to be merely a trading asset and not a political instrument. He therefore continued to supply all his Western trading partners, including South Africa and Israel, uninterruptedly until his downfall in 1978. For the USA and its Western allies the Iranian policy seemed to be more advantageous than a return to lower prices. As a result, once again they directed more of their political, military and diplomatic support to Iran within the 'twin pillar policy'. President Nixon ordered that Iran be granted licences to import any military hardware and technology below the nuclear level from the US. Saudi Arabia was only able to compete in the number of imports, but not in standard and quality of sophisticated weaponry.

The US government now saw the advantages of increased Iranian liquidity. Tehran was able to pay for its military imports immediately and to test the delivered weapons itself. This arrangement proved to be a bargain for the Americans. Unlike other allies, the gendarme of the Gulf was at least not in need of additional American financial help.

Despite these graphic examples of different Iranian and Saudi Arabian ambitions and policies, their partnership within the 'twin pillar' policy still worked better than predicted by many experts. Neither Saudi Arabia nor Iran went so far in their oil policy as to harm the other irreversibly. Both monarchs knew very well that they had no alternative but to reach a certain level of understanding in order to protect their capacity for oil production and their export markets. They shared the opinion that open confrontation would only strengthen third parties, be they leftist radical forces in the region or their alleged Eastern bloc supporters. As a result, during the 1970s common interests prevailed.

Both rulers were autocrats, reacting suspiciously and sensitively to any political change in the status quo and security needs therefore created a strong tie between them.

Any explanation of the source of this stability must in large part reflect Irani–Saudi co-operation, which in turn resulted from a basic coincidence of regional aims. Whatever anxiety Saudi leaders felt about Iran's ambitions and strength was allayed by the recognition that the two states shared many sources of security. Both opposed a major Soviet role in the region, and both were wary of any signs of radicalism regardless of its origin. Armed conflict in the region was to be avoided if possible, and oil production and sea lanes protected against interference or interruption . . . Iran, for all its military might, was never able to challenge Saudi legitimacy and leadership among Arab states, while Saudi Arabia, for all its economic and political influence, lacked the ultimate arbiter of military power.[25]

During the 1970s, the division of responsibility between Iran and Saudi Arabia became evident. In 1973 the Shah gave military support to the Sultan of Oman against the PFLOAG rebels. At the beginning of 1974 a combat-ready Iranian brigade was established in Oman on a permanent basis. There was a continual exchange of troops within this brigade to provide as many Iranian officers and NCOs as possible with combat experience. In addition, Oman became a very convenient testing ground for newly acquired American and other Western arms. The PFLOAG was defeated in 1975. In this case the division of labour between Iran and Saudi Arabia proved a success. Iran supported the Sultan in military terms, whilst Saudi Arabia gave economic, financial and diplomatic help.

In 1977, both countries harmonized their policies concerning the Horn of Africa to avoid a destabilization of their interests in the probable outcome of the Ogaden War between Somalia and Ethiopia.[26] The politics of the Baath leadership in Baghdad however, perceived as the most dangerous threat by both Mohammad Reza Pahlavi and Faisal, continued to be the main political reason for their cooperation. While the Shah was – at least temporarily – able to diffuse Baghdad's threat by urging Iraq into an accord in Algiers in 1975, Faisal invested heavily in the improvement of the military base at Hafar al-Batin near the border with Iraq. But he was not sure whether his country would be able to resist a serious military attack by Iraq without the help of Iran.[27] Iran in the 1970s appeared to be a military power at least nominally stronger than that of Iraq and Saudi Arabia put together.[28]

When King Faisal was murdered in April 1975, the Shah travelled to Riyadh for the third time in his reign to offer condolences to King Khalid on the death of his half-brother. Both agreed to continue the special relationship between their countries and the years up to the overthrow of the Shah were thus more or less distinguished by cooperation:

> It would be fair to say that Shah Muhammad Riza Pahlavi was at this time in full agreement with Saudi Arabia's policies on a wide range of issues, in particular the need to: (a) maintain the security and stability of the Arabian/Persian Gulf region; (b) secure an overall settlement of the Arab–Israeli conflict and the restoration of Palestinian rights; (c) ensure an Israeli withdrawal from Jerusalem; (d) promote Islamic solidarity among all Muslim nations and extend financial assistance to needy Islamic countries; (e) promote political, economic and military relations with the Western world, particularly the United States; and (f) combat communism and prevent its infiltration into the Islamic world, the Arab world and the African continent.[29]

Considering the results of the 'twin pillar' policy out of context, the downfall of the Shah and the subsequent Islamic revolution in Iran would render it a complete disaster. In the end the policy was not able to secure permanently the status quo in the region, nor to help American interests. However if one examines only the last decade of its existence, it must be recognized that it diminished the huge potential for conflict between Iran and Saudi Arabia and its Arab neighbours:

> So in the 1970s there remained a tacit division of labour, as it were, between Iran and Saudi Arabia, whereby the former dominated the Gulf militarily, and the latter dominated the economic affairs of OPEC.[30]

It was due to Faisal's sophisticated approach to policy and diplomacy that, despite his military and economic inferiority, he succeeded in containing the ambitions of the Shah. He achieved this by cleverly utilizing his superior reserves of oil and by exploiting the dynamic of the bilateral relations to mutual advantage. The relationship between Iran and Saudi Arabia was never to be as friendly and fruitful as it was between 1968 and 1979.

Pan-Iranism vs. Pan-Islamism

Relations between Iran and Saudi Arabia in the 1970s cannot be fully understood without considering the ideological parameters of their respective regional foreign policies during these years.

Like his father before him, the Shah tried to enhance the legitimacy of his rule by exploiting Persian history, culture and tradition. The population under his domination were to identify themselves with the dynasty by means of such key concepts as nationalism, Persianhood and the perception of an 'aryan' community. Mohammad Reza, unlike his father, was wise enough not to use such terms extensively in his foreign policy and propaganda, but he did permit a 'pan-Iranist' party to operate, under the leadership of Mohsen Pezeshkpour.

The use of words such as nation, language, race or ethnos to specify national identity is a feature of the twentieth century in Iran, although its roots can be found in the nineteenth century when the Iranian elite started to compare their country to Europe. The increasingly aggressive advance of European powers into the Middle East, including Iran, forced the educated and politically aware strata of Iranian society to look for the causes and motives behind European expansion and for the reasons for its economic, technical, and military superiority, in order to find some measure of self-defence. The protests against the Tobacco Régie in 1897 demonstrated that those Iranians who actively opposed European domination were largely influenced by the new Islamic ideology of al-Afghani and his followers. It also proved that nationalist feelings and ideas had to come under the umbrella of Islam.

During the period of the Constitutional Revolution, between 1905 and 1911, which also included strong anti-colonialist aspects, Islamic and nationalist elements in the proclamations and demands of the revolutionaries counterbalanced each other. Both forces cooperated in their struggle to reject any foreign tutelage and to limit the authority of the European dominated Qajar dynasty by establishing a constitution.[31] The Constitutional Revolution, together with the example of the Young Turks in the neighbouring Ottoman Empire, – at least till the end of the First World War – favoured those forces in Iran which sought in nationalism the ideal conditions for competing with European states on equal terms:

> It had something to do with economic backwardness and military weakness against the might of industry and empire in Europe; something to do with a sense of superiority about the past; something

to do with the contemporary power, success and prestige of Europe, and the decline, weakness and underdevelopment of Arabs and Turks who had conquered and ruled Iran in the past; something to do with the contemporary European theory and practice of nationalism, Aryanism and racism . . .[32]

The majority of Iranian intellectuals, artists and politicians developed their own world of ideas during the 1920s, the patriotic content of which broadly drew upon pan-Iranist emotions. By exploiting nationalist sentiment, Reza Chan, an officer in the Iranian Cossack brigade, had overthrown the Qajars in 1925 and founded his own 'Pahlavi' dynasty. Influenced by the politics of Kemal Ataturk, he planned to secularize the Iranian state and society and to modernize them, by force, according to Western standards.

The new ruler regarded secularization as a necessary means to close the gap with the West and to initiate his own legitimacy. In general he considered Islam an obstacle and he was only ready to grant it a folkloric role in Iranian culture. Nation and nationality were instead to have priority:

> The country's history was re-written to suit Aryanist/Persianist theory, and state education and propaganda created public amnesia among the younger generations about much of Iranian culture as it had been known by their fathers and grandfathers. Arabs and Turks were blamed for Iran's backwardness, and were described as being inherently backward, unintelligent, aggressive and uncivilised.[33]

Although Reza Pahlavi skilfully exploited the nationalist and pan-Iranist emotions of the intellectual elite of his country, he could not compensate for the weaknesses of this concept in a multi-ethnic country like Iran. Only about 65 per cent of the population in Iran identify themselves as Persians. The other 35 per cent class themselves as Turks, Arabs, Kurds, Azeris, Baluch and others. Even when Persian became the colloquial language, it was nevertheless not accepted by all Iranians as their mother tongue. Thus ethnic and linguistic diversity undermined national unity and the influence of nationalism. However, it should not be forgotten that affiliation to different religious confessions, not always congruent with membership of a particular ethnic group, influenced Iranian national feelings too.[34] In spite of this, Mohammad Reza Pahlavi not only continued the politics of his father but even intensified them.

He demanded legitimacy by claiming to embody the direct continuation of the Persian monarchical tradition from Cyrus the Great and the Akhamenids. In 1971 he celebrated 2,500 years of monarchy in Iran at Persepolis with great pomp, and accordingly orientated the Iranian calendar to the beginning of the Akhamenid rule.[35] Even more openly than his father, he dismissed Islam as backward and tried to pose as a progressive ruler in a region dominated by 'Islamic arrogance and ignorance', as he frequently called it.

It is clear therefore that an extreme contrast existed in the way Islam was regarded in Iran and in Saudi Arabia. The rule of the Al Saud over the Arabian Peninsula was ultimately only possible because of their symbiotic relationship with Wahhabi Islam. Since the alliance in 1744 between the founder of the Al Saud dynasty, Mohammad ibn Saud, and the Hanbali reformer, Ibn Wahhab, the higher echelons of the ulema had supported the rule of the Al Saud to their mutual benefit. Since the mid-eighteenth century it had twice been possible to establish a united state that extended beyond the borders of Najd under the leadership of the Al Saud. These efforts were successful for a third time with the foundation of the Kingdom of Saudi Arabia by Abd al-Aziz ibn Saud in 1932.

It may be an historic accident that Reza Shah, who had come to power seven years before, pushed his program of a secularized modernization in Iran at the same time that Ibn Saud declared Wahhabi Islam to be the exclusive state religion of Saudi Arabia. Nevertheless, Islam did not play the most important role in the foreign policy of Ibn Saud. It was used primarily for unifying the young Kingdom and for containing centrifugal tribal interests. Since Islam did not dominate Saudi Arabian foreign policy for several decades, it did not influence relations with Iran decisively; in other words foreign policy was shaped by other factors.

This situation changed only at the beginning of the 1960s, more precisely with the accession of Faisal in 1964. For King Faisal Islam became the most important single stronghold against pan-Arabism in the guise of Nasserism, with all its assumed and real political consequences.[36] As Crown Prince he invited more than one hundred Muslim notables, intellectuals and politicians from various Arab and non-Arab Islamic countries to a conference immediately after the hajj of 1962. They concluded their meeting on 20 May 1962 with the foundation of an organization called the World Muslim League. In all, 21 Islamic countries took part in this founding conference and it was decided to locate the new organization in Mecca.[37]

Encouragement and subtle pressure by Crown Prince Faisal was enough to convince many prosperous merchants and notables of the Hijaz to give financial support to the World Muslim League. The businessmen of Najd did not want to be left behind by their Hijazi counterparts and in the same year they created the financial basis for the foundation of a World Assembly of Muslim Youth.[38] By politicizing and ideologizing his conservative interpretation of Islam, Faisal succeeded in offering an alternative to the pan-Arab embrace. On the other hand, Saudi Arabia in the 1960s did not have the economic, political, and military means to unite all its partners and sympathizers under the flag of pan-Islamism.

The situation changed gradually after Nasser's defeat in the Six Day War. Faisal now felt himself strong enough to further promote his pan-Islamic concepts. In 1969 he proposed an annual meeting of all the leaders of Islamic states in order to openly discuss their problems and to close ranks against the non-Muslim world. A fire in the al-Aqsa mosque in Jerusalem in August 1969 created an opportunity for Faisal to insist on the urgency of an immediate meeting of Islamic heads of state. Eventually they met in Rabat and decided – completely in concurrence with the Saudi Arabian monarch – to institutionalize the meeting by founding the Organization of the Islamic Conference (OIC). Jerusalem was selected as its permanent residence.

But in view of the continued Israeli occupation of that particular city, Jedda was chosen as the temporary seat of the OIC. The first meeting at ministerial level in March 1970 saw the introduction of a process of frequent consultation and the passing of common resolutions within the organizational framework of the OIC – a triumph for Faisal's pan-Islamism. Saudi Arabia organized, via the OIC and in addition to it, a further series of institutions with specific functions, including the Islamic Development Bank. With Saudi Arabia's wealth rising by leaps and bounds throughout the 1970s, Faisal was able to emphasize his pan-Islamic concept via this financial pipeline and to increase his political stature.

In spite of the fact that both the Shah and King Faisal vigorously promoted their respective 'isms', they managed, amazingly, to avoid a confrontation in foreign policy. Pan-Iranism and pan-Islamism did indeed exclude each other, but ultimately did not compete for the same terrain. On the contrary, Faisal succeeded, step by step, in convincing the Iranian monarch of the usefulness of pan-Islamism in the struggle against Arab nationalism.

The Shah had already participated in the founding meeting of the World Muslim League in 1962. Then in 1965 Faisal visited Tehran, fostering among other things the Shah's conviction that the unity of Islamic states might become a successful way to resist the infiltration of communist ideas and radical Arab nationalism. At the end of that visit both rulers signed a communiqué which stated:

> It is necessary for the Islamic countries to study their problems, support their interests, develop their relationships and march unilaterally towards achieving the supra-Islamic goals for the prosperity of the Muslim nations, and to achieve social justice for them.[39]

Even at this early stage Mohammad Reza Pahlavi and King Faisal discussed the idea of a permanent annual meeting of Islamic heads of state. In December 1967, Faisal visited Tehran a second time and continued the exchange of views on ways and means to strengthen Islamic solidarity. It can be assumed that the King was well aware of the Shah's ambivalent attitude towards Islam. In 1963 the Shah had crushed a clergy-led revolt in Qom and Tehran by force, and one year later he exiled the undisputed leader and spokesman of that upheaval, Ayatollah Khomeini. He dubbed the Muslim clergy in Iran 'black reactionaries' and posed for the West as an enlightened statesman. On the other hand he recognized the usefulness of a stronghold of conservative Islamic states against an Arab nationalism fighting for social and political change. Nevertheless, he tried to convince King Faisal to emphasize all those components of Islam which appeared to give it a suitably progressive and modern appearance.

At any rate, Mohammad Reza Pahlavi continued cooperating with King Faisal. He took part in the founding meeting of the OIC and ordered the respective ministers of his government participating in the numerous special conferences to display general goodwill. Indeed the Iranian Shah did not just participate in or react now and then to the activities of the OIC, he several times came up with his own proposals such as the establishment of an Islamic Common Market. The high level of preparation and the organizational skill of the Iranian participation in the annual hajj adds to the impression that Iran at that time was keen to cooperate and live in harmony with Saudi Arabia. The Shah ordered a team of physicians and an ambulance to accompany the pilgrims and offered free medical care to pilgrims from other nations as well. Iranian pilgrims became known for their orderly behaviour and generosity.[40]

In conclusion one can say that the cooperative elements that Faisal and Mohammad Reza Pahlavi had managed to distil from the apparently contradictory concepts of pan-Iranism and pan-Islamism prevailed. It is further evidence of the common interests which, in general, dominated the bilateral relationship, binding the rulers of Iran and Saudi Arabia together until the Iranian revolution.

NOTES

1 For a detailed account of Iranian–Saudi Arabian relations between 1964 and 1975 see S.M. Badeeb, *Saudi–Iranian Relations 1932–1982* (London, Echoes, 1993), pp. 57–68.

2 N. Safran, *Saudi Arabia: The Ceaseless Quest for Security* (Cambridge, MA, Harvard University Press, 1988), pp. 134–5.

3 *Ettela'at*, Tehran, 8 January 1968.

4 Quoted in R. O'Brien, 'Oil Markets and Developing Countries', *Third World Quarterly*, 8:4 (1986), pp. 1312–3.

5 B. Baktiari, 'Revolutionary Iran's Persian Gulf Policy: The Quest for Regional Supremacy' in H. Amirahmadi and N. Entessar (eds.), *Iran and the Arab World*, (Basingstoke: Macmillan, 1993), p. 70.

6 K.L. Afrasiabi, *After Khomeini: New Directions in Iran's Foreign Policy* (Boulder: Westview Press, 1994), p. 102.

7 J. Calabrese, *Revolutionary Horizons: Regional Foreign Policy in Post-Khomeini Iran* (New York: St. Martin's Press, 1994), p. 45.

8 D.E. Long, 'The Impact of the Iranian Revolution on the Arabian Peninsula and the Gulf States' in J.L. Esposito (ed.), *The Iranian Revolution: Its Global Impact* (Miami: Florida International University Press, 1990), p. 110.

9 R. Litvak, *Security in the Persian Gulf: Sources of Inter-State Conflict* (Aldershot: Gower, 1981), p. 39.

10 Badeeb, *Saudi–Iranian Relations*, p. 61.

11 S. Chubin and S. Zabih, *The Foreign Relations of Iran: A Developing State in a Zone of Great-Power Conflict* (Berkeley: Los Angeles and University of California Press, 1974), p. 237.

12 J. Noyes, 'New Perspectives on the Persian Gulf' in *Hearings before the Subcommittee on the Near East and South Asia of the Committee on Foreign Affairs* (Washington DC: House of Representatives, 1973), p. 39.

13 S.K. al-Nowaiser, *Saudi Arabia's and the United States' Strategic Partnership in an Era of Turmoil: A Study of Saudi-American Political, Economic, and Military Relationship 1973–1983 – Dependence or Independence?* (Ann Arbor, University Press, 1988), p. 55.

14 R. Haass, 'Saudi Arabia and Iran: The Twin Pillars in Revolutionary Times' in H. Amirsadeghi (ed.), *The Security of the Persian Gulf* (London: Croom Helm, 1981), p. 153.

15 P.R. Odell, *Oil and World Power* (Harmondsworth: Penguin, 1986), p. 284.

16 US Arms Control and Disarmament Agency, *World Military Expenditures and Arms Transfers 1967–1978* (Washington DC, 1978).

17 *New York Times*, 10 May 1970.

18 Safran, *Saudi Arabia*, pp. 135–7.

19 F. Halliday, 'The Gulf in International Affairs: Independence and After' in B.R. Pridham (ed.), *The Arab Gulf and the Arab World* (London, Croom Helm, 1988), p. 106.

20 Haass, 'Saudi Arabia', pp. 153–4.

21 M.A. Hameed, *Saudi Arabia, the West and the Security of the Gulf* (London: Croom Helm, 1986), p. 3.

22 Safran, *Saudi Arabia*, p. 177.

23 N. Jeandet, *Un Golfe pour Trois Rêves; le Triangle de Crise Iran, Irak, Arabie* (Paris: Edition l'Harmattan, 1993), pp. 45–7.

24 Haass, 'Saudi Arabia', p. 156.

25 Ibid., p. 161.

26 Ibid.

27 M.A. Heller, *The Iran–Iraq War: Implications for Third Parties*, The Center for International Affairs Papers, no. 23 (Cambridge, MA, Harvard University Press, 1984), pp. 12–13.

28 D.R. Tahtinen, *National Security Challenge to Saudi Arabia* (Washington DC, Institute for National Strategic Studies, 1979), p. 21.

29 Badeeb, *Saudi–Iranian Relations*, p. 67.

30 M.E. Ahrari, 'Iran, GCC and the Security Dimensions in the Persian Gulf' in H. Amirahmadi and N. Entessar (eds.), *Reconstruction and Regional Diplomacy in the Persian Gulf* (London, New York: Routledge, 1992), p. 206.

31 S.T. Hunter, *Iran and the World: Continuity in a Revolutionary Decade* (Bloomington: Indiana University Press, 1990), p. 12.

32 H. Katouzian, 'Problems of Political Development in Iran', *British Journal of Middle Eastern Studies*, 22:1&2 (1995), p. 17.

33 Ibid., p. 18.

34 Hunter, *Iran*, p. 11.

35 C. Bina, 'Towards a New World Order: US Hegemony, Client-States and Islamic Alternative' in H. Mutalib (ed.), *Islam, Muslims and the Modern State* (New York: St. Martin's Press, 1994), p. 17.

36 See for example B.A. Mohabadian, *Fundamentalistische Bewegungen im Islam am Beispiel des Iran* (Marburg, Verlag der Universität Marburg, 1992), p. 87 and Nowaiser, *Saudi Arabia's*, pp. 52–4.

37 Badeeb, *Saudi–Iranian Relations*, p. 89.

38 Calabrese, *Revolutionary Horizons*, p. 66.

39 Quoted in Badeeb, *Saudi–Iranian Relations*, p. 87.

40 Ibid., pp. 88–90.

Part I

Bilateral Relations from the Islamic Revolution of 1978/9 to the Aftermath of the Second Gulf War

1

Iran's Islamic Revolution
and Saudi Arabia

_____

The Iranian Islamic revolution and Saudi Arabian reactions

> The revolution in Iran in 1978–9 was a watershed in the post-war politics of south-west Asia. It changed not only the politics and role of Iran in the region, but also underscored the profound transformation that had taken place between all the regional States and the United States.[1]

This statement by Sharam Chubin is only one of a large number of similar comments on the consequences of the Iranian revolution for the region which concentrate on the political and strategic results of the revolution. But it is necessary to analyse the revolution's economic, cultural and religious aspects too. This has also been attempted because of the Iranian revolution's tremendous importance as one of the very few real grass roots, mass revolutions of history.

Although during the post-revolutionary period the new leadership of Iran did sometimes refer to previous regional strategies, it soon became evident that attitudes to the West, particularly the US had also changed dramatically and its supposed or real regional allies had in fact changed completely. During the revolution Iran left the Central Treaty Organization (CENTO), a step which effectively paralysed the organization.

The new Iranian government appeared most consistent in its rejection of the pro-American foreign policy of the Shah, which was naturally going to affect relations with Saudi Arabia. The former policy of cooperation between the Shah and Saudi Arabia, within the American-initiated 'twin pillar' policy, had been a thorn in the side of the Iranian clerical leadership. 'The Iranian revolution was by its very nature calculated to cause unease among the Arab governments of the Persian Gulf. It was a revolution made in the name of Islam and the 'oppressed' Moslem masses and against the 'oppressors' and the powerful. It carried with it strong anti-American and anti-imperialist overtones . . . More significantly, Iranian leaders and clerics directly and indirectly called on their brother Moslems on the other side of the Gulf to follow the example set by revolutionary Iran. Khomeini often addressed his appeals not only to Iranians but to the people of the Moslem world in general; his denunciation of the role of the United States, the 'Great Satan', in the Moslem world, and of the Moslem governments that he believed furthered American interests, had implications for neighbouring countries and for the Persian Gulf states.'[2]

This new policy became especially evident during the hajj which, of course, took place in the heart of Saudi Arabia, in Mecca and Medina. In 1979, the first post-revolutionary year, Khomeini directed the following appeal to Iranian pilgrims:

> In this year in which Iran is the threshold of an Islamic Republic, and because of unjust propaganda of the foreigners, it is possible that Moslems from various countries not be informed of the depth of the Islamic movement in Iran. Therefore it is necessary that religious leaders, speakers and scholars, with whatever means that are available introduce this sacred movement. The other pilgrims must realise that the goal of the Iranian Moslems is to establish an Islamic government under the banner of Islam and under the guidance of the Holy Qoran and the Prophet of Islam so that our Moslem brothers will come to know that our only goal is Islam and we only think about the establishment of a just Islamic government.[3]

Iranian pilgrims were encouraged to publicize the slogans and demands of the Iranian revolution during the hajj and to appeal for its imitation. Furthermore Khomeini appointed several special envoys to propagate the Islamic revolution abroad, including the notorious revolutionary judge, Hojjat al-Islam Sadeq Khalkhali, and ordered Iranian embassies to coordinate their propaganda efforts in the interest of exporting the revolution.[4]

> An organised and expensive anti-Saudi propaganda campaign was carried out throughout the Arab and Islamic world. Daily newspapers were distributed free of charge, hundreds of books and booklets were published, video tapes and cassettes were produced and distributed in the Western world, and pamphlets and leaflets were distributed inside the mosques, particularly on Fridays – all in an attempt to discredit Saudi Arabia.[5]

Politicians of the Islamic Republic of Iran tried to surpass each other in their enthusiasm to export the Islamic revolution and to criticize Saudi Arabia, because only a frequently reiterated and proven revolutionary sentiment could create preconditions for a secure position in the still unstable political hierarchy of the young republic. Even President Abolhassan Banisadr, who was to flee the country in 1981, attacked Saudi Arabia in the strongest terms in 1979 and 1980. He called the Kingdom an American client, fearful of both the Iranian revolution and its own citizens. Regarding the Gulf states he declared:

> We do not consider them to be independent governments . . . and therefore do not wish to cooperate with them . . .; if the people in the Arab states . . . adopted the techniques developed by the Iranian revolutionaries, not one of these regimes would remain in existence, and they know it . . . All these overlords will be like dust in the wind.[6]

The monthly journal of the Pasdaran, the Revolutionary Guards, also gives an example of the vocabulary of Iranian anti-Saudi propaganda:

> Saudi Arabia, an Islamic country which is possessed of a centrality for Moslems of the world and must naturally serve as a promoter of the Islamic ideology, has so intermixed with the West that it can hardly be called independent. The entire resources of oil in Saudi Arabia are indisputably controlled by American trusts; and while the people there live in poverty, misery and ignorance, and one day's oil income of the country can cause a fundamental change in their situation, the government executes the West-dictated policies and strives to stabilize the economic situation of western industrialized countries which are the main exploiters of today's world.[7]

Many previously unknown problems confronted Saudi Arabia within a very short period of time. Not only did it have to appease Iranian pilgrims and neutralize their propaganda or explain away the 'sins' of following a pro-American foreign policy, but the Iranian clerical leadership was, by declaring Islam to be the basis of the Iranian republic and by propagating the establishment of an Islamic state in Iran, directly challenging Al Saud legitimacy. It should not be forgotten that one of the reasons for the relatively smooth relations between the Shah and Saudi Arabia was that the secular ambitions of the former did not compete with the Wahhabism of the latter.

The claims of the Al Saud to rule in alliance with the Wahhabi clerics, according to Islamic norms and traditions, and to look after the safety of the Holy places had been the central arguments for their legitimacy:

> This was an imperfect defence given the known hypocrisy and corruption of some members of the Saudi ruling elite, but it sufficed so long as no other regime of greater Islamic authenticity existed to challenge the propriety of Saudi rule. But when the Islamic revolution came to power in Iran . . ., the Saudis were faced with the danger of being undercut precisely on the issue on which they had themselves chosen to stand.[8]

There were additional challenges. While in exile in Iraq, Khomeini had developed his ideas regarding a future Islamic state, particularly regarding Velajat-e Faqih, the rule of the jurisprudent, and emphasizing the fatal role the monarchy had played in Iran. The leader of the Iranian revolution was convinced of the incompatibility of an Islamic state with any kind of monarchical rule. This conviction was central to the new Iranian republic and it became a part of foreign policy. The principle that monarchy was fundamentally unIslamic and that a republic was the only form of state acceptable to Islam thus became an additional challenge to the dynasties of the Arabian Peninsula, including Saudi Arabia.

The Kingdom had previously been a refuge for numerous fundamentalist Sunni spokesmen and ideologues escaping the social revolutionary and secular repression in Arab countries such as Egypt. Some of them showed their gratitude by their good behaviour and support for Saudi Arabian leadership, others however felt compelled to criticize the increasing westernization, corruption and decadence in their host country. The debate on which type of Islam was an adequate form of government began to intensify in Saudi Arabia.[9]

The government in Riyadh was taken unawares by the degree of Iran's hostility and by the problems the new situation caused. Continuing the tradition of a defensive Saudi Arabian foreign policy, those in power tried at first to find a discreet way out of this critical situation through talks with the Iranian leadership.[10] It seemed important to pacify their powerful opponent, encouraging a friendly approach and promoting propaganda minimizing any danger.

King Khalid sent his congratulations to Ayatollah Khomeini after the victory of the Iranian revolution expressing his satisfaction for an

'Iranian republic resting on a firm Islamic foundation.' Prince Abdallah concluded that 'from now on Islam will be the basis of our common interests and relations.' Other politicians of the Kingdom added that 'Islam and not heavy weapons would be the basis of the bilateral dialogue, by far more suitable to reduce the arsenal of tensions and dissatisfaction between both countries.'[11] Crown Prince Fahd blamed 'irresponsible persons' in Iran for criticizing his country and for spreading opinions not shared by the new Iranian leadership. 'We respect Imam Khomeini's convictions, and we will not change our attitude towards him or towards Iran,' he added.[12] It would appear that the Saudi Arabian leadership was trying to prolong the overall friendly relations of the 1970s by using revolutionary Islamic rhetoric on Iran.[13]

A contributory element in this illusion was the lack of coordination within the Iranian leadership immediately after the downfall of the Shah. There were still a number of moderates amongst the politicians in the provisional government, former supporters of the National Front and Mohammad Mossadegh (the Prime Minister between 1950 and 1953 who nationalized Iranian oil in 1951) or of the Freedom Movement of Mehdi Bazargan. Khomeini needed this political element during the first post-revolutionary months to secure the broadest possible support for his intended radical changes. Yet even in 1980, Foreign Minister Yazdi declared that whilst Iran had no intention of exporting the revolution beyond its borders, it could not prevent others being inspired by the revolution.[14] In the course of the Iranian internal power struggle the radical forces eventually won.

Encouraged by the irreconcilable attitude of Khomeini, the Iranian leadership intensified its anti-Saudi position. In addition to criticism that it was the lackey of the Americans, that, by still having a monarchy, it was unIslamic, and that it enforced a repressive policy in the name of Islam, Tehran now started to dispute the ability of the Saudi Arabian government to protect Mecca and Medina. Tehran proposed a Joint Islamic Committee to take over this function from the Al Saud.

This was the last straw for the Al Saud. The Saudi government began a counter-campaign which denounced the failings of the revolutionary regime in Iran, describing it as unIslamic. By the end of 1980, if not before, all the political signs in the Gulf region pointed to confrontation. Iran and Saudi Arabia, allies during the 1970s, became bitter opponents in the 1980s.

Exporting the revolution – a direct threat to Saudi Arabia

The confrontational aspects of the relationship between Iran and Saudi Arabia were not solely the result of the Iranian revolution. Rivalry for supremacy in the Gulf and the leadership of OPEC had already been a feature of the previous decade. They were, however, neutralized to some extent by the common interests of the two monarchies. The foreign policy initiated by the Islamic Republic of Iran had negated these common interests and made the old contradictions effective again. They were further intensified by a wave of new ideological and cultural contrasts.[15]

The Iranian revolution of 1979–80 is undoubtedly one of the major revolutions of modern times. All fundamental social and political change brought about through revolution, be it in 1789 in France or in 1917 in Russia, is characterized by universalist claims to a new set of norms for social, political and cultural behaviour with global validity.[16] It was Crane Brinton, in his classic work *The Anatomy of Revolution*, who made the now universal point that these 'great' revolutions 'as gospels, as forms of religion, . . . are all universalist in aspiration'.[17]

The stability of political structures in the immediate neighbourhood of Iran was a challenge to the revolutionaries. They wanted to bring about the same conditions there as in their own country. Their victory over their former rulers, previously considered invincible, was seen as a miracle which granted legitimization and supplied the incentive for successful action not only in the region but throughout the entire world. Since this miracle had only become manifest once previously accepted laws had been disregarded, the revolutionaries were now convinced that they had the legitimate right to operate outside the recognized norms of diplomacy and international law when pursuing their political aims. Depending on conditions, it became important to adapt the revolutionary struggle and fight for international civil liberties, socialism, or simply Islam as would best suit their aims.[18] 'For its part, postrevolutionary Iran saw its neighbours not as independent nation states but as parts of the Islamic world for which the 'Islamic republic' and 'Islamic revolution' had duties in mind which included what others would call 'intervention'.[19] Ayatollah Khomeini had unequivocally declared:

> The Iranian revolution is not exclusively that of Iran, because Islam does not belong to any particular people. Islam is revealed for mankind and the Muslims, not for Iran . . . An Islamic movement,

therefore, cannot limit itself to any particular country, not even to the Islamic countries; it is the continuation of the revolution by the prophets.[20]

Time and again Khomeini emphasized the responsibility of the Iranian revolution to spread Islam's message:

> The Islamic Republic intends to implement the ordinances of the Qur'an and those of the messenger of God in all countries. Iran is the starting point. It intends to demonstrate to all countries that Islam is based on equality, brotherhood and unity.[21]

By emphasizing the unity of all Muslims and making the umma the sole legitimate basis for Islamic politics, the Iranian leadership rejected the validity of any nationalist identity within Islam or even the validity of Muslim nation states whose identity is based on language, ethnicity or geography.[22] Muslims all over the world were to be awakened to the possibility of acting for their own benefit as interpreted by the Islamic Republic of Iran:

> Whereas the Muslim states should gather around this centre (the Islamic Republic) and incline toward Islam . . . they either do not pay attention or love of self . . . inhibits them from doing so . . . The Islamic Republic wishes that all Islamic countries, and their governments . . . would wake up from this benumbing dream.[23]

The independence of an individual Islamic state was an illusion; only a part of this 'benumbing dream'.

The struggle for the unity of the umma therefore became an important part of official Iranian policy as laid down in the constitution of the Islamic Republic:

> Based on the ordinances of the Qur'an, that 'Lo! that your community is a united one and I am your Lord, so worship me' (XX:92) the Islamic Republic of Iran is to base its overall policy on the coalition and unity of the Islamic nation. Furthermore it should exert continuous effort until political, economic and cultural unity is realized in the Islamic world.[24]

These sentiments were summarized in the concept of sudur-e enqelab, exporting the revolution, which became the overall credo of early post-revolutionary Iranian foreign policy.[25] It was Ayatollah Khomeini, once again, who was most outspoken in this regard:

> We should try hard to export our revolution to the world. We should set aside the thought that we do not export our revolution, because Islam does not regard various Islamic countries differently and is the supporter of all the oppressed people of the world. On the other hand, all the superpowers and all the powers have risen to destroy us. If we remain in an enclosed environment we shall definitely face defeat.[26]

Khomeini felt that the Islamic revolution was obliged to spread its ideas all over the world, to pave the way for an Islamic world order to be established at the end of time when the Mahdi, the Twelfth Imam, will appear. 'We will export our revolution to the four corners of the world because our revolution is Islamic. The struggle will be continued until there is everywhere the call: "There is no God but God, and Muhammad is his prophet". As long as people are being oppressed all over the world our struggle will be continued.'[27]

Khomeini repeated these ideas several times, directing them to different audiences, to ensure no misunderstanding, for instance telling a group of young Iranians about to travel abroad:

> Today we need to strengthen and export Islam everywhere. You need to export Islam to other places, and the same version of Islam which is currently in power in our country. Our way of exporting Islam is through the youth, who go to other countries where a large number of people come to see you and your achievements.[28]

However, the leader of the Iranian revolution did not assign this task only to young people but considered it the duty of every Iranian Muslim and of all Iranian institutions. Therefore it was not the exclusive responsibility of the Ministry of Foreign Affairs to pursue these political aims. In the early days of the revolution a so-called Liberation Movements Bureau was assigned to the Ministry to coordinate attempts to export the revolution. To increase its importance, the Bureau was soon put under the authority of the Supreme Command of the Pasdaran. The Pasdaran were created as a praetorian guard for the clerical regime and a counterbalance to the equivocal attitudes to the revolution amongst the regular forces. Fighting for the spread of Sharia rule throughout the world was, according to the constitution, one of their most important tasks.[29] Nevertheless, other individuals and organizations also continued their independent efforts to export the revolution by creating separate networks and structures.

In 1984, the Intelligence Ministry established yet another bureau from which to orchestrate Iran's religious activity in other countries.[30] Because Khomeini's version of the Islamic revolution did not recognize international laws and frontiers and emphasized the unity of the umma, he felt free to make use of existing links between different religious communities in the Muslim world, and to create new ones in order to establish a worldwide Islamic network with Iran at its centre. Revolutionary propaganda was therefore not only directed at the region immediately surrounding Iran, but also at communities in regions as far away as the Maghreb or even South East Asia, including Indonesia and the Philippines. Khomeini's policy also encompassed all possible means of enforcing revolutionary political ideology – arms, financial support, training, international congresses, radio programmes.[31] Nevertheless, even though Iran saw itself duty-bound to export the revolution and to support all peoples struggling for independence and freedom, Khomeini also reminded them that 'a right is something you have to fight for. The people must rise for themselves and destroy the rule of the superpowers in the world.'[32]

But it was not only radical idealism which drove the Iranian leadership to export the revolution. Pragmatic considerations had also led to the conclusion that a high degree of esteem for Iran within the Islamic world might safeguard the young revolutionary state which now felt exposed to a variety of internal and external challenges.

The more acutely the Iranian leadership felt the economic, political and military weaknesses of the Islamic Republic, the more it was compelled to conclude that successful export of the revolution would not be accomplished in one simple step or even within a short period of time. Furthermore, the reaction of the Muslims to whom the idea of exporting the revolution was addressed was not encouraging. This situation created further divisions in the Iranian leadership. As mentioned before, a purely nationalist or pan-Iranist approach under the slogan of 'Iran First' was seen as a remnant of the Shah's rule and therefore constituted political suicide, given the conditions of the Islamic revolution.

The first months of the revolution were undoubtedly dominated by a group of clerics and laymen who considered national borders simply the heritage of colonialism. In their opinion, the Islamic world, originally united, was broken up by the two aggressive elements in Western culture, nationalism and colonialism. This led to racial and national hatred between different Muslim nations and overshadowed Islamic cultural values. By espousing the powerful slogan 'Islam knows no borders', they could justify and legitimize their actions. Concentrating on the domestic development of the country alone would lead to the destruction of revolutionary values and the existing model of the Islamic revolution.

Therefore, continuous, fierce criticism of the values dominating the international system and the overthrowing of neighbouring regimes were their main objectives. They were ready to use military force, guerrilla warfare and espionage and to arm national liberation movements in order to destabilize unIslamic regimes. They would accept purely national development only as a step in the creation of revolutionary movements within the Islamic nations and as a threat to the international interests of the West.[33] But after initial enthusiasm had evaporated, a more moderate and pragmatic policy began to emerge. The export of the revolution was to be held in the balance between peaceful coexistence and opportunism. In other words, the Islamic Republic should inflict blows to hostile states if national interests required it and the situation allowed it; if not, it should continue to have peaceful relations with them.

Of course Ayatollah Khomeini and his followers could not openly promote this shift of emphasis in their policies. But they tried to downplay the threat contained in their public declamations to export the revolution without, however, disavowing it altogether. In late September 1982, Khomeini declared, 'by exportation of Islam we mean that Islam be spread everywhere. We have no intention of interfering militarily in any part of the world.'[34]

The Islamic Republic of Iran was to be an example for the Muslims of the world to follow. Its mere existence should convince other Muslims of their revolutionary responsibility and encourage them to follow suit and topple their respective dictatorial, pro-Western, unIslamic regimes. The revolution was to succeed internally first, thus preparing the ground for propagating its values and objectives internationally. The successful stabilization of the Islamic revolution in Iran would inevitably influence other suffering Muslims living in a world where everyone had access to advanced systems of telecommunication. 'When we say we want to export our revolution we mean we would like to export this spirituality and enthusiasm we see in Iran . . . we have no intention to attack anyone with swords or other arms . . .,'[35] Khomeini elaborated.

Once convinced of the greater value of this more sophisticated policy, Khomeini, for the time being, eliminated earlier, more aggressive overtones from the propaganda of the Islamic Republic. In 1981, he told a group of Iranian ambassadors and chargés d'affaires who had been recalled to Tehran for consultation:

> It does not take swords to export this ideology. The export of ideas by force is no export. We shall have exported Islam only when we have helped Islam and Islamic ethics grow in those countries. This is your responsibility and it is a task which you must fulfil. You should promote this idea by adopting a conduct conducive to the propagation of Islam and by publishing the necessary publications in your countries of assignment. This is a must. You must have publications. You must publish journals. Such journals should be promotive and their contents and pictures should be consistent with the Islamic Republic, so that by proper publicity campaigns you may pave the way for the spread of Islam in those areas.[36]

Other Islamic countries would thus gain the impression that living under threat of the export of the Iranian revolution meant books, journals, leaflets, radio and TV commentaries, conferences and mass rallies, but not tanks and missiles, not even guerrilla warfare.[37]

After the change in Khomeini's propaganda tactics, it was not surprising that other leading functionaries of the Islamic Republic followed suit. The President of the Republic, Hojjat al-Islam Ali Khamenei, whilst pointing out that 'the foundation and the idea of this revolution is not limited to our country and this nation',[38] also stated:

> Foreign Ministry officials are the apostles of the revolution. The nature of an official despatched abroad by a government demonstrates the nature of his government. If our diplomatic representative in all his dealings, including with people and government officials of the country to which he is despatched, adopts an Islamic approach, then he will be utilising the best method to demonstrate the role of the Islamic Republic of Iran.[39]

Later, when he had become the ruling Faqih, Khamenei announced at the Iranian Now Ruz in 1993 (21 March): 'The Islamic Revolution of Iran has taken place and was simultaneously exported throughout the world. The revolution was exported once, and that is the end of the story.'[40]

The Iranian Prime Minister during the 1980s, Mir-Husain Mussavi, announced in 1981:

> We have declared time and again that we have no intention of interfering in other countries' internal affairs, but what is shaking the Islamic world is a movement springing from this revolution among the Moslem masses of the world and, naturally, each people will shape their movement according to their own peculiar circumstances. They will force their governments to tread this path and, if not, naturally they will be confronted by the people's moves.[41]

Hojjat al-Islam Rafsanjani, Speaker of the Majlis and later President of the Republic, also pronounced on this issue. While agreeing with Khamenei in his declaration that 'from early on when the revolution succeeded we realised that a revolution is not a phenomenon which would stay limited within one border,'[42] he later specified: 'The phrase "exporting the revolution", if it is mentioned here, means that we introduce our revolution and (that) anyone who wishes to use our experience can do so. But interference and physically exporting (revolution) has never been our policy.'[43] There were even voices that legitimized the Iranian concept of exporting the revolution by pointing out the 'permanent Western approaches to export its value-system throughout the world'. The Iranian offensive was thus to be a simple countermeasure to Western pressure.[44]

But it may not have been mere pragmatism which led to this remarkable change in the policy of exporting the revolution. The 'reluctance to export the revolution by force of arms has deep roots in the Shia theory of war and peace, which holds that wars to spread Islam can only be waged by the Imams. And since the Shia world has been without an Imam since the Twelfth Imam was occluded, no expansionist wars can be waged.'[45]

Playing the Shia card

Although the revolutionary leadership in Tehran took every opportunity to ensure that its export of the revolution appeared an attempt to revitalize and reactivate Islam in general and thereby facilitate the expansion of the revolution beyond the national, cultural, geographical and denominational borders of Iran, it was unable to expunge the perceived stigma of Shiism. Since 1501, Iran has been the only country in the world where Shia Islam is the official state religion. The revolution of 1978–9 was fought under the leadership of a Shia clergy; the foundations of the Islamic Republic are based on the Shia confession. Despite numerous calls for Islamic unity, even Ayatollah Khomeini could not hide the fact that his vision of an Islamic state was based on Shia doctrine. It goes without saying that this must have had an impact on the concept of exporting the Islamic revolution.

Various scholars and politicians have tried to measure this impact. For example, Nikki R. Keddie came to the conclusion that:

> impact or influence, whether of ideas or of movements, is inherently unmeasurable. It is usually impossible to say whether a given individual, group, or movement which says it is influenced by another individual or movement would have experienced essential similar ideas and undertaken similar activities in the absence of the latter.[46]

But regarding the Iranian revolution she nevertheless stated:

> As a gross generalisation one may say that the Iranian revolution was, during its course and for many months after its victory, widely regarded as inspirational in the Muslim world, and more generally in the third world . . .[47]

This inspiration was clearly felt in the Sunni world. Many Sunni clerics, notables and even private individuals noticed that the revolutionary theories of Ayatollah Khomeini and of other leaders of the politicized Iranian clergy were influenced by the writings of famous Sunni fundamentalists such as Sayyid Qutb of Egypt and Mawlana Mawdudi of Pakistan. This also secured a certain sympathy and admiration for the Iranian revolution among Sunni Muslims. At first the unmistakably Shia arguments of Khomeini and his supporters, in addition to the nationalist sentiments which were broadcast and published, notwithstanding declared pan-Islamic beliefs embedded in the self-portrait of the revolutionary government, only slightly diminished their admiration.[48]

However, soon after the victory of the Iranian revolution, it became evident that the revolution would be most influential and would have the greatest chance of exporting its ideas and values among Shia Muslims. The Shia are an underprivileged and sometimes persecuted minority in almost every Arab country, and Khomeini's religious attraction was reinforced by his role as leader of a movement of the dispossessed.[49] But this appeal to the Shia did nothing to reassure the Saudi Arabian government. Although most of the population of Saudi Arabia belongs to the Wahhabi branch of Sunni Islam, there is a Shia minority of between 5 per cent and 10 per cent living in the eastern province of al-Hasa. Only the Persian Gulf separates the Saudi Shia from Iran. Yet this percentage would be negligible if the Shia were not concentrated in the heart of Saudi Arabia's oil industry, constituting between 40 per cent and 60 per cent of the workforce.[50] Most of them had been loyal workers of ARAMCO for decades, influenced less by nationalist or socialist ideas than by those of their Sunni environment.

But their loyalty was challenged when religious divisions were addressed, as happened after the Iranian revolution, and the Iranian leadership repeatedly called for people to rise up against any form of religious discrimination. Now the Saudi government's treatment of the Shia as second class citizens, frequently discriminated against and with a standard of living which was considerably lower than that of the Sunni population, took on another dimension. No Shia had ever occupied a position of real governmental influence, a cabinet post or its equivalent. It was an awareness of the increasing social, economic and political grievances of the Shia, resulting from widespread official and unofficial discrimination, that underpinned the Saudi fear of Iranian agitation. Probable Shia discontent represented a potentially mortal threat to the Saudi oil economy with its enormous revenues on which the whole Kingdom depended. From the Saudi perspective, the Shia challenge thus became the single most worrying socio-political problem facing the Kingdom during this period.[51]

And they were right to fear a worst-case scenario. Throughout the Kingdom, but especially in al-Hasa province, political discussions increased and intensified in the husainiyyas, the meeting places of the Shia. The discussions were fired by the daily Arabic broadcasts from Radio Tehran and from Radio Ahwaz designed primarily for Shia audiences on the other side of the Gulf.[52] By 1979 a so-called Organization of the Islamic Revolution for the Liberation of the Arabian Peninsula (Munazamat al-Thawra al-Islamiya li tahrir al-Jazira al-Arabiya) popularly called Al-Thawra al-Islamiya, 'the Islamic Revolution', began to operate in al-Hasa.[53]

In November the Saudi authorities had to face two crises. First, a group of some several hundred religious people, some of them allegedly Shia, seized the Great Mosque in Mecca attempting to force King Khalid to instigate fundamental change in his country. After a few days of seige, the insurrection was violently crushed by Saudi police and troops. Iran was quick to allege that American troops and advisers had helped in the operation.[54] But the Mecca incident galvanized the al-Hasa Shia. Nine days later, in defiance of the government's prohibition, the Shia clerics announced their determination to hold the processions commemorating the martyrdom of Imam Husain on Ashura, 28 November 1979. Thus some 90,000 Shia gathered in the town of Qatif on 28 November. They carried pictures of Ayatollah Khomeini and placards denouncing the House of Saud and America. They chanted anti-American slogans, and demanded that Saudi Arabia stop supplying the United States with oil and instead support the Islamic revolution in Iran. They also demanded a more equitable distribution of wealth and an end to discrimination. Others even demanded the establishment of an Islamic republic in al-Hasa.

When police attempted to disperse the large crowds, the Shia went on the rampage. The trouble spread from Qatif to Sayhat and other Shia settlements in the province. Even oil installations near Ras Tanura and Dhahran were sabotaged.[55] The riots lasted for three days and involved almost 200,000 Shia.[56] The government in Riyadh had to dispatch the National Guard to the region to restore control. These extreme Wahhabi Bedouin troops have no love for the Shia and are generally perceived by the Shia as being agents of Saudi repression. This mutual hatred brought an escalation in the fighting. In the end a total of 17 people, among them members of the National Guard, were killed, many more were wounded and hundreds arrested.[57]

But the situation could only temporarily be defused. More and more Iranian propaganda material flooded into al-Hasa calling for the Shia to continue denouncing the Saudi regime and demanding immediate reforms. Conditions remained volatile and in February 1980 riots again erupted in Qatif and other settlements in al-Hasa. The implications of these riots were also serious because the demonstrators demanded, '. . . that oil should remain in the ground since the revenues from its sale did not help alleviate the sufferings of the oil workers'.[58] Once again the Shia masses demanded the same legal status and the same living conditions as their Sunni compatriots and refused to continue working in the oil industry without adequate benefits.

The revolt was only suppressed by the use of substantial force. But unrest was again observed in al-Hasa in May 1981,[59] and these constant revolts forced the government in Riyadh to realize that it could not continue blatantly discriminating against the Shia. In the end the authorities decided to fulfil certain demands of the Shia population. King Khalid visited the province as early as November 1980 under the pretext of opening the Jubail naval base, but he made a special effort to meet Shia notables and listen to the grievances of the Shia community. He later ordered increased development spending in predominantly Shia areas.[60] One billion dollars were allocated for infrastructure, health and education projects in al-Hasa. All those incarcerated during the riots of November 1979 and February 1980 were pardoned and a general amnesty was proclaimed. The Ashura processions were legalized.

From 1980 to 1985 the eastern province experienced an intense pace of development, surpassing that of Najd and the Hijaz. Airfields, ports, hospitals, schools, roads and other facilities were constructed.[61] On the other hand, the government continued to mercilessly suppress any attempt at political emancipation by the Shia and generally regarded the behaviour of this section of the population with suspicion and anxiety. But the carrot-and-stick policy implemented in al-Hasa paid off in the end because the much feared large-scale, organized and well-armed revolution of the Saudi Arabian Shia did not materialize.

The Shia/Wahhabi dichotomy

Iranian efforts to initiate a change of power in Saudi Arabia by using the grievances of the local Shia had not been successful. But what about the Sunnis? Had not the Iranian revolution also set an example for Sunni groups wanting to seize power?[62] It should be made clear here that among the Sunnis of the Gulf region, and especially the Arabian Peninsula, there was little or no receptivity to any kind of Shia-inspired revolutionary movement.

> Whatever their political, social, or economic frustrations, the Sunni societies of the Gulf states are generally stable and do not look upon violence or revolution as a means of remedying their grievances.'[63]

This statement might not be completely valid for the 1990s, given the economic hardship experienced in the Gulf states, but at the end of the 1970s their rulers were still wealthy enough to simply buy off any dangerous social and political force incorporating as many individuals as possible into their regimes and suppressing those few left over.

Although these tactics provided a relative degree of stability, the Saudi Arabian government remained extremely wary of the continuous effort of the Iranian leadership to export the revolution. It was not at all certain whether Iranian assurances of not interfering militarily in other countries' affairs could be trusted completely. The Saudi Arabian government found itself in a situation in which 'the worst American legacy was that its Iranian arms transfer policy between 1972 and 1979 created an arsenal that could pose a security threat to other United States clients',[64] and in particular to Saudi Arabia itself. In light of the Iranian foreign policy creed, promulgated by Ayatollah Khomeini, of exporting the Islamic revolution, and also of the simultaneous weakening of American power in the Gulf after being expelled from Iran, the military inferiority of Saudi Arabia took on a much greater significance.

But even if Iran did not intend to wage a 'hot' war against its Arab neighbours, it was definitely attempting a 'cold' war by exporting the radical 'spirit' of its revolution. It is true that the Saudi Arabian government did not fear Wahhabi receptivity to Shia ideas. It was more upset about the fact that diplomatic rivalry had now shifted to the field of religion, an area it had previously regarded as its own monopoly.

Indeed, there are hardly any greater differences in Islam than those between Ja'fariya, or Twelver, Shiism, the state religion of Iran since 1501, and Wahhabism which gained virtually the same status in the centre of the Arabian Peninsula with the foundation of the first Saudi state in the mid-eighteenth century. But the contrast between the two forms of Islam did not lead to a permanent enmity.[65] Whilst the heritage of Arabian–Persian confrontation, discord in trade and economics, dynastic grudges and other matters had, for some time, characterized the relationship between Iran and Saudi Arabia, reflecting the specific character of post-revolutionary Iran, religion now became the most important tool in the struggle for hegemony in the Persian Gulf. The view of the Iranian leadership was that it had hit a 'bull's eye' with its decision to concentrate on religion.

Conflict in the field of Islam was a direct challenge to the legitimacy of the Al Saud stemming from the symbiotic relationship claimed for Wahhabism and Guardianship of the Holy places. Nobody could be allowed to surpass the Al Saud in matters of religion, and the claim of the Iranian revolutionaries that Arabs should acknowledge Iran's spiritual primacy as the 'Redeemer Nation',[66] that they were more committed to Islam than the Arabs and had a much more developed ability to interpret it, was an attack at the heart of the Al Saud's pretensions to power, more dangerous than Nasserist or Hashemite opposition earlier.

It should not be forgotten that Ayatollah Khomeini had several times clearly stated that Islam and monarchy were mutually exclusive and that monarchy is foreign to Islam, a deviation from its content and intention. For Khomeini the faith in Saudi Arabia was degenerate and he called it 'American Islam'.[67] This labelling was symptomatic of Khomeini's deep hatred of both superpowers, but especially of the United States. True Islamic states should sever all links with the superpowers, not in the sense of non-alignment, but simply rejecting the power of any external states: 'By definition they are oppressors, and any Gulf state with ties to one of them, must also be an oppressor and should therefore be eliminated.'[68] Saudi Arabia was one of the very few Islamic countries high up on his black list:

> Saudi Arabia is governed by the 'House of Saud', the family which has a great role in distortion of the Islamic spirit in Saudi society. Because of its self-seeking attitude on the one hand and its alleged 'crusade' against international communism and 'fear of Russian infiltration into the Persian Gulf area' on the other, the Saud monarchy has totally turned into an American satellite and Saudi Arabia has been rapidly becoming Americanized in every respect. Saudi riches such as oil and its domestic as well as foreign policy are employed to promote American interests.[69]

In 1985 Ayatollah Montazeri, for many years considered Khomeini's successor, asked rhetorically if the Wahhabis were true Muslims. In a series on Radio Tehran he declared:

> Wahhabism was originally established by mercenaries of foreigners whose main objective was to divert the Muslims, and to encourage them to fight each other . . . This sect is neither committed to Islam

nor to the Qur'an, it is rather interested in eliminating Islam and its history. Therefore Shi'ites as well as Sunnites are rejecting them.[70]

In 1987, the *New York Times* quoted Khomeini as follows: 'Mecca is now in the hands of a group of infidels who are grossly unaware of what they should do.'[71] The Iranian leadership tried to project an image of Wahhabism led by the Al Saud as an isolated sect, whilst the Iranian revolution represented authentic Islam.

Wahhabi clerics were, naturally, not excluded from this criticism. According to Iranian propaganda they were nothing more than puppets in the hands of the Al Saud. When Sheikh Abd al-Aziz ibn Baz, at that time the most prominent Wahhabi cleric, issued a fatwa in November 1981, rejecting the widespread tradition of celebrating the Prophet's birthday, calling it a 'blasphemous and heretic custom', Khomeini answered:

> this Mullah [Ibn Baz] is only a lackey of the Saudi Arabian court, eagerly trying to fulfil the wishes of the king . . . can it be blasphemy to respect Allah's prophet? . . . Ibn Baz is ignoring Islam in an extreme manner.[72]

But the Iranian leadership encountered significant obstacles when promoting its pan-Islamic approach. Two of the most important supranational Islamic organizations were situated in Saudi Arabia, the Organization of the Islamic Conference (OIC) and the Muslim World League (MWL). It was no accident, therefore, that the Iranian President Ali Khamenei denounced them as:

> reactionary tools of Western imperialism . . . lackeys getting orders from America.[73]

However this string of assertions, made without even a hint of a proof, was easily refuted by Saudi Arabian counter-propaganda.

No more subtle than their Iranian counterparts, the Saudi Arabian media labelled the Iranian leadership a 'corrupt bunch of thieves' which had created a 'slaughterhouse' in Iran and was now promoting a degenerate Islam. The 'Iranian butchers are a mentally distorted and ignorant gang, agents of Satan, who behave as if going nuts, like a fascist regime.'[74]

The tone, choice of words and general content of Saudi Arabian counter-propaganda betrayed the deep perplexity and sense of injury felt by the Al Saud regime. They were shaken by the constant assertion by the Iranian regime that the Saudi court could be compared with the Pahlavi monarchy. Iranian media repeatedly referred to the close alliance between the two monarchies during the preceding decade and their common alliance with the United States.

> The parallel drawn by Tehran between the Shah and the Saudi family heightened the anxiety, the more so as the similarities could not be denied: both royal regimes were conservative and pro-Western, ruling oil-rich Muslim countries caught in the middle of rapid modernisation and socio-economic transformation . . . the similarities were palpable enough to add their weight to the ongoing Saudi debate over the speed of modernisation.[75]

In general, it can be concluded that the distance between the official Islamic confessions of Iran and Saudi Arabia increased tension between them as propaganda claiming Islam to be the cornerstone of their respective statehoods intensified.

Utilizing the hajj

It is a matter of pride for the Al Saud to hold the guardianship of the shrines in Mecca and Medina. Taking responsibility for organizing the hajj endows them with prestige as well as legitimacy, not only in their own country, but throughout the Islamic world. Thus it was more or less inevitable that the escalating religious competition between revolutionary Iran and the Saudi Arabian Kingdom also affected the hajj, all the more so since it is one of the basic tenets of Islam.

Utilizing the hajj to export the revolution became an important part of the Islamic Republic's religious offensive. Claiming the legitimate right to extend its activities to other Muslim countries in order to propagate and defend Islam meant taking full advantage of the unique opportunity offered by the pilgrimage to Mecca and Medina. For the Iranian leadership the hajj was not primarily a traditional rite but a means of spreading its radical vision amongst millions of Muslims. Even if the Iranian revolutionaries had recognized international law and state borders, they still would have ignored them in the case of the hajj, arguing that it is one of the basic, common duties incumbent on all Muslims. For the radicals the hajj was more a matter of transgressing national sovereignty than a unique opportunity for Muslims to discuss their problems and to mobilize resources to fight their enemies.[76]

Ayatollah Khomeini and other Iranian spiritual leaders never kept their intentions to use the hajj as a vehicle for pan-Islamic agitation a secret and they regularly received Iranian pilgrims and instructed them in detail on the role expected of them.

For Iran the hajj thus became an act of immense political significance, whereas the Saudis preferred to view it as a common religious experience uniting all Muslims, not as an occasion for political confrontation.[77] To Ayatollah Khomeini and his followers a hajj where millions of Muslims simply came and prayed and then returned home was redundant. The reason for attending this sacred event was not just simply to acquire the title of Hajj. If the value of the hajj was purely personal then why did the Qur'an insist that the people gather from all over the world as one congregation at a given time?

> Muslims should talk about their affairs during hajj. They should familiarize themselves with the different communities of the Islamic nations. Hajj is the unique occasion wherein hundreds of thousands of Muslims from all races, linguistic backgrounds and countries come together. It is a huge Islamic conference in which all have come for the same objective. A Palestinian who has been expelled from his own homeland by the Zionists, an Afro-American Muslim who is fed up with the social discrimination imposed against him and others in the United States. An African Muslim whose wealth is being exploited by America. An Afghan Muslim whose land is occupied by Russians. An Egyptian Muslim whose pride and Islamic dignity has been sullied by the Camp David accord. All come to hajj to find a solution for their problems, Mecca and Madina are the focal points for Muslim unity.[78]

But Iranian intentions went further than this and included open denunciation of the enemies of Islam, above all the United States and Israel. Millions of Muslims were to be seen to articulate their opposition to the superpowers and to Western domination.[79]

These demonstrations, using the traditional form of *bara'at al-mushrekin* (liberation from infidels), were supposed to become an important part of the hajj.

> The ceremonies of bara'ah held during hajj are meant to express
> disgust with these powers . . . A duty that is made incumbent by
> hajj and its tawhidi rites upon every Muslim pilgrim is to express
> his bara'ah and disgust with all such things. This is the first step
> towards the realization of an Islamic will to negate these satanic
> phenomena and to establish the sovereignty of Islam and Tawhid
> over all Islamic societies.[80]

It was thought such rallies would bring about a fundamental change
in the character of the hajj. They would not only emphasize its overall
political significance, but would violate the neutrality of the host country.
How could the Saudi Arabian government convince its Western partners
that accusations shouted by millions of Muslims under its authority,
albeit temporarily, were not convergent with its own point of view?
The Saudi authorities therefore pronounced that attacking the 'enemies
of Islam' would be seen as a political gesture that did not belong at a
sacred event.[81] Sheikh Abd al-Aziz ibn Baz went so far as to issue a fatwa
stating that these Iranian rallies were heresy.[82]

The fatwa provoked a strong response from Ayatollah Khomeini:

> We hope that the Saudi government won't listen to the temptations
> of these clergies who have forgotten Allah and that they (the Saudi
> government) allow the Muslims, as it has promised, to freely parti-
> cipate in the hajj ceremonies and reject the infidels and polytheists.
> It (the Saudi government) should cooperate with them (the pilgrims)
> in this divine act, especially with the Iranian, Palestinian, Lebanese
> and Afghan pilgrims who have been aggressed upon by the infidels
> so that they, with one united voice, introduce the common enemy
> of all the oppressed to the world.[83]

The Iranian leadership must have been confident that such
statements would embarrass the Saudi Arabian government by exposing
the inherent conflict between their role as the protector of Mecca and
Medina and their secular interests, above all their close cooperation in
security matters with the United States. The Iranian statements were
also an attempt to disrupt the hajj in order to demonstrate that the Al
Saud were incompetent and unworthy protectors of the Holy shrines.[84]
The Saudi authorities saw the Iranian policy of 'boosting true Islam'
and behaving as if Iran was its sole defendant as a 'thin justification for
Iranian imperialism'.[85]

This particular strategy started to emerge as early as in 1979, when Iranian pilgrims demonstrated against the Saudi regime, seeking to influence other pilgrims, shouting their support for Ayatollah Khomeini and the Islamic revolution. These demonstrations were repeated in 1980 when thousands of Iranian pilgrims chanted the slogan: 'Allahu akbar va Khomeini rahbar (God is great and Khomeini is the leader)' and called for the overthrow of the Al Saud because of their deviation from the true Islamic path. The Saudi police found hundreds of leaflets and brochures containing, as officers called it, 'subversive Iranian propaganda which had nothing to do with the aims of the pilgrimage'.[86] The situation escalated further in 1981, when Iranian pilgrims organized yet more demonstrations, attacking the United States and Israel, calling for the unity of all Muslims and threatening a merciless revenge on the enemies of this unity. A number of skirmishes took place between Saudi police and Iranian pilgrims.

On 23 September, the Saudi authorities deported eighty Iranian pilgrims from Medina, accusing them of having violated the orders prohibiting political activity during the pilgrimage by distributing pictures of Khomeini and brochures containing Iranian propaganda. The next day, about twenty Iranian pilgrims were injured in a clash with security forces in Mecca when they and an accompanying television crew were not allowed to stay in the country.[87] On another occasion Saudi security units had to break into the Great Mosque, arresting many Iranians after dispersing demonstrators with the help of tear gas.[88] The Saudi government made official protests to Tehran about the behaviour of Iranian pilgrims but received only a sharp rejoinder from Khomeini who repeated that Islam makes no distinction between religion and politics, thereby making the pilgrimage as much a political activity as a religious one.[89]

The Iranian media started a new propaganda campaign, blaming the Saudi Arabian government for not cooperating with the Iranian pilgrims who, they said, embodied the new spirit of Islam.

When the world Muslims come to Saudi Arabia in order to perform the pilgrimage, from the outset they encounter the Saudi government's hypocrisy. They see that in the 'Motherland of Islam', the Islamic brotherhood and equality advocated by Islam is not everywhere manifest. Lack of Islamic characteristics in the Saudi government's treatment of the pilgrims as 'undesired foreigners' is indeed regretful. In the very Mosque of the Prophet in Madina, the pilgrims were very often harassed and beaten up by the Saudi security police . . ., only because they sympathised with the Islamic revolution . . . Despite the super powers' conspiracies to contain the Islamic revolution within the Iranian borders, the effects of the revolution over the Muslims the world over could be clearly felt in . . . hajj ceremonies. This could be seen in the form of demonstrations against the usurping Israeli regime and the two super powers and slogans in favour of the Islamic Revolution. Muslim pilgrims from different countries thus demonstrated their increasing awareness on both ideological and political matters, showing that for them there was no gap separating religion from politics.[90]

This conviction encouraged them to continue to use the hajj to spread the vision of Islamic revolution throughout the Islamic world and it was predictable that Iranian pilgrims would continue, and improve on, their work of Islamic propaganda in 1982. Indicating his strong commitment to their programme, Ayatollah Khomeini appointed Hojjat al-Islam Mohammad Musavi Kho'eniha, who had led the students invading the US Embassy in Tehran three years earlier, as his personal representative and coordinator of the Iranian pilgrims.

Once again Saudi forces clashed with large numbers of Iranian pilgrims who stuck revolutionary posters on walls, conducted marches confirming 'Islamic unity', during which portraits of Khomeini were displayed, and accused the Al Saud of collaborating with the United States and Israel. The clashes, during which the Saudi authorities used water cannon and tear gas, resulted in the arrest and expulsion of hundreds of Iranian pilgrims including Kho'eniha himself.[91]

Even after this experience the Saudi Arabian government was afraid of banning the Iranian pilgrims completely and instead limited their number for the hajj of 1983 to 100,000 and prevented an advance party coming from Iran to make special arrangements for them.[92] These steps, however, did not prevent Khomeini from appealing to that year's pilgrims

> to observe the orders of my representative, Hojjat ol-Eslam Kho'eniha, to consider all the Muslims as their brothers and (to) deal with them in a way which is appropriate for a concerned Muslim believer. It is hoped that the Saudi government will cooperate with the Iranian pilgrims who have always unmasked the oppressors who

invade and intervene in the Islamic countries. They, with co-operation and unity of expression, should condemn the aggressive infidels who invaded the limits of Islam so that this hajj . . . may be performed in such a manner which is acceptable to Allah and His Messenger.[93]

Despite the limit on the number of Iranian pilgrims the clashes and the disruption continued in both 1983 and 1984.

1985 was characterized by a temporary détente. In May the Saudi Arabian Foreign Minister, Saud al-Faisal, visited Tehran for discussions with his Iranian counterparts. At the end of the year the Iranian Foreign Minister, Ali Akbar Velayati, made a return visit to Riyadh. It seemed possible that the problem of the hajj could be resolved. Iran even removed Kho'eniha from the position of hajj coordinator as a friendly gesture towards the Saudis.[94] However the détente did not last. As early as 1986 Saudi Arabian security forces discovered huge amounts of arms in the baggage of Libyan and Iranian pilgrims.[95] The Ministry of Hajj and Awqaf in Riyadh later declared:

> The Iranian government during the pilgrimage season of 1986 brought into the Kingdom 95 cases in the bottoms of which C4-type explosives were concealed, in order to carry out terrorist acts with the aim of obstructing the pilgrimage. The Kingdom of Saudi Arabia dealt with that incident at the time with wisdom and far-sightedness so that the announcement of the news would not affect the pilgrims who had come to perform the pilgrimage and worship, and at the request of a number of heads of Islamic states who wished to contain the said incident.[96]

The tension between Iran and Saudi Arabia generated by the hajj reached its peak in July 1987. Khomeini's speeches during the preceding weeks had been very provocative. He urged the pilgrims once again to demonstrate and march 'with as much ceremony as possible' against the 'apostates of world arrogance headed by the criminal USA'.[97] This time the Iranian pilgrims not only carried portraits of Khomeini, leaflets and brochures, but it also became evident that their leaders at least were equipped with handguns. They demonstrated remarkable organizational skills in provoking clashes with different Saudi Arabian hajj organizers and security forces. They were also well aware that the capacity of the Saudi authorities to handle the hajj was stretched to the maximum given the numbers of people involved. In 1987 1.8 million Muslims participated in the hajj. In comparison, only 232,971 Muslims had participated in 1954.[98] However, it is unclear whether the demonstrators even intended or foresaw the outcome of their actions. About 402 people – 275 Iranians, 85 Saudis and 42 pilgrims of other nationalities – died on 31 July 1987 in Mecca after bloody collisions between pilgrims and the Saudi Arabian police; 649 people were injured.[99]

Tension, mutual encroachments, and disputes between the Iranian pilgrims and the institutions of the Saudi Arabian hosts had become endemic, but they had never before reached the magnitude of the summer of 1987. Nevertheless, the exact circumstances leading to the killings remain obscure. Both sides vehemently claimed to be in the right. The Iranians accused the Saudi government of ordering its police forces to open fire on the pilgrims. The local authorities in Mecca reproached the organizers of the Iranian pilgrims for having directed them straight towards the Great Mosque intent upon insurrection, giving the authorities no option but to fire on the crowd.[100] Iran welcomed its Shahia (martyred) pilgrims back as heroes. During demonstrations in several Iranian cities banners were shown with the slogan: 'Iranian pilgrims this year have gained the respect of the revolution through giving their blood and their lives.'[101]

But demonstrations alone were not enough. An angry crowd ransacked the Saudi Arabian embassy in Tehran in August. This organized 'people's furore' resulted in the burning of the embassy compound and in the death of one Saudi Arabian diplomat. Khomeini attacked the Saudi authorities for their 'brutal behaviour' and 'aggression in the House of God'. The Al Saud 'had forfeited the right, and indeed had demonstrated their inability, to rule over the holy places which belong to all Muslims'.[102] He declared Saudi Arabia Iran's number one enemy, even though Iran was in the midst of its war with Iraq. The Iranian leader also began referring to Saudi Arabia as the Hijaz, thus implying that the Al Saud did not have the legitimacy to rule in the birthplace of Islam.[103] The Speaker of the Majles (parliament), Hojjat al-Islam Rafsanjani, called for the Al Saud to be uprooted from the area:

> The martyrs' blood must be avenged by burning the roots of the Saudi rulers in the region. The revenge for [the spilling of Iranians'] sacred blood [in the Mecca riots] will be to divest the control of the holy shrines and holy mosques from the contaminated existence of

Wahhabis, these hooligans, these malignant people. The true revenge is to remove the colossal and precious wealth belonging to the Islamic world which lies under the soil of the Arabian Peninsula from the control of the criminals, the agents of colonialism. The Saudi rulers have chosen an evil path, and we will send them to hell.[104]

The following weeks were marked by the frequent exchange of similar threats by Iran and Saudi warnings against further such demonstrations during the hajj. During a meeting of Arab League Foreign Ministers in August 1987, the Saudi Arabian Foreign Minister, Saud al-Faisal lashed out, calling the Iranians terrorists and urging sanctions.[105] Leading media organs in Saudi Arabia revealed the 'secrets' of the Iranian hajj plan. They claimed that the Mecca riots were only the first step of a two-part plan to take power in Saudi Arabia. After seizing the Kaaba, a message from Khomeini would have been announced, followed by an attempt to incite a further uprising in al-Hasa. The supposed plan had been foiled thanks to a Saudi intelligence officer in Tehran.[106]

Other Saudi Arabian journalists maintained a less sensational approach. Mazher Hameed, a leading political analyst, wrote:

Those who consider the Iranian regime 'religious' must develop a tortuous logic to explain how the hajj, the holy pilgrimage, can be demeaned by political demonstrations. This is not extremism on behalf of religion; it is certainly not 'fundamentalism'; it is power politics without scruple. As in the use of masses of children to fight the war with Iraq, as in its resort to terrorism, the Iranian regime is extremist in the sense that it recognised no limits in acting to advance its own political interests.[107]

Fearing a repetition of events, Saudi Arabia broke off diplomatic relations with Iran on 26 April 1988, citing the attack on its embassy, Iranian raids on ships heading for or leaving Saudi Arabia, and Iranian involvement in terrorist actions, which in turn led Iran to boycott that year's pilgrimage. With the help of the OIC, the Saudi Arabian government also imposed a strict quota on the annual pilgrimage. Its representatives in the organization were successful in implementing a quota of 0.1 per cent of the population from each Muslim state.[108] Officially Riyadh declared that urgent repair and reconstruction work in the

Holy cities was overdue, and therefore the number of pilgrims had to be limited.[109] Thus only 45,000 Iranian pilgrims per year would be allowed to take part in the hajj, considerably less than the 150,000 which the Iranian authorities had calculated as a minimum. Saudi Arabia tried to sell this limited quota by stressing that it would still welcome the quota of Iranian pilgrims that the OIC had set, provided that the hajj was not disturbed.[110] However, these declarations influenced Ayatollah Khomeini's decision to prevent all Iranian pilgrims leaving for Saudi Arabia in 1988.

For Tehran the quota was a further piece of circumstantial evidence strengthening its belief that the OIC was dependent on Riyadh in its decision-making. The Iranian media sarcastically commented on every new proof it found displaying the inability of the organization to handle problems within the Islamic world, be it the Soviet invasion of Afghanistan, the Iraq–Iran war, the conflict in the Western Sahara or the civil war in Lebanon. These new attacks against the OIC could, however, only partially conceal the fact that Iran's success in establishing any alternative pan-Islamic organization was also limited.

The ceasefire signed on 20 August 1988 by Iran and Iraq ended the eight-year war between them. The end of the bitter fighting resulted, among other things, in a temporary strengthening of pragmatic elements in Tehran. When Saud al Faisal stated on 5 October that his government wanted a normalization of ties with Iran, and that King Fahd had regretted the absence of Iran at the OIC summit, Rafsanjani felt obliged to reply on 14 October saying that 'we feel there is no reason for us to quarrel with countries of the southern coast of the Persian Gulf – with any of them'.[111] Five days later, King Fahd ordered the Saudi media to stop attacking Iran. The 'problems with Iran are limited . . . and will be replaced with harmony, agreement and friendship'.[112] Both governments negotiated the many open questions of the hajj, Riyadh making it clear, however, that a resumption of relations was conditional on Iran's acceptance of the quota decision as well as confirmation that it would not use the pilgrimage for political ends. Rafsanjani nevertheless expressed his belief that diplomatic relations would be restored 'in the not too distant future'.[113] Yet both governments failed to solve the problem, despite the improved conditions in late 1988, adjourning it until 1989.

With the approach of the hajj of 1989, the quota dispute resurfaced. Saudi Arabia insisted on admitting only 45,000 Iranian pilgrims, whereas Iran made clear that it was not prepared to send less than 150,000. In the end Iran had to yield, if only to make the pilgrimage possible for Iranians at all. The hajj of 1989 was the scene of yet another disaster. On 10 July, two bomb explosions killed one pilgrim from Pakistan and injured another 16. Iran was quick to blame the Saudis, but shortly afterwards an organization called Generation of Arab Rage, located in Beirut, assumed responsibility for the bombings. Saudi Arabian security forces nevertheless arrested 16 Shia from Kuwait accusing them of having planned and carried out the attack, adding that they had obtained the explosives from Iranian agents. The Kuwaitis were executed in September 1989.

In the spring of 1990, it was time for another round of Iranian allegations. The new ruling Faqih, Ayatollah Khamenei, emphasized the following during a demonstration in Mashhad.

> As far as this revolution is concerned, God had perfected his proofs . . . One proof is the enmity of the evil people of the world towards this revolution. This is a yardstick. Wherever in the world you find a malignant individual or organization, someone who is evil, who perpetrates evil, who is the embodiment of the devil, who is the source of evil and corruption, whether in the East or in the West, whether among the developed countries of the world or whether among the under-developed countries, whether among the politicians or men of learning, writers and such like – wherever you find such an individual or organization you will see that they are against this revolution with their entire being . . . There are certain countries belonging to this group where the running of the affairs . . . is carried out without the slightest involvement of the people and their votes – governments with personal dictatorships, which have no parliaments and no elections, where the people have no representatives in the legislature, where they do not have a President that they elect. One person or one family has absolute rule over those countries, over the peoples of those countries, the wealth of those countries, the oil of these countries, and they do to the people of those countries whatever they wish, including massacre, suppression, imprisonment, torture and other forms of insults and calumnies against their nations.[114]

This was an obvious reference to Saudi Arabia but Khamenei ironically elaborated on it.

The Iranian government did not just repeat its general criticisms of Saudi Arabia but also frequently criticized the Saudi attitude to politicizing the hajj. Radio Tehran, for example, stated:

The Saudi government has once again blocked the path to the House of God for Iranian pilgrims even though the Islamic Republic of Iran spared no efforts to co-operate and show its goodwill. The Saudi regime is seeking to neutralise the political aspect of the hajj and prevent the airing of problems facing Muslims at this mammoth Islamic congress. No one, however, has the right to prevent Muslims from gathering for the political-ideological congress of the hajj and from performing their divine obligations . . . The political aspect of the political-ideological hajj obligation is diametrically opposed to the objectives of the colonialists and powers of oppression which seek to separate religion from politics, although the two are inherently indivisible. According to the late Imam of the Islamic umma (Khomeini), it is impossible for pilgrims to perform the hajj and not demonstrate against the powers of world arrogance. The disavowal of the pagans is one of their political duties, without which the hajj would be incomplete. By obstructing Iranian pilgrims from travelling to the House of God and preventing Muslims from expressing their beliefs and disavowing the pagans, the Saudi regime is not only ignoring the interests of the Muslims, but it has also pitched itself against all Muslims of the world. The Saudi regime's obstructionism of the past few years . . . confirm(s) that the Saudi authorities are not competent to administer the two holy mosques . . . Will the Muslims allow a regime which is completely subservient to the United States and indirectly subservient to international Zionism to rule over the two holy mosques? It is for this reason that now, more than ever before, the real nature of the Saudi regime has become the focus of attention for world Muslims. It is clear that the Islamic umma considers world oppression and international Zionism its real enemies and believes that they have planted their surrogates to rule over the Islamic world.[115]

The Saudi Arabian government reacted quickly and decisively to this new round of Iranian accusations. The Ministry of Hajj and Awqaf declared on 15 April 1990 that Saudi Arabia

has renewed its categorical rejection of the method of one-upmanship, bargaining and pressures being practised by the Tehran government in attempts which reaffirm the latter's place outside Islamic unanimity and its avoidance of a commitment to Islamic decisions on the pretext of false accusations being levelled by Iranian officials whenever the pilgrimage season approaches . . . Saudi Arabia, while renewing its adherence and commitment to the resolution of the 17th conference of the foreign ministers of the OIC . . . regarding the fixing of a specific proportion of pilgrims which is calculated as being the quotient of the population of a state over the number of Muslims in the world, found a total response and commitment to the resolution from all Islamic states except Iran, which continues to allow itself to break and violate this resolution for reasons which have become known and have been exposed to the Islamic world and its people.[116]

The statement further recalled the declarations of the Kingdom regarding Iranian practices manifested 'in the flagrant defiance of the feelings of Muslims'.[117] A few days later the Minister, Abd al-Wahhab Abd al-Wasi, added:

> The pilgrimage of the Iranians was suspended after the failure of indirect negotiations between the Kingdom of Saudi Arabia and Iran regarding an increase in the quota of Iranian pilgrims this year . . . The Iranians had insisted on the adoption of such methods as staging demagogic demonstrations, raising atheistic slogans, frightening the pilgrims and disrupting worship in the holy ritual sites. Such terrorist acts occurred in the recent years and the entire world saw all of them by satellite.[118]

The hajj of the following year was even more disastrous. On 3 July 1990 the Saudi Interior Minister, Prince Nayif, announced in a televised broadcast that about 1,426 pilgrims had died in the Mina tunnel in Mecca on 2 July when a crowd with an estimated total of more than 50,000 filled the tunnel, exceeding its capacity severalfold. A rush of pilgrims to the exit led to unbearable pressure, and the crowd panicked, with fatal results.[119] Iran took this event as a further opportunity to criticize Saudi Arabia. Radio Tehran commented:

> Many warn that the threat of similar incidents in the future exists because during the past years the Saudi regime's efforts to ensure the hajj's political security have been . . . generally geared towards the prevention of political activities such as (marches for) disavowal (of pagans) and not towards protecting the pilgrims from life-threatening situations.[120]

According to Tehran the inability of the Saudi authorities to organize the hajj properly was once again evident.[121] The Iranian press went even further. *Jumhuriye Islami* connected the incident to the general feelings of many pilgrims that they were not safe in Saudi Arabia: 'If the pilgrims had had confidence in the Saudi regime and its ability to administer the affairs of the holy shrines, they would not have been in such a hurry to leave the country.'[122]

One of the most notorious hardliners in the Islamic Republic's leadership, the former Interior Minister, Mohtashemi, declared that the tunnel disaster was part of a Western plan aimed at containing the traditional pilgrimage:

> The Saudi regime, whose leaders are themselves of Jewish origin, must counter the pilgrims ideologically and on security matters, to threaten them into giving up the pilgrimage . . . the Saudi government was charged by the West, namely the United States, to make the pilgrimage pass into disuse or short of that, make it controllable.[123]

Interestingly enough, the English version of *Kayhan*, usually geared to presenting an idealized image of the Islamic Republic to its international readership, repeated Mohtashemi's main ideas in an editorial entitled 'Joint Washington–Riyadh Conspiracy'.

The daily paper referred to the quota system as an American scheme and criticized the policy which barred Muslim youth from entering Saudi Arabia in order to allow the United States and Saudi Arabia to implement their conspiracies with greater ease. The Saudi quota was thus:

> in compliance with this plot and following direct orders from the US . . . there is a strong probability that the US wants to render the safe house of God insecure and ultimately make it a desolate place.[124]

These versions of the incident were frequently repeated by the Iranian leadership. Vice-President Mohajerani accused the Saudi government of having intentionally killed hundreds of pilgrims. As evidence he mentioned the 'contradictory statements made by the Saudi Interior Ministry officials, and most important of all, the haste and confusion of the Saudi King to hold the pilgrims themselves responsible for the catastrophe,' whereas he believed that:

> if the entrance to the tunnel had been open, and the exit had not been blocked, nothing would have happened . . . In any case

the fate of Mecca and Madina should not be linked to the political sovereignty of a government, because governments come and go, but Mecca, Madina and hajj remain forever. Today, world Muslims should decide about administration of Mecca and Madina, and supervise the hajj ceremony.[125]

A further escalation of the dispute was prevented only by the Iraqi invasion of Kuwait on 2 August 1990 which dramatically changed political alignments in the region. The hajj issue became unimportant. On 26 March 1991 diplomatic relations between Iran and Saudi Arabia were restored. After the reopening of the Iranian embassy in Riyadh on 1 April, the Saudi government allowed 110,000 Iranians to participate in the hajj that year, plus a further 5,000 relatives of those pilgrims who had died in the notorious hajj of 1987. The number was increased in 1993 to 115,000.[126]

NOTES

1 S. Chubin, 'Iran and its Neighbours: The Impact of the Gulf War', *Conflict Studies*, 10:204 (1987), p. 1.
2 S. Bakhash, *The Politics of Oil and Revolution in Iran* (Washington DC: Brookings Institution, 1982), p. 17.
3 'The Revolutionary Message and Historical Religious Decree (fatwa) of Imam Khomeini, September 20, 1979' in *Selected Messages and Speeches of Imam Khomeini* (Tehran: Ministry of Information and Islamic Guidance, 1980), pp. 37–8.
4 Bakhash, *The Politics*, p. 17.
5 S.M. Badeeb, *Saudi–Iranian Relations 1932–1982* (London: Echoes, 1993), p. 91.
6 *Al-Safir*, Beirut, 12 February 1980.
7 *Message of Revolution*, Journal of the Islamic Revolutionary Guards Corps, Tehran, 2:1 (1981), p. 46.
8 M.A. Heller, *The Iran–Iraq War: Implications for Third Parties*, The Center for International Affairs Papers, no. 23 (Cambridge MA: Harvard University Press, 1984), p. 13.
9 W. Ende, 'Die iranische Revolution: Ursachen, Intentionen und Auswirkungen auf die Arabische Halbinsel' in F. Scholz (ed.), *Die Golfstaaten: Wirtschaftsmacht im Krisenherd* (Braunschweig, Westermann-Verlag, 1985), p. 152.
10 G. Nonneman, 'Iraqi–GCC Relations: Roots of Change and Future Prospects' in C. Davies (ed.), *After the War. Iran, Iraq and the Arab Gulf* (Chichester: Carden Publications, 1990), p. 32.

11 *Saudi Arabia News Agency*, Riyadh, 2 April 1979, *Gulf News Agency*, Riyadh, 21 April 1979; 25 April 1979; *al-Hawadith*, Beirut, 6 June 1979.

12 *Al-Hawadith*, Beirut, 11 January 1980.

13 M. Khadduri, *The Gulf War: The Origins and Implications of the Iraq–Iran Conflict* (Oxford: Oxford University Press, 1988), p. 124.

14 *Bamdad*, Tehran, 16 July 1979, 3 September 1979; *Ettela'at*, Tehran, 18 September 1979.

15 H. Amirahmadi and N. Entessar, 'Iranian–Arab Relations in Transition' in H. Amirahmadi and N. Entessar (eds.), *Iran and the Arab World* (Basingstoke: Macmillan, 1993), p. 7.

16 B. Baktiari, 'Revolutionary Iran's Persian Gulf Policy: The Quest for Regional Supremacy' in ibid., p. 72.

17 C. Brinton, *The Anatomy of Revolution* (New York: Vintage Books, 1965), p. 196.

18 G. Sick, 'Iran: The Adolescent Revolution', *Journal of International Affairs*, 49:1 (1995), pp. 146–7.

19 S. Chubin, 'Iran and the Persian Gulf States' in D. Menashri (ed.), *The Iranian Revolution and the Muslim World* (Boulder: Westview Press, 1990), p. 74.

20 *Ettela'at*, Tehran, 3 November 1979.

21 Quoted in: F. Rajaee, *Islamic Values and World View. Khomeyni on Man, the State and International Politics* (Lanham, New York and London: University Press of America, 1983), p. 83.

22 S.K. Anderson, *The Impact of Islamic Fundamentalist Politics within the Islamic Republic of Iran on Iranian State Sponsorship of Transnational Terrorism* (Ann Arbor: University Press, 1994), p. 152.

23 Ayatollah Khomeini in *Kayhan*, Tehran, 26 July 1982.

24 *Constitution of the Islamic Republic of Iran* (Tehran: Ministry of Information and Islamic Guidance, 1979), Principle 11.

25 W.G. Millward, 'The Principles of Foreign Policy and the Vision of World Order expounded by Imam Khomeini and the Islamic Republic of Iran' in N.R. Keddie and E. Hooglund (eds.), *The Iranian Revolution and the Islamic Republic* (Syracuse Ill, Syracuse University Press, 1986), pp. 189–204.

26 *Foreign Broadcast Information Service (FBIS), Daily Report, Middle East and Africa*, 24 March 1980, vol. v, no. 058, supplement 070.

27 *Rahnemudhaye Imam* (Tehran, Vezarat-e Ettela'at va Ershad-e Islami, 1979), p. 28.

28 *FBIS, Daily Report, South Asia*, 9 March 1982, vol. VIII, no. 046.

29 G. Sick, 'Iran: The Adolescent Revolution', *Journal of International Affairs*, 49:1 (1995), p. 148.

30 J. Calabrese, *Revolutionary Horizons: Regional Foreign Policy in Post-Khomeini Iran* (New York: St. Martin's Press, 1994), p. 144.

31 F. Halliday, 'The Politics of Islamic Fundamentalism: Iran, Tunisia and the Challenge to the Secular State' in A.S. Ahmed and H. Donnan (eds.), *Islam, Globalization and Postmodernity* (London and New York: Routledge, 1994), p. 101.

32 *Bayanat-e Imam Komeini be monasabat yekom salgerd-e enqelab* (Tehran, Sazeman-e Ponzdahom-e Khordad, 1982), p. 5.

33 *Echo of Islam*, Tehran, 142/143 (1996), p. 42.

34 *Tehran Times*, Tehran, 30 September 1982.

35 Quoted in F. Rajaee, 'Iranian Ideology and Worldview: The Cultural Export of Revolution' in J.L. Esposito (ed.), *The Iranian Revolution: Its Global Impact* (Miami: Florida International University Press, 1990), p. 68.

36 *Soroush*, Tehran, March 1981, pp. 4–5.

37 M. Muhajeri, *Islamic Revolution. Future Path of the Nations* (Tehran: Jihad Sazandegih, 1983), p. 175.

38 A. Khamenei, *Chahar Sal ba Mardom* (Tehran, Sazeman-e Tablighat-e Islami, 1985), p. 354.

39 *FBIS, Daily Report, South Asia*, 11 March 1982, vol. viii, no. 048.

40 *Kayhan Hava'i*, Tehran, 4 April 1993.

41 *Tehran Journal*, Tehran, 10 October 1981.

42 *Peyam-e Shahedan*, Mashhad, n.d., p. 8.

43 *BBC SWB*, 3–4 February 1993.

44 I. Sanjar, *Nofuz-e Amrika dar Iran: Bar-rasi-ye siyasat-e khariji-ye Amrika va ravabet-e ba Iran* (Tehran, Sazeman-e Tablighat-e Islami, 1989), pp. 33–5, 59.

45 S.T. Hunter, *Iran and the World: Continuity in a Revolutionary Decade* (Bloomington: Indiana University Press, 1990), p. 41.

46 N.R. Keddie, *Iran and the Muslim World: Resistance and Revolution* (Basingstoke: Macmillan, 1995), p. 118.

47 Ibid.

48 W. Ende, 'Die iranische Revolution: Ursachen, Intentionen und Auswirkungen auf die Arabische Halbinsel' in F. Scholz (ed.), *Die Golfstaaten: Wirtschaftsmacht im Krisenherd* (Braunschweig, Westermann-Verlag, 1985), p. 152.

49 M.A. Heller, *The Iran–Iraq War: Implications for Third Parties,* The Center for International Affairs Papers, no. 23 (Cambridge MA: Harvard University Press, 1984), p. 14.

50 H. al-Hassan, *al-Shi'a fi'l-mamlaka al-arabiya al-Saudiya* (n.l., Mu'assasat al-baqi' li-ahya al-turath, 1993), vol. 2 (1938–1991), pp. 285–374.

51 R.K. Ramazani, *Revolutionary Iran: Challenge and Response in the Middle East* (Baltimore: Johns Hopkins University Press, 1986), p. 39.

52 D.E. Long, 'The Impact of the Iranian Revolution on the Arabian Peninsula and the Gulf States' in J.L. Esposito (ed.), *The Iranian Revolution: Its Global Impact* (Miami: Florida International University Press, 1990), p. 105.

53 M. Abir, *Saudi Arabia: Government, Society and the Gulf Crisis* (London: New York: Routledge, 1993), p. 77.

54 H. Amirahmadi, 'Iranian–Saudi Arabian Relations since the Revolution' in H. Amirahmadi and N. Entessar (eds.), *Iran and the Arab World* (Basingstoke: Macmillan, 1993), p. 147–8.

55 M. Abir, *Saudi Arabia*, p. 85.

56 M. Moaddel, *Class, Politics, and Ideology in the Iranian Revolution* (New York: Columbia University Press, 1993), p. 220.

57 M. Abir, *Saudi Arabia*, p. 85.

58 S. Holly, *Conflict in the Gulf: Economic and Maritime Implications of the Iran–Iraq War* (Colchester, 1988), p. 15.

59 *La Dernière Heure*, Brussels, 28 July 1981.

60 D.E. Long, 'The Impact of the Iranian Revolution on the Arabian Peninsula and the Gulf States' in J.L. Esposito (ed.), *The Iranian Revolution: Its Global Impact* (Miami, Florida International University Press, 1990), p. 107.

61 M. Abir, *Saudi Arabia,* pp. 87, 108.
62 A. Bligh, 'The Interplay between Opposition Activity in Saudi Arabia and Recent Trends in the Arab World' in R.W. Stookey (ed.), *The Arabian Peninsula* (Stanford, Stanford University Press, 1984), p. 75.
63 D.E. Long, The Impact, p. 105.
64 K. Krause, 'Constructing Regional Security Regimes and the Control of Arms Transfers', *International Journal,* 45:2 (1990), p. 405.
65 W.T. Tow, *Subregional Security Cooperation in the Third World* (Boulder: Westview Press, 1990), p. 14.
66 S. Holly, *Conflict,* p. 12.
67 *al-Shaheed,* Tehran, 25 November 1981.
68 S. Holly, *Conflict,* p. 12.
69 *Message of Revolution,* Journal of the Islamic Revolutionary Guards Corps, Tehran, 2:6 (1981), pp. 35–6.
70 *Radio Tehran,* 3 December 1985.
71 *New York Times,* New York, 9 August 1987.
72 *Ahbar al-'alam al-islami,* Tehran, 23 November 1981.
73 *Tehran Times,* Tehran, 7 May 1984.
74 *Radio al-Riyadh,* 19/20 November 1981.
75 J. Goldberg, 'Saudi Arabia and the Iranian Revolution' in D. Menashri (ed.), *The Iranian,* p. 161.
76 S.T. Hunter, *Iran,* p. 118.
77 Ibid.
78 *Voice of World's Islamic Movements* (Manchester, Islamic Republic of Iran's Consulate, 1984), p. 2.
79 A. Khamenei, *al-wahda al-islamiya: darura wa-hadaf. Min khutab Ayatullah Khamenei qa'id al-thawra fi 'usbu al-wahda al-islamiya li 'am 1410* (1989) (Tehran: Vezarat-e Ettela'at va Ershad-e Islami, 1989), pp. 21–30.
80 *Peyam-e rahbar-e mo'azem-e Enqelab va Valiye Amr Moslimin-e Jahan Hedrat Ayatollah Khamenei . . . (Message of Ayatollah Khamenei to Iranian Pilgrims, 18 May, 1993)* (Tehran: Vezarat-e Ettela'at va Ershad-e Islami, 1993), pp. 7–8.
81 *The Economist Intelligence Unit (EIU), Country Report Saudi Arabia,* 2nd quarter 1995, p. 11.
82 Ibid., 3rd quarter 1996, p. 10.
83 'Message of Ayatollah Khomeini to the pilgrims, 3 September 1983', *Message of Revolution,* Journal of the Islamic Revolutionary Guards Corps, Tehran, 4:21 (1983), p. 8.
84 D.E. Long, The Impact, p. 109.
85 S. Chubin, 'Iran and its Neighbours: The Impact of the Gulf War', *Conflict Studies,* 10:204 (1987), p. 2.
86 J. Goldberg, Saudi Arabia, p. 159.
87 M. Khadduri, *The Gulf War,* p. 128.
88 *Daily Telegraph,* London, 25 September 1981.
89 G. Linabury, 'Ayatollah Khomeini's Islamic legacy' in H. Amirahmadi and N. Entessar (eds.), *Reconstruction and Regional Diplomacy in the Persian Gulf* (London, New York: Routledge, 1992), p. 37.
90 *Message of Revolution,* Journal of the Islamic Revolutionary Guards Corps, Tehran, 2:6 (1981), p. 36.

91 J. Goldberg, Saudi Arabia, p. 159.
92 H. Gurdon, *Iran – the Continuing Struggle for Power* (Outwell, MENAS, 1984), p. 38.
93 'Message of Ayatollah Khomeini to the pilgrims, 3 September 1983', *Message of Revolution,* Journal of the Islamic Revolutionary Guards Corps, Tehran, 4:21 (1983), p. 8.
94 S.T. Hunter, *Iran,* p. 118.
95 L. Graz, 'The GCC as a Model? Sets and Subsets in the Arab Equation' in C. Davies (ed.), *After the War. Iran, Iraq and the Arab Gulf* (Chichester, Carden Publications, 1990), p. 8.
96 *BBC SWB*, ME/0740, 17 April 1990.
97 S. Holly, *Conflict*, pp. 15–16.
98 S.M. Badeeb, *Saudi–Iranian Relations 1932–1982* (London, Echoes, 1993), p. 83.
99 N.I. Rashid and E.I. Shaheen, *Saudi Arabia and the Gulf War* (Joplin MO, International Institute of Technology, 1992), p. 130; M. Khadduri, *The Gulf War*, p. 129.
100 P. Robins, *The Future of the Gulf: Politics and Oil in the 1990s* (Aldershot: Ashgate, 1989), p. 20.
101 S. Holly, *Conflict*, p. 16.
102 J. Goldberg, Saudi Arabia, p. 160.
103 H. Amirahmadi, Iranian–Saudi-Arabian Relations, p. 148.
104 Quoted in M. Mohaddessin, *Islamic Fundamentalism: The New Global Threat* (Washington DC: Seven Locks Press, 1993), pp. 94–5.
105 G. Nonneman, 'Iraqi–GCC Relations: Roots of Change and Future Prospects' in C. Davies (ed.), *After the War*, p. 42.
106 S. Holly, *Conflict*, p. 16.
107 M.A. Hameed, 'After Mecca: Saudi Arabia Is More Stable than It Looks', *Washington Post*, Washington DC, 9 August 1987. Quoted in M. Khadduri, *The Gulf War*, p. 129.
108 *Yearbook Iran 1989/90* (Bonn: Edition Ausland, 1990), p. 4–15.
109 G. Nonneman, Iraqi–GCC Relations, p. 47.
110 G. Nonneman, 'The GCC and the Islamic Republic: Toward a Restoration of the Pattern' in A. Ehteshami, and M. Varasteh (eds.), *Iran and the International Community* (London, New York: Routledge, 1991), p. 120.
111 Ibid., p. 119.
112 Ibid.
113 Ibid.
114 *BBC SWB*, ME/0722, 26 March 1990.
115 Ibid., ME/0763, 14 May 1990.
116 Ibid., ME/0740, 17 April 1990.
117 Ibid.
118 Ibid., ME/0759, 9 May 1990.
119 Ibid., ME/0808, 7 July 1990.
120 Ibid., ME/0809, 6 July 1990.
121 D.C. Barr, *Rafsanjani's Iran* (London: Gulf Centre for Strategic Studies, 1990), 3 vols., vol. 1, p. 104.
122 *Jumhuriye Islami*, Tehran, 8 July 1990.

123 *Kayhan*, Tehran, 8 July 1990.
124 *Kayhan International*, Tehran, 8 July 1990.
125 *Ettela'at*, Tehran, 14 July 1990.
126 G. Kemp, *Forever Enemies? American Policy & the Islamic Republic of Iran* (Washington DC: Carnegie Endowment for International Peace, 1994), p. 47.

2

Saudi Arabia in the
First Gulf War, 1980–1988

On 22 September 1980, at 2 p.m. local time, the Iraqi President Saddam Husain invaded neighbouring Iran, starting the First Gulf War. Initially, air raids were launched against key military and civilian targets in Tehran, Tabriz, Kermanshah, Ahvaz, Hamadan and Dezful, followed by further air attacks against the oil refinery in Abadan and the oil terminal at Kharq. Immediately after the air raids, nine Iraqi divisions crossed the Iranian border. The objectives of the Iraqi dictator can be summarized as follows:

- Economic weakening of Iran by destroying its oil industry and increasing of Iraq's own resources by occupying the province of Khuzestan, the centre of the Iranian oil production;
- Stabilization of personal power and liquidation of domestic opponents, be they religiously or politically motivated;
- Creating preconditions for the toppling of the Iranian revolutionary leadership and its replacement by a puppet regime. As early as the beginning of 1979 the Iraqi Foreign Minister, Tariq Aziz, declared that the government of Shapour Bakhtiar was the only legitimate government of Iran;
- Permanent weakening of Iran's military power;
- Iraqi hegemony in the Gulf region, and the upper hand in the power struggle with the Syrian branch of the Baath party for leadership in 'uniting the Arab homeland'.[1]

Officially Radio Baghdad announced four objectives on 22 September 1980:

1. Recognition of Iraqi sovereignty in its border region with Iran, in effect the return of the enclaves of Saif Saad and Zain al-Qaws to its control;

2. Recognition of sovereignty and legitimate rights of Iraq over the Shatt al-Arab, thus annulling of the Algiers Accord of 1975;
3. Return of the Gulf islands of Abu Musa and Greater and Lesser Tumb 'to the Arabs';
4. Renunciation by Iran of interference in the domestic affairs of Iraq and other Arab countries.[2]

It remains uncertain whether the Iraqi President had informed any foreign government in advance of his plans, but there are strong indications that he did so when visiting Saudi Arabia in the early August of 1980, bearing in mind that Iraq and Saudi Arabia had signed a security cooperation agreement in February 1979, followed by further security meetings during the first half of that year.[3] However, this alliance must have seemed strange to uninformed observers.

Since the second takeover of power by the Baath party in Baghdad in 1968 relations between Iraq and Saudi Arabia had not been cordial. The Al Saud were afraid of the pan-Arab, nationalist and proto-socialist approach of the Baath leadership, which was trying to gain support in the Arabian Peninsula. Verbal attacks by Baghdad against the Gulf monarchies and military and logistical assistance for underground groups in the Gulf region during the first half of the 1970s had not been forgotten. In fact, there had even been an alliance between Saudi Arabia and the Shah against Iraqi Baath ambitions during the 1970s. When Saddam Husain assumed the presidency in 1979 he tried to lead Iraq out of its regional isolation. Therefore he adopted new tactics, softening his tone towards the Gulf monarchies, weakening his ties with the Soviet Union and COMECON and even prosecuting Iraqi communists. But these measures were not sufficient to destroy suspicion amongst the monarchies of the Gulf and in the end only the Iranian revolution brought a change of attitude. Now that the Iranian policy of exporting the revolution seemed far more dangerous than the pan-Arab manoeuvres of Iraq, which had been successfully contained during the past decade, making use of the Iraqi war machine to minimize the chances of Iran exporting the revolution appeared an attractive option.

According to Radio Baghdad, King Khalid took the opportunity to pledge support to Iraq during a telephone conversation with Saddam Husain on 25 September 1980.[4] Radio Riyadh confirmed the phone call, but hastened to announce that King Khalid had only expressed his concern about the outbreak of war between two of his neighbours. Even during the very first days of the war Saudi Arabia tried to avoid being labelled an official ally of Iraq, fearing Iranian retaliation. There was no official statement that the government in Riyadh was formally siding with Iraq and the Saudi Arabian media was full of declarations that the war should be brought to an end through negotiation. But unofficially the Saudi government could not hide its enthusiasm over the benefits a quick Iraqi victory would have for Saudi Arabia. A change in the Iranian regime would be warmly welcomed.

Taking into consideration the reservations that Saudi Arabia had concerning the Iranian revolution, such a reaction was not surprising. According to J.D. Anthony, the reaction of Saudi Arabia to the Iran–Iraq war differed from those of other Gulf states.

> The Riyadh regime has been and remains profoundly disturbed by the Sunni–Shi'a character of the war. Not only has Saudi Arabia usually aligned itself with the traditionalist side of the Sunni Muslim camp, but the fundamentalist foundation of its own regime is the repository of a very different ideology, although in the eyes of many, it is a no less radical interpretation of Islam. Thus, on the sectarian level, Saudi Arabia is especially concerned about the potential of the Tehran government to undermine the Kingdom's regional role.[5]

Testing the limits of formal neutrality, Riyadh granted permission for Iraqi aircraft to be stationed on Saudi airbases, decreasing their vulnerability to attack by the Iranian air force, which was still intact, and allowing them to attack Iranian targets from even more directions.[6] But apart from sheltering Iraqi aircraft, support remained limited during the first week of fighting. More did not appear necessary, and nobody within the Saudi leadership was really interested in strengthening Iraq more than necessary.

Of course, the war diverted the attention of both Iraq and Iran from Saudi Arabia. It seemed to erode the power of Khomeini and also led to a change in the radical Arab camp, allowing Baghdad to woo the Gulf monarchies and eventually to improve its relations with Washington. 'The war also provided the Saudi regime with a golden opportunity to improve its image in the Kingdom and in the Arab world, badly tarnished in the late 1970s.'[7] In this respect the war was welcomed by Riyadh, though it did not relish an overall victory for Iraq since the result would be an undisputed Iraqi ascendancy in the Gulf. However, the course of the war ultimately dispelled Saudi concerns.

The Iraqi offensive stalled in November 1980, after Khorramshahr and some one hundred square miles across the border had been conquered. The Iraqi situation in the Gulf was not much better. Iranian naval control made Iraqi ports unusable and virtually choked Iraqi oil exports. It now seemed possible that Iraq could lose the war, not through reversal on the battlefield but because of its faltering economy. At this point substantial Saudi Arabian help for Iraq began to materialize. Riyadh took the lead in mobilizing Arab financial support for Iraq and contributed the largest share itself. This financial assistance was complemented by logistical support. Saudi Arabia made its Red Sea ports available to receive both civilian and military imports destined for Iraq, and by 1981 Qadimah, a port north of Jedda, had become the terminus of the single most important supply route for Iraq. The Saudi media added its share, frequently denouncing the Iranian war effort and justifying the Iraqi cause.

The Al Saud were nevertheless reminded, from time to time, of their own vulnerability. When Iranian aircraft successfully attacked the Kuwaiti terminal of Umm al-Aysh, Iraq was promptly requested to recall aircraft stationed in Saudi Arabia.[8]

Nevertheless it was during this period of stalemate in the Iraq–Iran war between November 1980 and September 1981, that Saudi Arabia gave substantial help to Baghdad. The shipment of military as well as civilian supplies amounted to US$ 6 billion up to April 1981 and another US$ 4 billion between May and December 1981. It was also at this time that Saudi Arabia agreed in principle to construct a crude oil pipeline to the Red Sea to give Iraq a chance to export substantial amounts of oil, despite the blockade of its Persian Gulf ports.[9]

The Al Saud considered their support for Iraq even more justified when an attempted coup in Bahrain was uncovered in late 1981. Both the Bahraini and Saudi governments were sure that it had been initiated by Iran. The Saudi Interior Minister, Nayif ibn Abd al-Aziz, attacked Iran as the 'terrorist of the Gulf' and urged other Arab countries to follow the Saudi example and increase their support for Iraq.[10]

The Saudi government also made use of its strong position in OPEC to harm Iran. Due to the destruction of its oil installations, Iran was keen to get a high price for the limited amount of oil it was now able to export. In 1981, OPEC set an export quota for Iran of 1.2 million barrels per day without the possibility of raising prices. This quota was intended to seriously reduce Iran's capacity to earn the foreign exchange needed to keep its war machine going.[11]

Tension further increased in late 1981 when Iran started a fully-fledged counter-offensive. By the spring of 1982 Iranian forces had successfully pushed the Iraqi invaders back to the border and beyond. The complete collapse of Iraq seemed a real possibility and would have meant the loss of the Iraqi buffer between Kuwait and Saudi Arabia on the one hand and Iran on the other. A direct military conflict with Iran would thus become likely. Both countries, therefore, increased their financial support to Iraq, pouring between US$ 20 and 27 billion into the Iraqi war effort by the end of 1982.[12]

The Saudi regime was all too aware that it was unable to withstand an Iranian attack. It furthermore realized that its gigantic oil industry was located on the Gulf side of the Kingdom:

> rendering its vital oil installations and terminals more vulnerable to Iranian threats in three major ways. First, the hub of the Saudi oil industry, at the Ras Tanura terminal, is about sixteen minutes from Bushehr via Iranian Phantom jet. Second, the centre of the Saudi oil industry also happens to be the region in Saudi Arabia inhabited largely by Shia Muslims . . . Third, the bulk of Saudi oil exports still has to be shipped through the Iran-dominated Strait of Hormuz.[13]

Saudi Arabia, therefore, did its utmost to prevent an overall Iranian victory, short of actual military participation in the war. There was not only the danger of a direct confrontation with Iran on the battlefield but also of a defeated Iraq turning to Khomeini-style fundamentalism which would create the possibility of a war on two fronts – not necessarily a military war but definitely an ideological and political war.

When Iraq's other enemy, Syria, closed the pipeline from Iraq to the port of Banyas on the Mediterranean, the newly constructed pipeline, running from Rumailah in Southern Iraq to the Saudi Arabian port of Yanbu on the Red Sea, went into operation transporting two million barrels of crude oil per day.[14] Furthermore, Saudi Arabia continued to overproduce oil, resulting in low prices. During an OPEC ministerial meeting in December 1982, the Saudi delegation defeated an Iranian initiative to set production quotas determined by each member country's need for foreign exchange, the size of its population, the capacity of its oil reserves and the quantity of its petroleum exports in the preceding decade. In addition, it successfully organized opposition to the election of an Iranian Secretary-General for OPEC during that meeting, although it was Iran's turn to fill the post. Saudi Arabia was so determined to prevent an Iranian victory that it was ultimately prepared to risk the 1986 oil market crash, caused by its own overproduction.[15]

When Iranian forces directly threatened Basra and Fao in Southern Iraq in the late spring of 1982, a sense of sheer panic was evident in Riyadh. Although support for Iraq had proved very costly, the overall result, a weakening of the Gulf giants Iran and Iraq, had seemed worthwhile. But now the balance had swung in favour of Iran. The Saudi rulers therefore quickly changed their tactics and offered Iran US$ 25 billion in reparations in order to end the war.[16] Avoiding a military clash with Iran was now more important than any gain derived from further bleeding Saudi Arabia's two major rivals in the region. Saddam Husain also gave in and proposed an immediate ceasefire, but Khomeini refused.

Fortunately for Saudi Arabia, the war took a fresh turn after 1982. The Iranians had been successful in regaining control of their own territory, but then failed to conquer Iraq. Once again it became the Saudi government's main objective to enable Iraq to withstand Iranian attack. From February 1983 onwards, Saudi Arabia and Kuwait began selling 330,000 barrels of oil per day to Iraq, keeping the Iraqi war economy alive.[17] The inability of either Iraq or Iran to win the war militarily and Iran's flat refusal to accept less than the complete surrender of its adversary resulted in another stalemate. There were only minor changes in the front line, but the war now became known as the 'war of the cities' and the 'war of the tankers'.

The former meant the bombing of large urban agglomerates in enemy territory with long-range missiles, the latter, blockading enemy trade. Iraq besieged the main Iranian terminal at Khark, whereas Iran tried to prevent any Iraqi tanker, or tankers from other countries allegedly transporting Iraqi oil, from passing through the Straits of Hormuz. The tanker war, which began in earnest on 26 April 1984, also directly affected the economies of the Gulf Arab states, most of all Saudi Arabia.

The Kingdom now became even more involved in the Iraq–Iran war. It was only a matter of time before the first direct military clash between Iran and Saudi Arabia occurred. On 5 June 1984 Saudi aircraft ambushed Iranian fighters as they prepared to attack two tankers leaving

Saudi Arabian ports. With the aid of an American AWACS intelligence plane, a Saudi Arabian F-15 fighter shot down an Iranian Phantom jet near the Saudi island of al-Arabiya, about 60 miles north-east of Jubail. Later that day a second stand-off between eleven Iranian F-4s and eleven Saudi F-15s took place, but the Iranians decided to withdraw. Soon after the Saudi government established an air defence interception zone, the so-called Fahd line, that extended beyond the control zone for commercial traffic and the 12 mile-zone for territorial waters.[18]

These incidences also led to a new wave of Iranian anti-Saudi propaganda. The Iranian media condemned the 'reactionary, deceitful, filthy Saudi regime for fighting Islam in the robe of Islam'. How could a regime pretending to speak on behalf of Islam 'support the Baathists, who do not believe in religion, in their war against the Islamic revolution in Iran?'[19] Tehran repeatedly threatened to treat Kuwait and Saudi Arabia as parties to the war if they continued supporting Iraq. Both states therefore pressurized the GCC to denounce Iran's behaviour and the organization sponsored a UN resolution condemning Iranian attacks.[20]

The above picture of a bitter cold war between Iran and Saudi Arabia in the 1980s is coherent but not entirely appropriate. Looking for solutions, even in the depths of crisis, was always part of skilful and experienced regional diplomacy, avoiding a hopeless, unmovable situation. It should not be forgotten that the Al Saud, although they benefited from the war through the weakening of two rivals and the reduction of attacks on their legitimacy,[21] were not traditionally known for a tough and uncompromising foreign policy. It was the powerful antipathy displayed by Iranian radicals, and by Khomeini above all, that contributed to the uncharacteristically firm anti-Iranian stance of Saudi Arabia, reflected in its stridently pro-Iraqi position.[22] Nevertheless, Saudi Arabia followed tradition, and began looking for ways of avoiding any further deterioration in its relationship with Iran. As early as September 1984, only three months after the clash in the air over al-Arabiya, King Fahd personally invited Hojjat al-Islam Rafsanjani to take part in the hajj; Khomeini, however, blocked the attempt at rapprochement.

Rafsanjani, nevertheless, became the spokesman of a group within the heterogeneous Iranian regime that sought to improve relations with Saudi Arabia and to coax the Kingdom away from its one-sided support for Iraq. In 1984 secret negotiations were conducted between Iran and Saudi Arabia, when the Saudi side tried to discover under what conditions

Iran would accept a ceasefire. This rapprochement was assisted by the revelations of Irangate in 1985–6 – which indicated that Iran would cooperate even with its worst enemy – and the weariness of the Al Saud, paying Iraq's ever-increasing war costs. Saud al-Faisal visited Iran in May 1985 and offered to help end the war.[23] There were hints that the Saudi Foreign Minister had suggested Riyadh should shoulder the bulk of the Iranian reparation demands and that he did not exclude the possibility of asking Saddam Husain to step down if Iran began serious negotiations. But the Iranians insisted on Saddam's initial departure and demanded 'observer rights' in Mecca and Medina. The Saudi side had no choice but to reject these points.[24]

Although Saudi Arabia made a second attempt during the GCC's summit in November 1985 to develop a more even-handed policy towards Iran and Iraq, and followed this by inviting the Iranian Foreign Minister, Ali Velayati, to visit Riyadh in December, these efforts did not produce any agreement on ways to end the war. It was obvious, once again, that each fresh setback in relations was caused by elements within the Iranian regime who could not accept that exporting the revolution had failed. In the end, this was a brief 'honeymoon' in relations between Iran and Saudi Arabia during the First Gulf War and the government in Riyadh then returned to its previous policy of more or less unconditional support for Iraq. In the second half of 1986, it approved another US$ 4 billion 'loan' (in fact a donation) to Iraq and allowed Iraqi planes to land and refuel in Saudi Arabia after sorties against Iranian oil facilities in the southern Gulf. Terrorist bomb attacks in Kuwait in April, May and June of 1987, allegedly organized by Iranian agents, reinforced the Saudi position.[25]

1987 seemed to prove that Saudi Arabia had backed the winning horse since it marked the turning point of the war. A major offensive launched by Iran in February seriously threatened Basra but ultimately failed to attain its objective. Tehran had reached the limits of its military capacity. In addition, due to its own inflexibility and its continual attempts to export the revolution, the Iranian regime was trapped in isolation. The constant endeavour of Iraq to internationalize the war now, at last, became effective. In 1984, claiming a responsibility to secure free trade in the Gulf, America joined other Western countries in sending naval forces to the area. By August 1987, 40 American ships carrying 20,000 troops were patrolling the Gulf waters. By 1988 the total number of ships of foreign navies had increased to 90 with 50 of them American. In all they carried 40,000 men. This show of strength was completed with the reflagging of Kuwaiti vessels and tankers to protect them from Iranian attacks. Because Iraq had repeatedly shown a readiness to start negotiations, these measures could only result in confrontation with Iran, the party that continually rejected offers of negotiation. On 18 October 1987, the first American–Iranian clash occurred when a tanker under American colours was hit by an Iranian missile. In retaliation four destroyers of the US Navy damaged two Iranian drilling platforms.[26] Further incidents followed.

Internationally isolated, cut off from its supply routes, and challenged by a population increasingly tired of war, the Iranian leadership had to withstand heavy pressure to end hostilities. This pressure increased tremendously when the UN Security Council issued Resolution 598, calling for a ceasefire between Iraq and Iran, which was accepted immediately by Iraq. Iran's government, however, was still not ready to comply. Under these conditions Iraq, not unexpectedly, regained the upper hand on the battlefield. On 26 April 1988, Iraqi forces recaptured Fao, pushed towards the border, and even crossed it in several places. Without doubt, Saudi Arabia was now on the winning side. Its London-based newspaper, *al-Sharq al-awsat*, even advocated the removal of the Iranian leadership. On 7 May, Taha Yassin Ramadan, a member of the Iraqi Revolutionary Command Council, described the viewpoint of his country and that of Saudi Arabia as 'identical'. Nine days later, King Fahd praised the Iraqi leadership in his Eid al-Fitr message for having successfully withstood the forces of 'oppression and tyranny'.[27]

The war seemed to have returned to the same point it started from eight years earlier, and in the end Iran had to accept a ceasefire which went into effect on 20 August 1988.

Almost immediately after the signing ceremony, the Saudi government modified its policies towards Iran. The neighbour on the other side of the Persian Gulf had been tremendously weakened by the war and the danger of its exporting revolution was diminished considerably. On the other hand, Saddam Husain was behaving as if he was the undisputed winner and was flexing his muscles. The Iraqi victory had changed the balance of power in the Gulf region. The Saudi government was therefore no longer interested in further weakening Iran. Step by step King Fahd tried to placate his Iranian neighbour. Even after Khomeini's boycott of the pilgrimage in 1988, the Saudi monarch merely regretted the absence of Iranian Muslims. In an interview with the Kuwaiti News Agency on 3 May he declared:

> We cannot change the geographic reality of Iran and Iran cannot change our geographic reality . . . On our side, we do not ask Iran for anything more than mutual respect and good neighbourliness, which are the same things that Iran requests.[28]

Despite severed diplomatic relations, indirect talks continued, using Pakistan as an intermediary.[29]

Some years later, after the Iraqi invasion of Kuwait, Saudi justifications for siding with Iraq against Iran in the First Gulf War almost sounded apologetic. In February 1991, King Fahd declared:

> Allah knows that when we helped Iraq, the intention was not to harm any country, and I refer here to Iran, but the primary aim was to preserve Iraq. It is widely known that Iraq cannot occupy Iran . . . As I said before, we do not want to make trouble for Iran or harm it, but we also do not want Iraq to be occupied by any country because it is an Arab country and a neighbour.[30]

On another occasion he clarified his position by claiming that his country had had only two possibilities during the Iran–Iraq war, either to allow an Iraqi defeat or to support Iraq, in spite of the fact that the objectives and principles of Saddam Husain were dubious.[31] However, Saudi Arabia's role as the de facto ally of Iraq throughout the First Gulf War was enough to delay normalization in relations with Iran for an indefinite period of time.

The role of the Gulf Cooperation Council (GCC)

The idea of closer cooperation between the Gulf states dates back to the late 1960s when the British announced their intention of withdrawing from the region by 1971, abrogating their responsibility for the defence, finance and foreign affairs of Bahrain, Qatar and the seven sheikhdoms known as the Trucial States. But London failed to create a single federation out of all nine emirates because Qatar and Bahrain opted for independence, leaving the Trucial States to establish the United Arab Emirates

(UAE). The Shah's attempts to present himself as successor to the British, guaranteeing the security of the smaller Gulf Arab states, were also unsuccessful, due to their fear that Iran would dominate any structure or organization of which they were members. Numerous differences between the states of the Arab Peninsula further prevented the establishment of security structures.

Nevertheless the idea persisted and, in November 1976, strengthening of regional cooperation was put on the agenda of the meeting of Gulf Foreign Ministers in Masqat. After lengthy discussions the proposal floundered over the representation of Iraq and Iran. Iraq was seen as the propagator of nationalist radicalism and, as mentioned before, Iran was simply not trusted.[32]

It was to take yet one more event to pressure the Gulf Arab states into rethinking their reluctance to foster cooperation among themselves. In 1979, the Iranian Islamic revolution provided such an event, completely reshaping the balance of power in the Gulf region and causing a much higher level of instability than in the preceding decade. The threat of exporting the Iranian revolution was feared by all Gulf rulers, though Saudi Arabia was Iran's main target because of its sheer size, the deep-rooted Shia–Wahhabi dichotomy, Saudi control of Mecca and Medina and the traditional rivalry between them for hegemony in the Gulf region. But this Iranian focus on Saudi Arabia did not mean an exoneration of the smaller Gulf states. None of them could attempt to compare their military strength with that of Iran, even after the near dissolution of the regular Iranian army following the revolution. In addition, they had the Shia factor to consider. There are Shia living in almost all Gulf Arab countries, constituting between four per cent of the population in Oman and 72 per cent in Bahrain. In addition, over 300,000 Iranian Shia emigrants had settled in Kuwait, Bahrain, the UAE and Qatar. Both elements, indigenous and immigrant, together represented a significant extension of the Islamic Republic's ability to foment unrest or even revolution on the Arabian Peninsula.[33]

In 1980, Saddam Husain tried to utilize this concern by proposing a security treaty comprising Iraq and the six Gulf states of the Arabian Peninsula. He sought to placate the Gulf states, trying to convince them of fundamental changes in his regime and the cessation of his interference in the domestic affairs of his neighbours. He felt himself strong enough to assume a leading role in the Arab world after Egypt's isolation following the signing the Camp David Agreement. He wanted initially to regain control of the entire Shatt al-Arab and then, in a powerful position, start negotiations with Kuwait on shared control of the Kuwaiti islands of Bubjan and Warbah which blocked the access to the only Iraqi deep water port, at Umm Qasr. He therefore had to outmanoeuvre an Omani proposal, made a year earlier, to share responsibility for security in the Gulf with the main importers of Gulf oil in the West. Implementation of that proposal would have conclusively undermined Iraqi aspirations to dominate the pact.

Saddam Husain sought every possible opportunity to participate in various economic and financial ventures sponsored by the Gulf Arab states and generally tried to present himself as a pioneer of Arab glory and Arab pride. Although most Gulf states were ready to accept an Iraqi shield against Iranian Shia expansionism, they rejected the idea of a dominant role for Saddam Husain. Right from the start he was excluded from any serious attempts to establish the pact.

The foundation of the GCC

Despite these Iraqi initiatives, the Gulf Arab rulers felt they had to react independently to the new situation. In November 1980, the Saudi Interior Minister, Nayif ibn Abd al-Aziz, revealed that there were plans for achieving Gulf security which would soon result in agreement: 'Saudi Arabia is trying to have a unified agreement on Gulf security.'[34] Shortly afterwards, King Khalid told the Emir of Kuwait that, from his point of view, the security of the Gulf was indivisible and that, therefore, the security of Kuwait and Saudi Arabia were one. On 10 December 1980, the Saudi Defence Minister, Sultan Ibn Abd al-Aziz, declared that a joint defence strategy had to be formulated.[35]

Fully aware of the large number of subversive acts already perpetrated by Iranians in the Kingdom, the Saudi leadership concluded that the Kingdom's susceptibility to those acts might mean the vulnerability of all the Arab states of the Gulf region and vice versa. After reaching this conclusion they wasted no more time. In January 1981, at the Islamic Foreign Ministers' meeting in the Saudi city of Taif, six Gulf Arab states, Kuwait, Saudi Arabia, Bahrain, Qatar, the UAE and Oman agreed in principle to form a Cooperation Council. Its main purpose would be the containment of Iraqi power, Iranian hegemony and radical Islam.

The establishment of the Council was certainly accelerated by the course of the Iraq–Iran war, which had reached its first stalemate after the early successes of Iraqi forces. At the beginning of 1981 the outcome of the war could not be predicted, but an Iranian victory, with all its implications, did not seem impossible. The First Gulf War therefore became the major catalyst in the creation of the Gulf Cooperation Council (GCC), which officially came into existence on 26 May 1981, when the rulers of the member states met in Abu Dhabi.[36]

But there were also other, more general, motives. 'The member states of the council simply felt vulnerable after the apparent failure by the United States to react more aggressively towards both the Iranian Revolution in 1978–9 and the Soviet intervention in Afghanistan the following year. In addition, all the member states were apprehensive at the growing Soviet–American rivalry which threatens to turn the Gulf area into the battlefield of the superpowers.'[37]

On the surface, the new organization tried to downplay its security or military aspects. It proclaimed a strictly neutral position regarding the Iraq–Iran war, asserting that its main objectives were the strengthening of political, social, economic, cultural, legal and administrative harmony among the members. But greater military cooperation was definitely a goal as well. Saudi Arabia submitted a proposal on collective security measures to the other members that envisaged an independent military force, at the same time encouraging them to strengthen the battle capabilities of their armies. The Saudi proposal ultimately envisioned the creation of a GCC Rapid Deployment Force that could be used in times of emergency.[38] It was an open secret that military cooperation was also intended to improve the internal security of the member countries, since the RDF could also, ultimately, be deployed in the case of domestic unrest.

Despite these prospects the Saudi proposal was not wholeheartedly welcomed by the other GCC countries who jealously defended their complete independence of action in matters of internal security. The Saudi initiative was therefore seen as an attempt to patronize them and although common sense prevailed the process of military harmonization proceeded very slowly. It lasted until 1985, when the RDF was officially created. Kuwait, for example, joined the mutual defence agreement of the organization only at the end of 1986.[39] This cautious approach lasted until 1993 when the military leaders of the GCC agreed to earmark certain naval and air force units for joint operations under a single military command, thus making the small RDF more effective.[40]

Although the GCC tried to downplay its military aspects, its creation was viewed by Iran as an affront. Tehran saw it primarily as an anti-Iranian military pact, because there was no reason to believe that it was directed against Israel. Iran was also concerned about the exclusive nature of the GCC, viewing it as a ploy to keep Iran out of Persian Gulf affairs. Since the GCC portrayed itself as simply a part of other pan-Arab projects, Iran felt isolated and excluded from the economic and political life of the Gulf region. It was poor consolation that the enemy, Iraq, was also excluded.

In addition, Iran was convinced that the GCC was merely a cover for the expansion of Saudi influence, and was designed to lead to total Saudi control of the smaller Gulf states. Furthermore, the GCC could be used as an instrument of American policy in the Persian Gulf. Iran could not dismiss the thought that the Council, influenced by American interests, might develop aggressive anti-Iranian intentions. Only a few Iranian officials preserved a conciliatory approach, saying that they did not object to the GCC as long as it remained a defensive organization and was willing to accept the existence of the Islamic Republic.[41]

Balanced politics during the Iraq–Iran war

There were clear indications that these moderate remarks did not go undetected on the other side of the Gulf. Despite constant Iraqi war propaganda claiming to fight for the Arab cause against the Persian arch-enemy, and despite the necessity of confronting Iranian attempts to export its revolution, the GCC kept the lines of communication to Tehran open, trying to persuade the Iranian government to pursue a more conciliatory path. Indeed, during the first months of the GCC's existence there were, even in Saudi Arabia, some elements within the oligarchy, led by Crown Prince Abdallah, who approved the Islamic zeal of the new Iranian regime and admired its anti-Western and anti-Israeli stance.

This position was fostered by the strong pro-Syrian attitude of Abdallah, Syria being one of Iran's closest allies in its war against Iraq. Only after Tehran had escalated its attacks on the Al Saud, and Wahhabism in general, did these elements have no other choice but to turn their backs on Iran.[42] Led by Saudi Arabia, the whole GCC gradually changed its policy towards Iran from 1981 onwards. Although officially maintaining a neutral position, it supported Iraq both diplomatically and financially.[43]

The main objective was to prevent an Iranian victory. Altogether the GCC spent about US$ 50 billion on Iraq during the course of the Iraq–Iran war, either as cheap credit or as outright donations. Kuwait alone contributed US$ 15 billion.[44] However the burden of supporting Iraq financially was more or less tolerable for the GCC during the first months of the war. The lack of Iranian and Iraqi oil on the world market pushed the oil price up to US$ 30 per barrel, resulting in record earnings for the GCC in 1980–1. The Council earned further money by rendering a number of services to both parties to the war.

But when it became obvious that the war could last for years and that the oil price would not maintain a high level, continued financial support for Iraq became a painful burden. As early as 1982, the GCC began looking for the means to bring an end to the war, all the more so when Iranian forces had driven the Iraqi army out of territories occupied in 1980. In December 1982, the GCC secretly offered to pay Iran between US$ 25 and 30 billion in reparations in exchange for an Iranian guarantee to end the war.[45] The offer turned out to be fruitless. On the one hand the Iranians demanded about US$ 100 billion in reparations, and on the other they were simply unwilling to give in so soon after their first taste of victory.

The GCC thus had no other choice but to continue its support for Iraq, despite worsening financial conditions. But there were remarkable differences between the official Saudi policy toward the Iraq–Iran war and that of the GCC in general. The latter had to take the military weakness of its smaller members into consideration, which made them more vulnerable than Saudi Arabia to Iranian military superiority. Therefore, whilst support for Iraq continued, it was reasonably discreet from 1982 onwards.

Nevertheless, there were differences within the GCC on further political measures. Whereas the three northern members, Saudi Arabia, Kuwait and Bahrain, whose territories were nearer the front line, increased their aid to Iraq, the southern three, the UAE, Qatar and Oman, did not feel so involved in the conflict and tried to keep in touch with Iran, even during the worst moments of the war. Certain states profited tremendously from the conflict. Dubai in particular was noted for its continuing, indeed increasing, trade with Iran. When Saudi Arabia tried to come to better terms with Iran in the mid-1980s, the political weight of the southern members of the GCC had increased. The GCC summit in November 1985 in Masqat brought a neutral, more even-handed approach to the conflict. The Iranian government was quick to note the change and encouraged it.

Ali Velayati referred to 'friendly gestures', newspapers saw it as the 'beginning of the road' and an Iranian radio commentary declared that the change in the stance of some of the littoral Gulf states indicated the development of a more realistic attitude toward events in the region.[46] These remarks, however, were not in line with the usual comments by Iranian politicians and media on the subject of the GCC. As mentioned above, the creation of the organization was seen, at best, as an 'unfriendly gesture' and when the Council's support for Iraq became obvious, Iran began directing open threats at the other side of the Persian Gulf.

President Khamenei, for example, declared:

> we urge them [the GCC states] to put pressure on Iraq to stop its warmongering in the Gulf – or to stop supporting Iraq if it will not listen. We have nothing against them and do not wish to fight them . . . [Iran] would not be indifferent if they helped Iraq.[47] The Iranian Prime Minister, Mussavi, put it even more directly, emphasising: Our policy is to deal a stronger blow against any blows. We have repeatedly warned the Persian Gulf states against linking their fate with that of Saddam. We issue the same warning right now.[48]

The 'honeymoon' between Iran, Saudi Arabia and the GCC did not, therefore, last long. Iraq became increasingly successful at internationalizing the war, involving the GCC states in the tanker war. The increasingly frequent attacks on ships belonging to GCC member states, or plying to and from their ports, were as difficult to ignore as the Iranian capture of the Fao Peninsula.[49] On the other hand, the Iranian government did not respond to GCC mediation offers with any substantial measures and showed no desire to compromise. The GCC then developed a symbiosis with the United States, causing the latter's direct intervention in the war on the side of Iraq and, as a consequence, Iran's relations with the GCC dramatically deteriorated.[50] The Iranian Foreign Minister, Ali Velayati, known to be relatively moderate, issued a strongly worded warning to the GCC: 'Any country which supports

Iraq is subject to our retaliatory measures.'[51] On the other hand, the anti-Iranian statement of the 1987 Arab summit in Amman was complemented that same year by a GCC declaration stating that 'any aggression against any member country of the Council is an aggression against all the members'.[52]

Under these conditions there was an increased readiness among nearly all GCC members to accelerate the process of unifying their forces, or at least to rethink some of their reservations concerning the creation of a Rapid Deployment Force. In fact, the Saudi quest to purchase the Airborne Early Warning and Control System (AWACS) from the United States dated back to 1981. This went hand in hand with the Kingdom's willingness to permit American access to onshore military facilities in the event of a major escalation of the war. But it became obvious that the American shield had to be strengthened by regional military input. Thus, in October 1985 the GCC–RDF was created in an embryonic form.[53] The military aspects of the Council not only increased, but became more visible than ever before.

Saudi Arabia as the leading force in the GCC did not welcome this development wholeheartedly. On the one hand, it had pushed for the militarization of the Council right from the beginning, on the other hand, it became increasingly afraid of being trapped into using military force. The Al Saud was most reluctant to become militarily involved in the Iraq–Iran war. Consequently, they formulated the conditions under which they were willing to react militarily with extreme caution. They would only take offensive measures in the event of an attack on their own territory or if there was an attempt to close the Straits of Hormuz, the major export outlet of Saudi Arabia.[54] The Al Saud possessed enormous military potential, but they also had a tradition of not overreacting and resorting to military force only under extreme conditions. In the end, this caution kept Saudi Arabia and the other GCC members out of the war, without completely destroying their ability to mediate between their warring neighbours, Iraq and Iran.

Saudi Arabia and the GCC

The foundation and forming of the GCC can be assessed as one of the greatest foreign policy successes of Saudi Arabia in recent years. Its leadership of the Arabian Peninsula became more effective than ever before.

Iraq was in no position to challenge that dominance, and furthermore, the external danger constituted by Iran drove the small littoral states to look for protection to the larger and more powerful Saudi Arabia. The Al Saud were thus able to impose their own perspective on security matters on the smaller sheikhdoms.[55] Since 1981 the Saudi government had been able to prevent any major development on the Arabian Peninsula – with the exception of Yemen – contrary to their interests. 'They [the Saudis] were the "superpower" of what would become the Six, with more people and wealth than their five colleagues put together.'[56] Saudi Arabia was not one of the small, vulnerable, albeit wealthy emirates, but an active regional player, involved in Arab politics long before its transformation by the oil bonanza.[57] But there were also numerous other advantages in comparison to the smaller sheikhdoms.

The sheer size of Saudi Arabia provides it with a certain strategic weight unavailable to the smaller Gulf states. The Saudi government also possesses a degree of stability unknown in some of the sheikhdoms and benefits from an acceptance of its legitimacy that probably exceeds that of any other Gulf Arab state and, indeed, most states in the region. Leadership is of course also, conferred on the Kingdom by virtue of its giant oil resources which far surpass those of the other GCC members, and which ensure Saudi influence in the West. As a result of oil exploitation it is able to benefit from financial strength through subventions to a number of other states. Finally its leadership is conferred by its religious standing amongst Muslim nations as the guardian of the Holy places in Mecca and Medina.[58]

Many observers, therefore, thought that the GCC was little more than a fig leaf disguising Saudi ambitions to dominate the Gulf. The choice of Riyadh for the headquarters of the GCC reinforced the theory of a Saudi-dominated league with a system of minor satellites, similar to the relationship between the Soviet Union and the countries of Eastern Europe. Saudi Arabia provides the major part of the GCC's budget. In addition to the normal obligations of a host country, Saudi Arabia has also donated 126,000 sq. m. of land to the GCC and added the Secretariat building to it. This was more than a symbolic gesture. According to Arab customs and traditions the host holds a special position. With the Secretariat in Riyadh, a great number of second tier meetings automatically take place there. The Secretariat staff is also, quite naturally, largely Saudi, except at the very highest levels.[59] It was only to camouflage this dominance that the Kuwaiti Bishara was elected the first Secretary General of the GCC.

Despite the many advantages to the Kingdom in being a member of the GCC, the Saudi government had to pay careful consideration to the mood of the other members in order to ensure the viability of the organization. Mutual perceptions are strongly affected by the actions of the Kingdom in regional matters. The leadership in Riyadh largely succeeded in maintaining a delicate balance between a too obvious desire to dominate the other member countries and abjuring its former quest for power. When founding the GCC, the Al Saud were fully aware of the fears of smaller littoral Gulf states that they could be merely exchanging the hegemonic quest of Iran during the 1970s for dominance by Saudi Arabia in the 1980s.

They skilfully appealed to the common values and traditions of the monarchies of the Arabian Peninsula, avoided imperialist gestures and projected a relationship with the other members of the Council 'which could be compared with that of the United States and Western Europe'.[60] They liked to conceive their position within the GCC as *primus inter pares*.[61]

With the First Gulf War ending in a draw, Saudi Arabia started a new offensive to accelerate the integration process within the Council, particularly on military matters,[62] though the results of this offensive also revealed the continuing ambivalence in the relationship between Saudi Arabia and its partners in the GCC. Pure self-interest forced the smaller Gulf states to cooperate with Saudi Arabia, though they insisted on the preservation of all the necessary attributes of their sovereignty. Thus a number of them readily agreed to defence regulations with the United States and other NATO states. Saudi Arabia's common border with the other states on the Arabian Peninsula is not undisputed and harbours some latent conflicts.

The relationship between Saudi Arabia and Kuwait contains many of the elements which typify this type of conflict. On the one hand there is the common origin of both reigning families, deriving from the Utaiba tribe. The Al Saud has never forgotten the asylum and friendship they were granted by the rulers of Kuwait in the final years of the nineteenth century when they had to flee the constant attacks of the Al Rashid, and Kuwait was the launching point for the reconquest of Riyadh by the founder of Saudi Arabia, Abd al-Aziz ibn Saud, in 1902.

In the aftermath of the Anglo-Ottoman convention of Constant-inople the territorial boundaries between Kuwait and the fast-expanding state of the Al Saud were first marked out in 1913. Although there were repeated attacks by the militant Ihwan militias against Kuwait in the following years, Ibn Saud successfully convinced the ruler of Kuwait that he could contain the extreme behaviour of his storm-troopers. A degree of bitterness entered relations in 1922 when Kuwait was forced under the treaty of Uqair to hand over large areas on its southern borders, though these were later partly included in the Neutral Zone separating the Emirate from Saudi Arabia. Nevertheless, both states agreed, without great difficulty, to share the profits when considerable deposits of oil were discovered in the Neutral Zone in 1954.

In 1961, just after Kuwait had received its independence from Britain, the Al Saud, in return for Al Sabah assistance nearly a century earlier, contributed some 3,000 troops to help withstand the first Iraqi attempt to occupy the Emirate. In 1963 both governments started negotiations to cancel the provisions in the Uqair treaty on the Neutral Zone. On 7 July 1965 they agreed to divide the Neutral Zone equally between themselves. But it would take four years before the division was actually complete.[63]

On the other hand, although this has never been officially admitted, the Al Sabah were concerned that their southern neighbour might overwhelm them in a strong embrace and ultimately impair their sovereignty. For their part, the Al Saud had been observing the efforts, albeit timid and inconsistent, at political liberalization in Kuwait with similar suspicions, viewing its cosmopolitan atmosphere as a dangerous virus which could infect other Gulf monarchies. Kuwait, furthermore, had had a degree of trade relations with COMECON states since the 1960s, later enhanced by diplomatic ties.

Since Saudi Arabia did not have official diplomatic relations with any communist country, it made use of Kuwait at certain crucial periods of the Cold War to initiate discreet contact with the Eastern bloc. But the Al Saud would have preferred to abstain from all such contacts, if Kuwait would have only relinquished its dangerous flirtation with the East. The tolerance of the Al Saud was certainly exceeded when the Kuwaiti government announced its intention in 1976 to buy weapons from the Soviet Union. The supply would include modern tanks and artillery, air-to-air and air-to-surface missiles, amounting to US$ 400 million, and would be accompanied by Soviet advisors.[64]

In reaction, the Saudi Arabian government stepped up the dispute over the maritime borders of the Neutral Zone, as well as the offshore continental shelf and island regions, unresolved since 1969. Saudi Arabian troops occupied the islands of Qaru and Umm al-Maradim in June 1977. The outraged Emir of Kuwait branded this an act of aggression. Nevertheless, he was forced to recognize the superior power of Saudi Arabia. The Soviet supply of arms was reduced to air-to-surface missiles which would be installed by Egyptian specialists. After this incident he avoided any dispute with Saudi Arabia, which kept Qaru and Umm al-Maradim.[65]

Although the Al Saud remained outraged about many aspects of Kuwaiti behaviour, for example the relatively easy entry of pilgrims into Saudi Arabia via Kuwait without paying the obligatory fees,[66] the First Gulf War brought about a closer cooperation between the two states which survived after it had ended. It was no accident that the Al Sabah fled to Saudi Arabia when Iraqi troops invaded their country on 2 August 1990. Although there were some points of disagreement between them, for example their different positions on military treaties with Western states and the permanent presence of foreign troops on their soil, it cannot be denied that Saudi Arabia and Kuwait have drawn closer together in the face of many challenges in the late 1990s and the common threats they have confronted in the recent past.

This state of affairs is an exception in Saudi relations with other GCC states. More than twenty years after its formal settlement, the conflict over the Buraimi oasis still underpins relations with Oman and Abu Dhabi. In 1925, Wahhabi tax collectors turned up in the Buraimi oasis, which is situated between Abu Dhabi and Oman, demanding tribute – albeit in vain. But the conflict only escalated when rich oil deposits were discovered in the oasis after World War II. In 1952, Saudi troops occupied Buraimi only to be forced to withdraw under British pressure three years later. The conflict was decisively influenced and prolonged by the various owners of oil concessions backing the conflicting parties. The conflict also had numerous negative repercussions, Saudi Arabian interference in Oman's civil war, waged between the Imam of Nazwa and the Sultan of Masqat, being but one example.

After lengthy negotiations and various attempts at mediation, including those of the UN, the conflict was settled at the end in 1974 when Saudi Arabia recognized an agreement signed by Oman and Abu

Dhabi in 1966, according to which Oman gained control of three villages south of al-Ayn including their vital water wells, but the rest of the oasis came under the control of Abu Dhabi. The approval of Saudi Arabia was achieved when the ruler of Abu Dhabi, Sheikh Nahayan, proposed the creation of an additional access route to the Persian Gulf for the Kingdom between Qatar and Abu Dhabi. A more detailed discussion of the complicated issues of the Buraimi conflict would exceed the limits of this study.[67]

Memories of the humiliation Oman suffered due to Saudi Arabian arrogance still prevail. They provoke arguments about the exact border-lines in the Rub al-Khali, as well as about the ownership of exceptionally valuable water resources like the Umm Zamul well. Nevertheless, both King Fahd and Sultan Qabus tried to improve bilateral relations and signed a border agreement in March 1990.

The reigning family of Abu Dhabi also felt periodically humiliated by Saudi Arabia. Tribes in the Buraimi oasis had for decades declared their loyalty to the Emirs of Abu Dhabi. Nevertheless, Sheikh Nahayan was forced into far-reaching compromises in 1974 when he saw the danger of being crushed between the millstones of Saudi Arabia and Oman. ARAMCO had discovered remarkable deposits of oil in 1970 in the Liwa oasis, which lies between Abu Dhabi and Saudi Arabia. On 29 July 1974, the Saudi Arabian government forced Abu Dhabi to accept a regulation linked with the Buraimi agreement preventing exploitation of deposits in the Liwa oasis although they clearly belonged to Abu Dhabi.[68]

The additional access route to the Persian Gulf port of Khor al-Udaid created for Saudi Arabia in 1974 had, of course, affected relations with their other immediate neighbour on the corridor, Qatar. The Al Thani, the ruling family of Qatar, had themselves frequently tried to gain control of Khor al-Udaid. In December 1965, in spite of British opposition, they signed a secret agreement with Saudi Arabia which included Qatar renouncing its claim on Khor al-Udaid in exchange for a small piece of Saudi territory on its southern borders. The rulers of Qatar recognized too late that they had thus cut their border with Abu Dhabi, leaving Saudi Arabia as their sole neighbour on the mainland. For the Al Saud this meant further strategic protection of the economically vital province of al-Hasa. However, to date they have refused to fulfil their part of the 1965 agreement. The Al Thani have waited in vain for the transference of the stipulated Saudi Arabian territory to their control but have been too weak to insist on their demands.

The latent tension in these unresolved conflicts became manifest once more in 1992, when a bitter argument flared up between Saudi Arabia and Qatar. On 30 September 1992 an armed incident occurred at the border checkpoint of al-Khofus, resulting in the deaths of two Qatari border guards and an unidentified insurgent from Saudi Arabia. Qatar revoked the agreement of 1965, reproaching Saudi Arabia for having neglected its obligations and for attempting, furthermore, to shift the border with Qatar in its favour. The Saudi Arabian territorial claims end, after all, at a line south of the port of Umm Said.[69]

Saudi Arabia has been most successful at maintaining balanced relations with Bahrain. On 22 February 1958 both countries signed an initial agreement concerning their maritime borders, thus ending a long quarrel over the control of the Fasht Abu Safah oilfield. Bahrain abstained from exploiting the field and was satisfied with a guarantee of 50 per cent of the profits from it. The limited oil resources of Bahrain led to an early decision by its government to establish a sophisticated oil-processing industry which was also used by Saudi Arabia. By the end of the 1980s a gigantic bridge between Saudi Arabia and Bahrain had been completed, underlining their symbiotic relationship, a relationship which, to give one example, paid off politically for Bahrain when Iranian attempts at infiltration were foiled with the help of Saudi Arabia.

Iran's relations with the smaller GCC states

The problems attendant on having a large Shia minority not only influences Iran's relations with Bahrain but also with the majority of the other Gulf states. Since the Iranian revolution all the Gulf's Arab potentates have been carefully watching to see whether that dramatic political transformation could affect the unstable structures of their own states. As the price for quick economic modernization, the Gulf littoral states were forced to take in large quotas of foreign workers. Although they had no political rights, by the end of the 1980s these workers constituted 73.2 per cent of the residents in Qatar, 69 per cent of those in the UAE and 61.2 per cent of the population of Kuwait.[70]

The reaction of these foreign workers to external revolutionary impulses remained unknown for a long time. It is within this context that the Gulf monarchies' fear of Iranian desires to export the revolution can be understood. Indeed, although not a numerical majority in all Gulf Arab states, the Shia and immigrant Iranians further reduced the number of recognized citizens, who were clearly a minority among the overall population of those countries. Like the al-Hasa Shia, the majority of Shia in the smaller Gulf states had sufficient reason to denounce the humiliations of the past and demand a legal, political and economic status equal to that of their Sunni compatriots. Though only 11.53 per cent of the people living in the UAE declare themselves to be Shia, their share amongst citizens amounts to 41.39 per cent. In Qatar almost 80 per cent are Shia, whilst 23.29 per cent of its citizens are of Iranian origin.[71]

But a decade or more after the Iranian revolution it became obvious that the fears of the Gulf monarchs were not going to materialize. Nevertheless, there are some remarkable differences between the experiences of the northern and the southern members of the GCC. Iranian attempts at infiltration were partially successful in the northern GCC states of Kuwait, Bahrain and Saudi Arabia, whereas they failed completely in the southern member countries of Qatar, the UAE and Oman. A high percentage of Shia in the population in general and in the citizenry in particular did not prove an adequate basis for the existence of a pro-Iranian rebel movement. The social heterogeneity of the Shia population undoubtedly affected their behaviour. Shia notables and businessmen in Qatar, Oman, Sharjah and Dubai have for generations been closely linked to the ruling families. They participated in the economic boom, and were therefore unwilling to risk change, least of all by violent means. But their position caused the southern GCC states to take a more moderate attitude than their northern partners towards Iran during the Iraq–Iran war.

However, a degree of common interest between prosperous Shia immigrant Iranians and the traditional establishment was also visible in the northern member states of Kuwait and Bahrain. Nevertheless, tensions did become obvious. In Bahrain, the Shia make up only 49 per cent of the overall population, but 72 per cent of the citizens.[72] The island state, therefore, belongs to the few neighbours of Iran – besides Iraq – with a clear Shia majority. In the case of Bahrain the conflictive relations with Iran also arise from latent Iranian territorial claims.

These claims refer back to the rule of the Akhamenids and, more recently, the inclusion of the island in the province of Fars between 1235 and 1507. A Portuguese intermezzo ended in 1622, and Bahrain was affiliated to Fars once again. Even when the Al Khalifah took possession of Bahrain in the mid-eighteenth century, they had to respect Persian supremacy. A protection treaty between the Al Khalifah and the British East India Company finally ended Persian dominance in 1820. However, the expansionist Gulf policy of the Pahlavi Shahs included the recovery of Bahrain. The plans, however, had to be withdrawn, at least temporarily, after the Guiccardi mission and a referendum organized by the UN in 1971 in which a majority of the inhabitants voted for independence.

Even though Khomeini condemned the essential components of the Shah's policy, he excluded the Iranian claim to Bahrain from his criticism. Between 1979 and 1981, Ayatollah Ruhani, on orders from Khomeini, organized an underground network in Bahrain from his headquarters in Qom with the ultimate goal of toppling the Al Khalifah. With the conspiracy's failure in 1981, Iran's activities became known. Whilst focus on Bahrain had eased Iranian pressure on Kuwait and Saudi Arabia, it turned the rulers of Bahrain into the most determined opponents of Iran during the First Gulf War. They provided naval bases for the US in the Gulf after 1987 and by 1988 Bahrain had become an important base for anti-Iranian activities on the part of the international community in the Persian Gulf.

Unlike Bahrain, Kuwait had not been the object of Iranian territorial claims. The Al Sabah had maintained intensive diplomatic contacts with Iran since the independence of their country in 1961 and there was no visible deterioration – at least for a while – after the Iranian revolution. Kuwait is the GCC state geographically closest to Iran. The border between both states is drawn on the continental shelf and the governments of Iran and Kuwait had reached an agreement with regard to its marking-out as early as January 1968, including Iranian sovereignty over the island of Charq and Kuwaiti sovereignty over the island of Failaqah.

Iranian–Kuwaiti relations deteriorated rapidly, however, after the beginning of First Gulf War. As in Bahrain, Iran's clerical leaders tried to incite the Shia population against the rule of the Al Sabah. In 1979 Khomeini appointed a Shia Friday preacher for Kuwait, but the appointee was denied entry. Iranian goals regarding Kuwait, however, were only part of its strategic objectives in the war. A Shia Islamic Republic of Kuwait was to embroil Iraq in a second front in the south, thereby increasing Iranian chances of conquering Basra. Of course, for the rulers of Kuwait this distinction had hardly any meaning. The 'mistaken' Iranian air-raids on Kuwaiti oil installations in November 1980 and June 1981, as well as the expansion of the Shia terrorist movement within the Emirate, which was responsible for a series of bombings prior to December 1983 and a failed attack on the Emir in May 1985, strengthened the determination of the Kuwaiti government to grant Iraq every possible assistance against Iran. As shown above, Saudi Arabia and Kuwait became the most important single creditors of Iraq. The Kuwaiti government's request to put its tanker fleet under the protection of the American flag opened up the last phase of the Iraq–Iran war, internationalizing it with corresponding consequences for Iran.

The degree of difference in the relationship of the southern Gulf states to that of the northern ones with Iran is clearly demonstrated by the relations between Oman and Iran. Like Kuwait in the north, Oman is the GCC member in the south of the Persian Gulf closest to the Iranian mainland. But this is the only similarity. The Omani–Iranian border extends for 125 nautical miles on the continental shelf of the Persian Gulf, from the Straits of Hormuz in the north to the Gulf of Oman in the south. Respective border agreements between the two states were completed on 25 July 1974 and became effective on 28 May 1975.[73] On the Gulf 22 markers refer to a near retention of the principle of equidistance. The northern end of the common border was not yet marked because Oman, along with Ras al-Khaimah and Sharjah, had made claims on Musandam.

The Straits of Hormuz constitute, without doubt, the most sensitive part of the Omani–Iranian border because all tanker traffic in and out of the Gulf proceeds through them. During the time of the Shah's rule both countries agreed to mutually ensure the smooth functioning of the Straits for regional oil exporters and Western importers. After the Iranian revolution, with its anti-Western and anti-royalist tendencies, both the states of the Arabian Peninsula and the Western industrial nations were hopeful that Oman would fulfil its unique function as guarantor of free naval access via the Straits.

This assumption put Oman in a complicated situation. The country itself was not dependent on the export route running through the Straits because the majority of its ports lay to the south, on the Gulf of Oman. Why then should Sultan Qabus endanger his good relations with Iran in favour of third parties? Iran's assistance in crushing the rebellion in Dhofar in the 1970s, which was solidly supported by Iraq, had not been forgotten by Oman. The force needed to suppress the Dhofar revolt had far exceeded the military capabilities of the Sultan and the Al Saud had found themselves also unable to shoulder that responsibility.[74]

The excellent commercial relations which had been established between Iran and Oman remained intact after 1979. Moreover, Sultan Qabus had little reason to fear the export of the Iranian revolution since 75 per cent of his citizens are followers of Ibadism and 20 per cent declare themselves to be Sunni. Only 4 per cent of inhabitants with civic rights are Shia.[75] The First Gulf War also took place in areas remote from the coasts of Oman. These factors explain the sometimes considerable difference of interest between Oman and its northern partners in the GCC.

Only the excellent relations of the Sultanate with Great Britain and the United States (air and naval bases of the Rapid Deployment Force (RDF) and later the Central Command were based in Oman) induced Sultan Qabus to accept the reflagging of Kuwaiti tankers in 1987. But the attempt that same year by GCC headquarters to station a common military force in Kuwait failed because of his veto.[76] Oman allowed the use of its territorial waters for the search for Iranian sea mines only in individual cases and did not react to occasional incursions by Iranian destroyers in the course of their engagements with international naval units after 1987.

It must be added, however, that relations between Oman and Iran are not completely devoid of tension. Educated citizens of Oman are well aware that in the past Persia has occupied parts of Oman's coastal region. Is it impossible to imagine Iranian rulers in the future laying claim to Oman?[77] But though these fears may be latent, they do not influence the behaviour of either government at the moment.

Though not as good as those with Oman, relations between Iran and the UAE were also balanced up to the summer of 1992. The border agreements between them were first violated by the Iranian occupation of the islands of Tumb and Abu Musa. At least Abu Dhabi and Dubai had already signed a border agreement with Iran,[78] which Dubai eventually ratified in 1974. But while Ras al-Khaimah, owner of the Tumb islands, was compelled to stand by helplessly when the Iranians occupied it, Sharjah, the owner of Abu Musa, came to a profitable agreement with Tehran on 30 November 1971, the very day of the Iranian occupation.

In the early 1970s Iran bore the cost of the development of the Mubarak oilfield which lies offshore of Abu Musa and offered the Al Qasimi 50 per cent of the projected profits. In addition, the Shah granted the rulers of Sharjah a say in the local affairs of Abu Musa and gave settlement rights to the citizens of Sharjah. The Al Qasimi soon came to value the advantages of cooperation with Iran – which included status in the disputes within the UAE – more highly than absolute sovereignty over Abu Musa.

Dubai also profited from her extensive commercial relations with Iran, though business was not exclusively controlled by the 80,000 Iranian residents of the Emirate and large numbers of Arab merchants also participated. Even the First Gulf War could not interrupt these lucrative connections but on the contrary the considerable requirements of Iran, now cut off from its traditional commercial partners, expanded them. In 1986, re-exports from Dubai to Iran reached the sum of US$ 350 million, thus topping re-exports from the Emirate to its next most important trading partner by over one hundred per cent.[79] The Al Maktum were also clever enough to utilize their good relationship with Iran in the constant disputes within the UAE.

The border between Qatar and Iran on the continental shelf was agreed in the bilateral treaty of 20 September 1969 which became effective on 10 May 1970. Both sides insisted on the principle of equidistance and no islands were included in the agreement. Marking out the border was radically simplified by this approach, which was interrupted only at the point where the common border between Qatar and Bahrain remained disputed.

But Qatar's efforts to achieve fruitful relations with Iran also have a thoroughly pragmatic background. In view of the numerous challenges within the GCC, be it the policies of Saudi Arabia, Bahrain or Abu Dhabi, it is important for the Al Thani to be able, albeit unofficially, to threaten to give support to Iran, even when the feasibility of such aid would appear impossible under the prevailing circumstances. However, in the end, it is usually more useful for Qatar to bet on the GCC than on Iran. Qatar, therefore, agreed to all the organization's resolutions on the Iraq–Iran war, with the Al Thani retaining anonymity behind these collective decisions.

On the other hand, there was a frequent exchange of official delegations between Tehran and Doha between 1980 and 1988, and the

Al Thani refused to provide naval bases and other logistical facilities for US Marines in 1987. In the final stages of the Iraq–Iran war they even refused to allow the installation of a naval supervisory system, paid for by the government of Japan, at the northernmost point of Qatar, merely to avoid possible provocation of Iran.

The ceasefire

Immediately after the signing of the ceasefire with Iraq on 20 August 1988, Iran launched a charm offensive to improve relations with the Gulf Arab states, excluding Saudi Arabia. The Iranian leadership was obviously not prepared to concede the Saudi Arabian role in convincing the Iraqi President to halt his military offensive. It was thus the smaller GCC states that were the main target of the Iranian diplomatic initiative. And Tehran got an encouraging response.

Oman's Foreign Minister visited Iran twice in August and September. The second visit took place just after the GCC Foreign Ministers' meeting held between 4 and 5 September 1988 when a desire for 'friendship between all the peoples of the Islamic nation' was expressed. As a result of pressure from its smaller members, the GCC decided to examine opportunities for improving relations with Iran and to send envoys to both Iraq and Iran in an attempt to break the deadlock in the peace talks which were being held in Geneva. According to radio stations in Iran, the Omani Foreign Minister had even stated that the GCC saw no obstacles to including Iran and Iraq in a GCC meeting once the main differences between them had been resolved.

Sultan Qabus implicitly took Iran's side in an interview in December when he suggested that 'forces' should withdraw behind their own borders, in order to establish trust, which clearly referred to Iraq holding on to Iranian territory after signing the ceasefire. Qabus promised that the GCC would establish closer relations with Iran once a real state of peace was achieved. His Minister of Commerce and Industry went to Tehran in late December to negotiate and sign a wide-ranging accord on economic cooperation, including the establishment of a joint economic–industrial commission.[80]

Qatar had stuck to its own traditional, low key pragmatism throughout the war and continued to do so after August 1988. Al Thani disillusionment with Saudi behaviour over the still unresolved border problem led them to keep lines of communication to Tehran open. Even when some Iranian officials presented a claim to a part of the gas field lying off Qatar in March 1989, the government in Doha did not react officially.

Without making any grand announcements the UAE also continued to develop their economic relations with Iran. Although with the end of hostilities Dubai had obviously lost its profitable position as one of Iran's very few trading partners, the UAE as a whole tried to build on the favourable conditions that Dubai had established.

Even Bahrain responded to the new situation. On 10 October 1988 Manama announced that an agreement had been reached with Tehran to upgrade bilateral relations to the level of chargé d' affaires and Bahrain's Foreign Minister, Sheikh Mohammad ibn Mubarak, confirmed that his government intended to resume relations at ambassadorial level soon.[81] All these activities more or less confirmed the idea that the smaller GCC states feared a victorious Saddam Husain once again trying to change the balance of power in the Persian Gulf.

NOTES

1 H. Fürtig, *Der irakisch–iranische Krieg 1980–1988: Ursachen, Verlauf, Folgen* (Berlin, Akademieverlag, 1992), p. 43.

2 P. Rondot, 'Irak gegen Iran: Krieg ohne Entscheidung', *Europaarchiv*, 36:3 (1981), p. 68.

3 C. Wright, 'Iraq – New Power in the Middle East', *Foreign Affairs*, 58:2 (1979/80), p. 259.

4 M. Khadduri, *The Gulf War*, p. 125.

5 J.D. Anthony, 'Regional and Worldwide Implications of the Gulf War' in M.S. al-Azhary (ed.), *The Iran–Iraq War* (London: Croom Helm, 1984), p. 113.

6 W. Quandt, 'Reactions of the Arab Gulf States' in A.E.H. Dessouki (ed.), *The Iraq–Iran War: Issues on Conflict and Prospects for Settlement* (Princeton: Princeton University Press, 1981), pp. 39–41.

7 M. Abir, *Saudi Arabia*, p. 126.

8 M.A. Heller, *The Iran–Iraq War*, pp. 14–15.

9 G. Nonneman, The GCC, p. 105.

10 G. Nonneman, Iraqi–GCC Relations, p. 37.

11 H. Amirahmadi and N. Entessar, 'Iranian–Arab Relations in Transition' in H. Amirahmadi and N. Entessar (eds.), *Iran and the Arab World* (Basingstoke: Macmillan, 1993), p. 9.

12 H. Gurdon, *Iran*, p. 36; G.H. Jansen, 'The Attitudes of the Arab Governments towards the Gulf War' in M.S. al-Azhary (ed.), *The Iran–Iraq War*, p. 86.
13 R.K. Ramazani, *Revolutionary Iran*, p. 8.
14 N.I. Rashid and E.I. Shaheen, *Saudi Arabia*, pp. 121–2.
15 H. Amirahmadi and N. Entessar, Iranian–Arab Relations, p. 9.
16 *Jerusalem Post*, Jerusalem, 2 June 1982.
17 G. Nonneman, Iraqi–GCC Relations, p. 37.
18 R.K. Ramazani, *Revolutionary Iran*, pp. 9–10.
19 J. Goldberg, Saudi Arabia, p. 157.
20 G. Nonneman, Iraqi–GCC Relations, p. 38.
21 S.K. al-Nowaiser, *Saudi Arabia's and the United States' Strategic Partnership in an Era of Turmoil: A study of Saudi–American political, economic, and military relationship 1973–1983 – dependence or independence?* (Ann Arbor: University Press, 1988), p. 146.
22 G. Nonneman, The GCC, p. 116.
23 N. Jeandet, *Un Golfe pour trois rêves: le triangle de crise Iran, Irak, Arabie* (Paris: Edition l'Harmattan, 1993), pp. 56–60.
24 G. Nonneman, The GCC, p. 107.
25 G. Nonneman, Iraqi–GCC Relations, pp. 40–1.
26 H. Fürtig, *Der irakisch–iranische Krieg*, pp. 93–4.
27 G. Nonneman, Iraqi–GCC Relations, pp. 47–8.
28 *FBIS-NES-89-085*, 4 May 1989.
29 P. Robins, *The Future*, p. 20.
30 Quoted in S.M. Badeeb, *Saudi–Iranian Relations*, p. 126.
31 *Saudi Arabian Bulletin*, London, March 1991, p. 2.
32 D.E. Long, The Impact, p. 113.
33 F.A. Khavari, *Oil and Islam: The Ticking Bomb* (Malibu, 1990), pp. 100–1.
34 Quoted in S.R. Grummon, *The Iran–Iraq War: Islam Embattled* (New York, Westport, London: Praeger, 1982), p. 54.
35 Ibid., pp. 54–5.
36 D.E. Long, The Impact, p. 113.
37 S. Holly, *Conflict*, p. 21.
38 S.M. Badeeb, *Saudi–Iranian Relations*, p. 124.
39 M. Abir, *Saudi Arabia*, p. 127.
40 S. al-Mani, 'Of Security and Threat: Saudi Arabia's Perception', *Journal of South Asian and Middle Eastern Studies*, 20:1 (1996), p. 79.
41 S.T. Hunter, *Iran*, pp. 120–1.
42 M. Abir, *Saudi Arabia*, pp. 127–8.
43 For a more detailed account of the GCC's support for Iraq see ibid., pp. 128–44.
44 E. Wirth, 'Irak und seine Nachbarn' in *Die Golfregion in der Weltpolitik* (Stuttgart, Berlin, Cologne, Kohlhammer-Verlag, 1991), p. 33.
45 *Monday Morning*, Beirut, 670 (1985), p. 26.
46 S. Chubin, Iran, p. 12.
47 *Daily Telegraph*, London, 9 June 1984.
48 *The Guardian*, London, 21 May 1984.
49 L Graz, The GCC, p. 8.

50 C. Bina, 'Farewell to the Pax Americana: Iran, Political Islam and the Passing of the Old Order' in H. Zanganeh (ed.), *Islam, Iran & World Stability* (New York: St. Martin's Press, 1994), p. 122.
51 *International Herald Tribune*, Paris, 29 July 1987.
52 *Arab News*, Jiddah, 21 October 1987.
53 M.E. Ahrari, 'Iran, GCC and the Security Dimensions in the Persian Gulf' in H. Amirahmadi and N. Entessar (eds.), *Reconstruction and Regional Diplomacy in the Persian Gulf* (London, New York: Routledge, 1992), p. 204.
54 Ibid.
55 S. Holly, *Conflict*, p. 21.
56 J.W. Twinam, 'Reflections on Gulf Cooperation with Focus on Bahrain, Qatar and Oman', *American–Arab Affairs*, 18:3 (1986), p. 17.
57 G. Salamé, 'Perceived Threats and Perceived Loyalties' in B.R. Pridham (ed.), *The Arab Gulf and the Arab World* (London: Croom Helm, 1988), p. 249.
58 M.A. Hameed, *Saudi Arabia, the West and the Security of the Gulf* (London: Croom Helm, 1986), p. 10.
59 L. Graz, The GCC, p. 6.
60 D.E. Long, 'Saudi Arabia and its Neighbors: Preoccupied Paternalism' in H.R. Sindelar and J.E. Peterson (eds.), *Crosscurrents in the Gulf* (London, New York: Routledge, 1988), p. 183.
61 Ibid., p. 185; M.A. Heller, *The Iran–Iraq War*, p. 15.
62 *al-Riyadh*, Riyadh, 8 November 1990; 16 November 1990.
63 R. Litvak, 'Sources of Inter-State Conflict' in S. Chubin (ed.), *Security in the Persian Gulf* (Aldershot: Gower, 1981), 3 vols., vol. 2, pp. 36–40.
64 L.G. Martin, *The Unstable Gulf. Threats from within* (Aldershot: Gower, 1984), pp. 53–4.
65 *Qatar News Agency*, Doha, 19 June 1977; 21 June 1977.
66 H.F. Eilts, 'Foreign Policy Perspectives' in H.R. Sindelar and J.E. Peterson (eds.), *Crosscurrents*, p. 25.
67 More detailed information in R. Litvak, Sources, pp. 52–5; A.R.S. Abu-Dawood, *International Boundaries of Saudi Arabia* (New Delhi, Galaxy Publications, 1990), pp. 49–51.
68 *Arab Report and Record* (London, 1974), p. 307.
69 A.R.S. Abu-Dawood, *International*, p. 47, Map 9.
70 R.K. Ramazani, *Revolutionary Iran*, p. 33.
71 Ibid.
72 Ibid.
73 R. Litvak, Sources, p. 69.
74 M.A. Conant and R. King, *Consequences of 'Peace': The Iranian Situation and Outlook* (Washington DC, Conant and Associates, 1988), p. 65.
75 W.T. Tow, *Subregional Cooperation*, p. 20.
76 P. Robins, *The Future*, p. 61.
77 H.F. Eilts, Foreign Policy, pp. 26–7.
78 R. Young, 'The Persian Gulf' in R. Churchill and J. Welch (eds.), *New Directions in the Law of Sea* (London: Croom Helm, 1973), 3 vols., vol. 3, p. 233.
79 *Süddeutsche Zeitung*, Munich, 21 April 1992.
80 G. Nonneman, The GCC, pp. 117–8.
81 Ibid.

3

Détente during the
Second Gulf Crisis, 1990–1991

Iran's leadership tests the gains of neutrality

In 1988, the Iranian leadership had to conclude that, after ten years of revolutionary zeal and eight years of war with Iraq, its foreign policy had failed. It was also directly or indirectly involved in many other conflicts during that time, in Afghanistan, in the Central Asian republics of the faltering USSR, Armenia and Azerbaijan, and in Kurdistan. But vehement anti-Americanism and a policy of exporting the Islamic revolution had isolated Iran to such a degree that its involvement in all these conflicts turned out to be disastrous. In 1988 Iran stood alone, its economy was shattered, the American navy was patrolling its maritime borders – something had to be done.

It is debatable whether Iran's acceptance on 18 July 1988 of UN Security Council Resolution 598 calling for an immediate ceasefire was simple capitulation or the positive outcome of a new, more pragmatic foreign policy. In any case, Iran was forced to take this decision because of its desperate military and economic situation and more or less complete political isolation. This observation is important because it allows conclusions concerning the depth of change in the Iranian policy to be drawn. The assumption that a more pragmatic foreign policy had been adopted seems a reasonable one in view of the fact that the acceptance of 598 was accompanied by Khomeini's appointment of Hojjat al-Islam Rafsanjani as Commander-in-Chief of Iranian armed forces in 1988. This appointment indicated a change in the self-image of the Islamic Republic which was confirmed by the election of Rafsanjani as President of the Republic a year later. The change was felt by many observers, both inside and outside Iran, to be so profound that they associated 1988 with the creation of a second Islamic Republic.

While for Ayatollah Khomeini the success of Islam had always enjoyed priority over worldly matters in all areas of life, Rafsanjani could now assert his stance vis-à-vis the ageing Khomeini and his belief that, after losing the war with Iraq the Islamic Republic now risked being paralysed unless it could safeguard its economic survival.

After the decision to accept the resolution was taken, it developed its own dynamic. The reconstruction of the country, for which cooperation with potential regional and international partners was necessary, now received priority. Within days after the ceasefire, high-profile economic delegations from Japan, Australia, Italy, India, Pakistan, Kuwait and Turkey arrived in Tehran to compete for an extensive list of reconstruction tenders. South Korea alone received construction orders worth US$ 15–16 billion between 1988 and 1993.[1] Spie-Batignolles of France and the Bechtel Company from the hated United States received the order for the construction of an ultra-modern refinery at Arak near Bandar Abbas.[2]

At any rate, the desire of the international community to become economically active in Iran was only one side of the coin. For its part the Iranian government had to guarantee its ability to respect agreements and to create the right political conditions for peaceful trade and reconstruction in order to re-establish credibility.

The minimum requirement for economic credibility was the elimination of the constant threat to export the revolution. Since Rafsanjani 'showed no real interest in the pursuit of Khomeini's messianic goals and he appeared to want to limit his attachment to these goals to the rhetorical level',[3] the religious factors which had played so vital role in Iran's foreign policy during the First Gulf War were now less visible.

Politicians such as Rafsanjani, Khamenei, Velayati, Nabavi and others publicly stated that it was necessary to reassess the priorities of the Islamic revolution and to produce a climate more favourable to economic reconstruction. 'Reconstruction has become our nation's slogan',[4] Khamenei announced, thus, in a sense, setting priorities.

Thus, at least temporarily, the purely national interests of Iran gained the upper hand over the radical philosophy of the revolution. Iranian politicians and media alike abandoned propaganda exporting the revolution. There was a general desire to improve relations with the neighbouring states, reflecting the specific intent of the Iranian government. As early as November 1988, with the knowledge of Ayatollah Khomeini, Rafsanjani expressed regret for past Iranian behaviour toward certain Arab states: 'If Iran had demonstrated a little more tactfulness, they [the Arab States] would not have supported Iraq.'[5]

Iranian policy experts were even more frank:

These foreign policy outlooks and demands [the export of the revolution], though well intended, original and constructive, were unrealistic and lacked strategic substance. They disregarded the deep dependencies of the Arab world and the historically-accumulated misperceptions between Iran and the Arab state system. In their historical interactions, Iran and the Arab world have not experienced long durations of peace and constructive relationship. Major Arab states and Iran have stood by each other as competitors in trade, territory, religious assertiveness, political power and regional status.[6]

Rafsanjani and his supporters now interpreted export of the revolution primarily as an obligation to strengthen the revolution in Iran according to the new creed: if the Islamic Republic became attractive to other Muslims, the revolution would spread by merely setting a successful example.[7] The Foreign Minister, Ali Velayati, supported the President by asserting that future Iranian foreign policy must take into consideration the international balance of power in order to secure the economic and political survival of the Islamic Republic, and should pursue the fulfilment of its spiritual and religious duties by setting an example and not by interfering in the internal affairs of other countries.[8]

Only if Iran regained some sort of strength and stability would it be able to protect, and later to spread, the ideals of revolutionary Islam. Of course, the hardliners around Khomeini still thought that radical political acts should be carried out abroad, but after their master changed his mind, they had to accept that absolute priority should be given to the security of the revolutionary Iranian state.[9] The previous decade of intransigence, nonconformity and isolation really could not be called a success by anyone. Thus new foreign policy practices had to be shaped to ensure foreign appraisal of Iran as moderate and cooperative. Only if these practices were established would foreign governments and business be ready to participate in Iran's long-term recovery. Apart from economic reconstruction, the Iranian government also pursued two related goals: the restoration of its position in the Gulf and the stalling of Iraq's reconstruction and acquisition of weapons.[10]

Victorious Iraq had to be contained by all possible means available. The Iraqi President had prolonged the peace negotiations in New York and Geneva. Even when the ceasefire was established and the threat of renewed hostilities had receded, Iraq continued to rearm extensively, thus widening the military gap between itself and Iran. Saddam Husain seemed determined to maintain supremacy over Iran and to be the heir of the late Shah, adopting his role of regional policeman in the Persian Gulf and aiming at becoming the most powerful ruler in the Arab world. These goals must have been viewed by Iran as a serious threat to its national security and a severe constraint on its regional diplomacy[11] until the Iraqi occupation of Kuwait in August 1990.

In April 1990 Saddam Husain sent strongly-worded, somewhat polemical letters to Rafsanjani and Khamenei asking for negotiations at the highest possible level to promote peace 'not only between Iran and Iraq, but between Iran and the Arab Umma'.[12] He suggested that negotiations take place a mere six days later in Mecca. Rafsanjani's answer, dated 2 May 1990, was equally polemical and harsh in tone, referring to the 'imposed, unwanted war' and declaring that Iran had no problem with the 'Arab Umma'. He argued further that the continued occupation of Iranian territory by Iraqi forces would certainly prove a major obstacle to the successful conduct of negotiations and reiterated his full support for UNSC Resolution 598.

Saddam Husain answered this letter on 19 May, merely reiterating the points made in his first letter. Rafsanjani's response of 18 June agreed to negotiations at the highest level, but rejected Mecca as a meeting place because of the hostile attitude of the Saudi government to Iran.[13] The slow pace of the Iraqi–Iranian reconciliation formed the background to an Iranian quest for partners to help contain Saddam Husain.

The increasingly expansionist foreign policy of Iraq after 1988 was also viewed as dangerous by the majority of the GCC members. Iran, therefore, sought to drive a wedge between Iraq and its erstwhile supporters in the GCC. A precondition for this policy was a new image for Iran, one serious about turning over a new leaf in foreign relations. Iraq must no longer be seen as a necessary bulwark against Iran's export of the revolution. Rafsanjani looked for cooperation with the Arabs and the strengthening of political and economic relations. He denied any Iranian intentions to once again play the policeman of the Persian Gulf.[14]

Taking into consideration the strategic interests of Iran in the challenging period which included the ceasefire, the death of Khomeini, who had been the revolution's undisputed leader, and the beginning of the Second Gulf War, there were several reasons why its new leadership should want to court the GCC. First of all, GCC goodwill was essential for solidarity within OPEC when trying to secure stable oil production and prices. Since the Islamic Republic earns over 90 per cent of its foreign exchange by exporting oil, OPEC's ability to operate had absolute priority. Secondly, the Gulf Arab states offered a good prospective market for other Iranian exports, being relatively large and having considerable consumer power. Given the high per capita income in the littoral states and their need for agricultural and light consumer products, Iran has a twofold advantage – it is a competitive producer of these goods and it can expect favourable market conditions. Thirdly, the traditional ties between Iran and the southern sheikhdoms are a real asset to Iran since the ports of Dubai and Sharjah handle a significant portion of trade to and from the region. Fourthly, the financial surplus of the smaller Gulf Arab states could be invested, at least partly, in Iran, if the Islamic Republic could ensure the necessary preconditions. Fifth and finally, Iran would have the opportunity – as mentioned before – to use the GCC as a mediator between itself and Iraq.

A peace settlement would have allowed Iran to cut its defence budget substantially, freeing money that could then be redirected into economic reconstruction. Given the troubled relations between Iran and the GCC during the First Gulf War, it was clear, however, that the Islamic Republic would have to work hard to regain the trust of the Gulf Arab states and of potential investors and financiers.[15] Fortunately for the Iranian leadership, most of the GCC states welcomed the changes in Iran's foreign policy and were ready to give them a chance. The preconditions for a normalization of relations, at least between Iran and the smaller Gulf Arab states, had been created.

At first, it was hard for the leadership in Tehran to normalize relations with Kuwait after 1988 but the jubilation, expressed by the Kuwaiti government, press and public alike, over Iranian acceptance of UN Resolution 598 was an inducement. When Rafsanjani, at least verbally, abandoned the idea of exporting the Islamic revolution, the Al Sabah had less reason to mistrust their own Shia subjects. The Iranian government successfully requested an upgrading of its diplomatic relations with the Emirate. A Kuwaiti official told the *Washington Post* on 28 September that his government was prepared to resume friendly relations with Iran, emphasizing that he saw no need to consult Iraq before doing so.[16] By the end of September 1988, Kuwait had resumed full diplomatic relations with Iran. Yet it was the Second Gulf War and the common hostility to Iraq that led to a permanent improvement of mutual relations and a dwindling of the ill-feeling left over from the Iraq–Iran War, although the events of the former decade continued to have an effect.

Iran opposed the security agreement between Kuwait and the US vehemently[17] because it jeopardized plans to re-establish Iranian influence in the Gulf area. At the time, however, an improvement in relations with Iran was important for the Kuwaiti government and Kuwaiti officials asked their Iranian counterparts to 'consider the extraordinary vulnerability of Kuwait' and invited Rafsanjani to a summit in the Emirate to negotiate still existing 'discrepancies'.[18]

The change in Iranian foreign policy was also welcomed by other GCC members. Iran's Deputy Foreign Minister, Mohammad Ali Besharati, visited Bahrain in September 1988 and negotiated an upgrading of diplomatic relations, with an exchange of chargés d'affaires on 16 October 1988.

The Iranian foreign policy offensive was even more successful among the southern members of the GCC. As already mentioned, these states did not break off contact with Tehran during the First Gulf War. Due to their greater distance from the focal points of the war they could afford to continue lucrative commercial relations with Iran. These experiences were, therefore, very useful in the period after the First Gulf War. When Qatar's Emir assumed chairmanship of the ruler's council within the GCC after the war, he used this position to smooth the way for a further approach to Iran by the GCC.[19] He may have been encouraged to do so after meeting Mohammad Ali Besharati in September 1988.

The improved relationship also survived the Second Gulf War. At the end of 1991, a Qatari government delegation headed by the Crown Prince spent several days in Iran and had numerous conversations with leading Iranian politicians about the details of further political and economic cooperation.[20] The most important single project they agreed upon during the negotiations was the construction of a freshwater pipeline from the Karun river in Iran to Qatar, with an investment volume of US$ 13 billion.[21]

The UAE also welcomed the change in Iran's foreign policy as a 'turning point', and President Sheikh Zayed al-Nahayan spoke of Iran's courage in reaching that decision.[22] Ali Velayati tried to further improve relations by visiting the UAE in December 1988.

It goes without saying that the Omani reaction was similar, largely because Iran's relations with Oman have always been good, except for a few brief years immediately after the revolution. Oman has always looked on Iran as a counterweight to Saudi Arabia, since towards the latter Oman has had misgivings. The government in Masqat was even ready to mediate, along with Pakistan, between Iran and Iraq.[23] Before the Second Gulf War there was talk of a summit between Presidents Rafsanjani and Saddam Husain in Oman. An Iranian naval vessel made a courtesy visit to Oman, and the two countries concluded a number of agreements concerning economic and cultural cooperation.[24]

Iraq and Saudi Arabia were very concerned about Iran's approaches to the smaller Gulf Arab states. After all in the spring of 1988 the Saudi press was still supporting the renewed Iraqi push into Iranian territory, sometimes even going so far as to advocate the removal of the Iranian leadership.[25] But when the partners of the Al Saud in the GCC wholeheartedly welcomed Iran's revised foreign policy and acceptance of UN Resolution 598, the Saudi leaders became aware they were risking a breach in the hitherto solid cohesion of the GCC. In the summer of 1988, the Saudi government thus started to pressurize the Iraqi leadership to show some flexibility towards Iranian demands following the ceasefire.

The more conciliatory atmosphere emerging between Iran and Saudi Arabia in the autumn of 1988 brought an end to mutual attacks in the press, and expectations were made public that relations would be normalized in the not too distant future. Mohammad Besharati referred to Saudi Arabia when he stated: 'We are prepared to sit down, talk and overcome the great misunderstanding between us . . . neighbourhood is unchangeable . . . our holy shrines . . . and our Ka'ba are there. The Prophet is buried in Saudi Arabia. Can we ignore it?'[26]

But it soon became clear that the gap between Iran and Saudi Arabia would be far less easy to bridge than that between Iran and the smaller Gulf Arab states. The Mecca riots, Iranian intransigence over the quota for Iranian pilgrims, which had led to a rupture in diplomatic relations, and, indeed, continuing Saudi–Iranian competition for regional influence, made it quite natural that relations would take longer to mend.[27] Khomeini's hostility to the Al Saud was uncompromising, expressed even in his last Will and Testament. When Khomeini died, on 3 June 1989, there was hope on the other side of the Gulf that an improvement in relations might now occur. But despite Rafsanjani's and Khamenei's pragmatism, their hold on power was still tenuous and they were unable to shake off Khomeini's legacy of antagonism to Saudi Arabia.

The hardliners within the leadership were only temporarily silenced. They continued to hold powerful positions in government, wielding an influence that could not be ignored. They viewed every step of the new government with suspicion, ready at any given time to criticize it for unIslamic behaviour, even for surrender to the enemies of Islam. Such accusations could result in a fall from power if not death in the Islamic Republic of Iran.

Ali Velayati was frequently in trouble when responding to questions in the Majlis or from the press on Iran's contacts with unIslamic regimes, previously denounced as a matter of principle. He explained almost apologetically to the Tehran weekly *Soroush* that the resumption of diplomatic relations did not imply friendship or the resolution of differences. With skilful arguments he justified the approach of Iran towards the member states of the GCC:

> We have always considered Saddam Husain is an aggressor who earns no confidence at all. At least his military potential to wage a new aggression has to be destroyed . . . today the West and the states of the region have officially or unofficially confirmed the truth of our assessment.[28]

This was a reiteration of his argument made in 1988 in which he had stated that: '. . . the objective of the slogan "Neither East nor West" is the negation of alien domination and not [the] snapping of communications'.[29]

The first real test of the seriousness and stability of Iran's new foreign policy came with the Iraqi aggression against Kuwait on 2 August 1990. The new elements in this policy now became particularly significant since these important events next door forced the government in Tehran to explain its new foreign policy objectives in more detail.

Iran's neutrality and support for the UN, accompanied by its vociferous condemnation of the Iraqi invasion of Kuwait, gained it considerable international credit during the Second Gulf War. Its support for Kuwait's sovereignty was taken by the Gulf Arab states as proof of a genuinely new approach in Iranian foreign policy and confirmed that their acknowledgement of that change had paid off. Iran's recognition of the legitimacy of the Emir of Kuwait's rule was of particular significance, considering Iran had once tried to secure the overthrow of the Al Sabah by supporting dissident Islamic forces in Kuwait.[30]

But considering also the prevailing power of radicals within the Iranian leadership, this policy of neutrality also contained enormous risks for Rafsanjani and Khamenei. They came under frequent attack for allowing the return of substantial Western military influence to the Gulf. By supporting and implementing successive UN resolutions, the Iranian pragmatists tried 'to avoid any regional and international measures that represented an attempt to monopolize the Persian Gulf region under a unilateral US-imposed regime . . . The United Nations was regarded by Tehran as a preferable, if still unsatisfactory, forum for the resolution of the crisis.'[31]

On the other hand, the Iranian regime could not ignore the anti-Western atmosphere in neighbouring states after the start of the allied counteroffensive:

> Seeing themselves as the centre of the world Islamic movement, the Iranian leaders had no alternative but to support this populism in the Arab world . . . Ayatollah Khamenei responded by calling for resistance to the American and allied presence in the Gulf.[32]

Fortunately for Tehran, it received further opportunities to prove its usefulness to the international community at the same time as its Islamic credibility. Thousands of refugees, initially Pakistanis, Palestinians, Bangladeshis, Filipinos and Kuwaitis, escaped to Iran after 2 August 1990. Later Iran sheltered those fleeing the allied bombing of Iraq, including many diplomats and businessmen from all over the world, unable to escape from Iraq by air because of the embargo. Finally, it provided a safe haven for the Iraqi Shia fleeing from southern Iraq and Iraqi Kurds fleeing from the north after their failed attempts to overthrow Saddam Husain.[33]

Nevertheless, it was the Iraqi President who, involuntarily, handed the Iranian leadership their greatest success. According to increasingly reliable evidence, Rafsanjani realized that the Iraqi President would be willing to make almost any concession in return for assurances concerning further military operations. A few days before he invaded Kuwait, Saddam Husain sent a letter to Rafsanjani proposing that all disputed issues between the two states be put on the agenda for negotiation. His own proposals included the exchange of all prisoners of war and the withdrawal of all forces to internationally recognized borders within two months. On the issue of the Shatt al-Arab the Iraqi President suggested that future discussions should centre on the principles of fishing and navigation rights, dividing the revenues equally between both countries, and that the entire problem should be put up for arbitration, the results of which should be binding for both sides.[34]

In the months following the invasion Saddam Husain went even further. He held out the prospect of accepting the full implementation of UN Resolution 598 and renewing the validity of the 1975 Algiers Accord, conceding half of the Shatt al-Arab waterway to Iran.

Thus, in the course of the Second Gulf War, with apparently no hesitation, the Iraqi President surrendered what he and his country had so bitterly fought for over eight years, with a loss of hundreds of thousands of Iraqi lives, and at a cost of so much suffering for the civilian population. Due to his serious miscalculation of reactions to the invasion of Kuwait, the Iraqi President had little choice but to try and buy the tolerance of his former enemies.

In a statement on 11 December 1991 Javier Perez de Cuellar, the UN Secretary-General, named Iraq as the aggressor, the party responsible for starting the Iraq–Iran war. This statement fulfilled one of the key Iranian demands in negotiations over UN Resolution 598. This concession was not just a matter of prestige, but had profound legal implications on the issue of war reparations that the guilty party would be required to pay and which Iran calculated at over US$ 300 billion. But the Iraqi government reached the depths of humiliation when it sent its most valued military aircraft to Iran to save them from destruction.[35]

Thus, in the Second Gulf War, Iran belatedly won the First Gulf War, and without firing a shot. In addition, the efforts of the Iranian leadership to find a peaceful solution to the crisis in the months between August 1990 and January 1991, in order to save Iraq from destruction, helped its relations with many other Arab and Muslim states. Iran renewed diplomatic ties with Jordan, Tunisia and Morocco, and normalized its relations with Egypt, reopening interest sections in their respective capitals.

Iranian efforts to improve its relations with the member states of the GCC also included Saudi Arabia. Rafsanjani recognized that any improvement of the Iranian position in the Gulf area would depend upon a détente with Saudi Arabia. As early as December 1988, referring to Saudi Arabia, he declared:

We and they both have the desire to resolve problems pertaining to
bilateral relations . . . we did not have expansionist intentions from
the beginning, just as our southern neighbours do not have aggressive
designs . . . We urge our southern neighbours . . . to cooperate with
us in order to resolve existing issues concerning the oil markets,
maritime laws and Resolution 598.[36]

The Iraqi invasion of Kuwait and the radically altered balance of
power in the Gulf region after the Second Gulf War acted as catalysts
improving exchanges between Iran and Saudi Arabia. Iraq now proved
to be an even greater threat to Saudi Arabia than it had been during the
1970s. Iran's leadership followed the dictum that the enemy of my enemy
is my friend and the détente with Saudi Arabia thus became one of its
most remarkable successes during the Kuwait crisis, with full diplomatic
relations between both countries being restored on 19 March 1991.

Although the Iranian government repeatedly expressed disapproval
at the presence of Western troops in the heart of the Islamic world,
Tehran and Riyadh nevertheless managed to agree that both general
stability and securing their own power required a minimum degree of
partnership between them. Although there were disagreements over Shia
and Wahhabi missionary activity in Central Asia or – indirectly – in the
Afghan civil war, a series of remarkable diplomatic exchanges began in
the spring of 1991.

The Iranian Foreign Minister, Ali Velayati, paid an official visit to
Saudi Arabia in April 1991. On his arrival he was quoted in a semi-official
Saudi Arabian press bulletin as having said that the present positive
development in the relationship between the two countries was the result
of a deep and realistic understanding of the situation which prevailed in
the Gulf region.[37] In two rounds of lengthy negotiations, both Foreign
Ministers discussed a variety of issues ranging from Gulf security matters
and economic cooperation to the ongoing disputes over the hajj, OIC
and OPEC policies. During an audience with King Fahd it was decided
to convene a joint Iranian–Saudi economic commission. After the talks,
Velayati stressed that Iran and Saudi Arabia, as the two leading countries in
the Persian Gulf, had decided to pursue close, strategic and comprehensive
cooperation in order to ensure regional security. He added that during the
meetings he had insisted that regional security could not be maintained
without the participation of regional states, in particular the Islamic
Republic of Iran.

Saud al-Faisal, his Saudi Arabian counterpart, was quoted as saying that his country agreed with Iran that it was necessary for the two countries to cooperate in international organizations but was careful to point out that 'on the international scene, Saudi Arabia considers itself in the same rank as Iran'.[38]

Saud al-Faisal returned the visit in June 1991 accompanied by the Minister for Oil, Hisham Nazir. The negotiations covered almost the same issues as those discussed during Velayati's trip to Riyadh. Disagreements over the hajj were also resolved, to the satisfaction of both governments. For the first time in four years Iranians were given the unrestricted right to perform the pilgrimage. Rafsanjani actively urged Iranian pilgrims do all they could to guarantee a smooth hajj in 1991 and to avoid a repetition of the events which had led to the rupture of relations.[39] Problems would not come from Iranian pilgrims but from their leaders, still strongly influenced by the line of the Imam. Ayatollah Meshkini, Speaker of the Assembly of Experts, declared in Friday sermons in Qom that Iranian pilgrims still had a duty to denounce pagans during the hajj.[40] Khamenei reiterated this duty in a lengthy message to the pilgrims, but he was statesman-like enough not to make it a requirement of the forthcoming hajj.[41]

So Rafsanjani had good reason to fear that Iranian agitators would threaten the process of normalization with Iran's neighbours by their activities during the pilgrimage and that once again the international community would view the Islamic Republic as a lawless regime.[42] However, the Saudi government was astute enough to permit the Iranian pilgrims to demonstrate against America and Israel and restraint on both sides ensured that the demonstrations were orderly and no anti-Saudi slogans were chanted by the participants.[43] Both regimes agreed to an expansion of economic ties and to cooperate within OPEC[44] and the media of both countries widely covered the Foreign Ministers' visits.

In a lengthy commentary, Radio Tehran discussed the visits and assessed the current atmosphere:

> The Tehran–Riyadh ties, which resumed recently in the wake of an announcement that the Saudi Arabian authorities have agreed to Iran's request on the dispatch of hajj pilgrims, are improving rapidly and it is expected that, thanks to the existing understanding and the developments which have taken place in the region, the two countries' relations will be upgraded . . . Iran and Saudi Arabia, as

two countries of the Persian Gulf region and two oil-exporting states, have many points in common, although these have not led to the same outlook or stances in recent years. Within the framework of bilateral relations, the developments of the past decade and the Iran–Iraq war, in the course of which Saudi Arabia remained one of the financial backers of the Iraqi regime, were considered the main obstacle to an all-embracing link between the two countries. During this period a tense and unstable atmosphere dominated bilateral ties, so much so that any issue which somehow involved the two countries had no fate but confrontation and opposition. This confrontation was always conspicuous in OPEC, in the security issues of the Persian Gulf, in the presence of the foreign forces in the region, in the hajj and in international Islamic issues . . . In this connection one should not evaluate the visit of Saudi Arabia's Foreign Minister as a solution to all the existing disputes between Tehran and Riyadh; rather this visit is worthy of consideration within the framework of a fresh look at the problems and a different approach to them.[45]

The official Saudi Arabian government bulletin *Saudi Arabia* was more optimistic in characterizing the visits as a 'breakthrough' in bilateral relations.[46] A possible contributing factor to this euphoric assessment may have been a promise, given to Saud al-Faisal during his visit, that the Islamic Republic would no longer give support to opponents and 'dissenters of any colour' from member states of the GCC.[47] This then was the real turnaround in Iran's foreign policy that Uthman al-Umir, Editor-in-Chief of the Saudi Arabian daily *al-Sharq al-Awsat*, had observed, and that would complete the development of the Islamic Republic from a revolution to a state regime.[48]

In June 1991, Iran and Saudi Arabia upgraded their ties by appointing respective ambassadors. In September during the annual session of the United Nations General Assembly the Foreign Ministers of the GCC countries met Ali Akbar Velayati at the Iranian embassy in New York.[49] They discussed issues related to Gulf security, including Iran's role in it, and cooperation between Iran and the GCC. The GCC Foreign Ministers were encouraged by the meeting to propose negotiations to 'establish a framework for the strengthening of their relations'.[50] After the first meeting, Saud al-Faisal told reporters that if the current positive trends in Iran's diplomacy continued, Iran and the GCC could develop mutually beneficial relations during the 1990s. Later it became known that King Fahd had extended an invitation to Rafsanjani.[51]

In November 1991 the king presented Rafsanjani with a piece of the holy curtain of the Kaaba as a gesture of goodwill. The Iranian President took this opportunity to not only express his gratitude but to welcome the expansion of mutual relations 'in all the existing fields . . . We hope that thanks to the wisdom and the efforts of Islamic personalities, we will emerge from the present era in such a way as to remain proud before history and the Muslim people of the region.'[52] The rapprochement between Iran and Saudi Arabia culminated in Rafsanjani's visit to Riyadh in December 1991.

These gestures, however, should be viewed with scepticism. Despite the remarkable improvement in Iranian–Saudi Arabian relations, it should be pointed out that a number of important issues remained unresolved at the beginning of the 1990s. These included the future leadership of and security in the Persian Gulf area and the traditional sources of tension between Arabs and Iranians. Both countries continued to see each other as ideological enemies.

Rafsanjani's rejection of the ideology of exporting the Islamic revolution, which had clearly reached a dead end, and the priority given to Iran's national interests[53] also resulted in a revitalization of the traditional relationship between Iran and other neighbours such as Turkey and Pakistan.

The Regional Cooperation for Development (RCD), a trilateral economic pact between Iran, Turkey and Pakistan, which had been dissolved after the downfall of the Shah, was revived in 1990 with the establishment of the Economic Cooperation Organization (ECO). In establishing the ECO, the three states had ambitious intentions. The ECO was to create a bridge to the GCC, with the hope of an eventual merger between the two organizations. These ideas were discussed at some length when the Turkish President Özal met Rafsanjani in Tehran on 10 November 1990. After the negotiations Rafsanjani told the press: 'In the meeting with President Targut Özal, the expansion of collaboration through the ECO was emphasized. The ECO can be used as a framework for a common market and other countries can join in, if they wish to do so.'[54] However, the most remarkable response to this offer came from Central Asia and not from the GCC. Although these new Central Asian members strengthened the ECO, they also created certain difficulties for Iran and Turkey, who were both competing for influence in those regions of the former Soviet Union.

Whilst political relations between Iran and Turkey remained ambivalent, the improvement of relations with Pakistan absorbed a good deal of Iran's attention. Top politicians of both countries regularly exchanged opinions on bilateral, regional and global matters and the Centres for Strategic Studies in both countries coordinated their programmes on 17 August 1991.[55]

In addition to its dealings within the ECO, the Iranian government also tried to make use of the favourable conditions created by the Kuwait crisis to enhance its relations with other organizations including the United Nations and, in particular, the OIC. In October 1991, revolutionary Iran appointed a permanent envoy to the OIC (S. Zanganeh) for the first time, thus increasing its weight in the Islamic world.

But Rafsanjani and his followers had further ambitions to reintegrate Iran into the world market, naming South Korea and Turkey as successful examples for Iran to emulate in the period after the Second Gulf War.[56] They were fully aware that such a reintegration presupposed an improvement in relations with the West. Given the dominant position of the United States in the West, Rafsanjani needed to develop an effective approach to the United States, without, however, creating an impression in his own country and in the Muslim world generally that he was surrendering to America. Iran also sought better relations with Europe, encouraging the European Community to participate in the reconstruction of Iran's economy. The prospects for such a policy were hopeful, largely due to the increased international stature of Iran.

Iran was, however, primarily interested in negotiating a new regional order with the GCC states. Rafsanjani intended to securely establish the new image of the Islamic Republic in the minds of its neighbours in order to better the position of his country in the post-war order. On the one hand and despite his approaches to the American government, he made tremendous efforts to keep the United States out of any future regional security arrangements, on the other hand he insisted that Iran was integral to such arrangements.

To this end he emphasized the GCC's own concepts of self-reliance, hoping that such a strategy would reduce the GCC's dependency on foreign powers and on America in particular. Iran would then be able to secure its image as the guardian of autonomy and conscience in the GCC.[57] Only by removing the high-profile Western, and especially American, military presence in the region, would Iran be able to strengthen its own position and fulfil its ambition to become the regional replacement of the West. Having removed Western military presence from the Gulf, Iran could again attempt to assert itself as the dominant power and the only one equipped to ensure peace in the region:

> Thus what may have started as a short-term Iranian policy of isolating Iraq though rapprochement with the West and its Gulf Arab allies was to blossom into a new framework of reference to guide Iran's foreign policy after the ceasefire.[58]

But Iran's efforts were not met with success in either regard.

The revitalized prospect of cooperation over security between Iran and the GCC alarmed Washington. Only the American military protection of the Gulf Arab states could legitimize the permanent presence of the United States in a region President Carter had declared in 1977 to be of vital interest to the US. The American government had never forgiven the Islamic Republic for the indignity bestowed upon the US with its defeat in the revolution of 1978–9. In the absence of a bellicose Iraq, American policy portrayed Iran as the main regional threat to the sheikhdoms. Washington presented the GCC with its own terms for regional security, offering official security treaties to each of the interested parties. Wary after the experience of the Second Gulf War, the majority of the GCC states agreed. Regardless of the future results of the policy, the United States, for the time being, was successful in convincing its allies of the advantages of a dual containment of both Iraq and Iran.

Tehran was naturally annoyed that, despite the 'honeymoon' after the ceasefire in 1988, the GCC states preferred to look for a counterweight to Iran's rising power rather than to develop a strategy of cooperation and collective action. Furthermore, it failed to convince the West that its endorsement of cooperation with the GCC could be seen as proof that it no longer sought to overthrow the Gulf regimes or to disrupt the flow of oil from the region.[59]

Iran's disappointment became even more evident when the 'Gulfanization' of future security arrangements was replaced by an 'Arabization'. The Arab states still feared that if Iran was allowed to become a full member of any Gulf security arrangement it would inevitably become the dominant partner. A number of the Arab participants of Desert Shield and Desert Storm met between 5 and 6 March 1991 in Damascus and issued the Damascus Declaration on Gulf security, signed by the Foreign Ministers of Egypt, Syria and the six GCC member states. The so-called 6+2 formula directly threatened the Iranian strategy of involvement in any future security arrangement. Tehran immediately dispatched Ali Velayati and Vice President Habibi to Damascus to express Iran's displeasure at its apparent exclusion from this security scheme. They privately expressed their dismay to the Syrian President, who had been Iran's strongest ally in the 1980s, that Iran's views had not been taken into account when the security arrangement was formulated.[60]

The possible deployment of Egyptian and Syrian military forces in the Persian Gulf, as envisaged by the accord, was interpreted by Iran as a serious attack on its legitimate interests in the region and its security strategy. In response to the 6+2 formula, the Iranian government called for the inclusion of both Iraq and Iran in the GCC. Of course, Iran was aware that as long as Saddam Husain remained in power, Iraq's inclusion would remain a contentious issue. As might be expected, the GCC did not respond directly to this demand but instead sought a de-escalation of the matter by offering participation of Iran and Turkey in a broader, non-military union. This proposal however did not satisfy Iran's expectations. On the contrary, Iran became particularly concerned about the apparent attempts by Egypt to present itself as the main guarantor of security for the GCC states, in other words for the Gulf as a whole.[61]

It was of no help to Tehran that the 6+2 arrangement lasted no more than a few months, outmanoeuvred by the mutual defence agreements between several GCC states and the United States. Therefore, one must conclude that the new Iranian foreign policy had failed with respect to security in the Gulf, making the policy as a whole only partially successful.

However, relations with the Arab world, and in particular with the GCC, remained a priority in the new Iranian foreign policy for three reasons: oil, the location of the most important religious centres of Islam, and the American military presence. Iran continued to try and reach a *modus vivendi* with the Gulf states, trying to prove that, in the long run, there could be no security in the region without Iranian involvement.[62] Despite set-backs, Iran's neutral policy during the Second Gulf War turned out to be a remarkable success for the Islamic Republic.

Saudi Arabia – a military winner, but an economic loser

The prominent position of Saudi Arabia as one of the most important members of the alliance against Saddam Husain in the Second Gulf War failed to result in political success after the war had ended. Although the Al Saud were able to survive the danger of being swept away by Iraq's superior war machine, they came under frequent attack from Islamists both inside and outside the country for having accepted the presence of large numbers of Western soldiers on the soil of the most holy places in Islam. Securing a military victory over Saddam Husain became a costly burden for the Al Saud with lasting consequences in the post-war period. The cliché of an immensely rich Saudi Arabia was first established in the 1970s. When the world price for oil rocketed in 1973 from less than US$2 per barrel to more than US$11 per barrel, it meant unbelievably high foreign currency incomes for the producer countries almost overnight. As the biggest Arab producer of liquid hydrocarbon, Saudi Arabia was the main beneficiary of this financial boom.

In spite of the tremendous drive to economic modernization pursued by King Faisal, Saudi Arabia was initially unable to absorb this level of foreign currency inflow. The government in Riyadh therefore invested extensively in the industrial countries. The international media, especially the financial press, was filled with reports of billions of Saudi Arabian petrodollars floating through the Western financial markets. But in general Saudi Arabia was more interested in the safety of its foreign investments, and only to a much lesser degree in achieving the highest possible interest rates.[63] Two consequences arose from this: On one hand, large portions of Saudi Arabian foreign capital could not be liquidated because of long term investments, and on the other hand, the inflation rate in the deposit countries frequently exceeded obtainable interest and it would have been more economic under such conditions to leave the oil in the ground. But due to various interests within OPEC this was not an option for Saudi Arabia.

Since his assumption of power in the early 1960s, King Faisal had been, as has been said, exceptionally interested in economic modernization. In addition to his many other merits he had put the economic development of his country on the right track, from 1973 until he was murdered in 1975, increasing the government's capacity to handle the cash flow within the country's borders. The government's Five-Year Plans now began to give serious consideration to the previously unknown financial power of Saudi Arabia. Within a few years a modern infrastructure and an effective and sophisticated communications network were created and modern enterprises were established, not only within the oil industry but within other branches of the economy, particularly in the building and construction industries. New educational institutions, hospitals and social service facilities were established, whilst others were redeveloped or replaced.

The economic boom influenced further differentiation within Saudi Arabian society as big merchants, industrialists and commission agents multiplied their profits. But a unique division of responsibilities emerged during the boom. Whereas the state took care of the costly preconditions for economic development, particularly in the infrastructure, the higher echelons of private enterprise were only interested in making a profit, although always with the involvement of the Royal court. In the overheated economic atmosphere this specific dependency of the private economic sector on the state was created and nepotism and corruption flourished more than ever before. But the treasury was so amply filled that even workers, smaller businessmen and craftsmen participated in the boom, without really questioning the extremely inequitable distribution of wealth. Even the lowest echelons of Saudi Arabian society, the Bedouin amongst others, now an uprooted and urbanized rural population, received a small, albeit much welcome, portion of state welfare.

Until the end of the 1970s, this development had hardly any serious setbacks. In 1980 alone, the Saudi Arabian state earned US$ 102.2 billion from oil exports.[64] In 1981 the result was nearly repeated when US$ 101.2 billion in oil export earnings filled the pockets of the Saudi government. This constituted nothing less than an increase by a factor of 53 in the Saudi oil export income within a single decade.[65] In the same year the foreign currency reserves of Saudi Arabia reached a level of US$ 150 billion.[66] But it peaked at that amount.

Like all product markets the international oil market is subject to certain cycles, and it was quite natural that after the long, unbroken boom of the 1970s a recession would set in during the 1980s, lasting almost as long as the preceding economic trend. The export earnings of Saudi Arabia decreased rapidly. In 1982 only US$ 76 billion flowed into the Saudi treasury. In 1983 the amount was hardly more than US$ 37 billion.[67] The weaknesses of the Saudi Arabian economic development plan became visible, including the almost complete dependence of production on revenue generated from oil, the expenditure-oriented strategy of the government primarily driven by political motives to ensure the dominance of the state but lacking a sound economic base, the weak roots of the economic elite in the productive sphere with assignment of essential productive functions to foreign capital and a foreign workforce and an unprofitable structure of products with a potential for export, particularly products of the first processing level of crude oil.[68]

Even the most important source of Saudi Arabia's income before the oil era, the profits from the pilgrimage to Mecca and Medina, had almost disappeared. An average of two million pilgrims per annum, staying from two to seven weeks in Saudi Arabia, clearly spent considerable amounts of money, but the money was earned by Hijazi merchants and businessmen, whilst the state actually incurred losses through the cost of its responsibility for the infrastructure and services.

In the end, therefore, only reliance on reserves and acceptance of a budget deficit remained as options for the government. In April 1983, the Saudi budget foresaw expenditures of US$ 73.2 billion for the fiscal year 1983–4, while expecting an income of US$ 63.9 billion. Reserves would balance the budget. As it became clear, in the course of the year, that actual earnings would not exceed US$ 53.2 billion, some government projects were stopped and others were delayed. Through these measures expenditure was lowered to US$ 63.1 billion. This situation occurred again in April 1984. For the fiscal year 1984–5 planning figures were set at US$ 60.9 billion in income and at US$ 73.8 billion in expenditure, which meant drawing on state reserves to the extent of almost US$ 13 billion.[69] However, worse was still to come. In 1986, Saudi Arabia only earned US$ 28.5 billion from oil exports.[70] Due to constant draining, Saudi Arabia's financial reserves fell to approximately US$ 50 billion by the end of the decade. The fall in oil income forced a novel economic course on the Saudi Arabian government.

Economic programmes were reduced or the periods for their realization were prolonged. Even military procurement programmes were subject to revision. It became increasingly harder for the Al Saud to maintain the standards of the comprehensive state welfare system established in the 1970s.

They were also aware of the fact that the growing contradictions within society could only be handled through buying off latent political opposition. Whilst recognizing the skilful management of internal affairs by the Al Saud, the success of the welfare system in appeasing social discontent should not be overestimated. As K. McLachlan pointed out:

In real terms, the country made rapid improvements in areas of human welfare but stayed relatively in the lowest international rank. Oil income singularly failed to buy those improvements in human conditions that are not susceptible to instant cures. The dichotomy between material wealth and physical facilities *vis à vis* the low educational and health status of a large proportion of the Saudi Arabian people was a constant source of social friction both among the Saudi Arabians themselves and between Saudis and better-educated foreigners whom they employed.[71]

But, full of hope, the Saudi Arabian government awaited the end of the recession in the world oil market and an increase in prices in the second half of the 1980s. It enthusiastically welcomed all forecasts that predicted a 'clear relaxation of the international demand for oil accompanied by increasing prices as of about 1988'.[72] Market and prices, however, actually stagnated until the outbreak of the Second Gulf War.

Panic, uncertainty and the loss of Iraqi and Kuwaiti oil caused the world market price to soar from US$ 16 per barrel to more than US$ 30 per barrel in the second half of 1990. Spot market prices even topped US$ 40 per barrel.[73] A few weeks after the ceasefire, however, the prices evened out again to a level somewhere between US$ 15 and US$ 18 per barrel, and it became obvious that the unbridled expenditure of the 1970s would remain an unique event.

The Saudi Arabian government had to adjust its policies to accommodate these facts. The enormous financial losses during the Kuwait crisis marked the final point in a decade of pecuniary descent. The Gross Domestic Product (GDP) of Saudi Arabia in 1991 equalled only one third of the GDP of 1981,[74] and a state debt of US$ 55 billion had accumulated since 1983.[75] This situation was only partially corrected by the short-term tripling of oil income in the second half of 1990.

Of course, spot market prices of US$ 30–40 per barrel and the simultaneous increase of the Saudi Arabian production level from 5.4 million barrels per day (bpd) to approximately 8 million bpd must have improved the balance sheets. But – according to its own statistics – the Saudi government contributed a total of US$ 69 billion to Desert Shield and Desert Storm,[76] and had to pay out US$ 30 billion for American military hardware alone. Only in January of 1994 did the governments in Riyadh and Washington agree upon the prolongation of a repayment rate of US$ 6 billion for the coming financial year.[77] At any rate, the short-term surplus profits of 1990 were not enough to solve the increasing financial problems of Saudi Arabia resulting from both Gulf Wars; the enormous Saudi payments to Iraq during the First Gulf War must also be taken into consideration.

In fact frequent financial deficits continued. Due to the war, no regular state budget was fixed for 1991. In 1992–3 the government expected a deficit of US$ 3.9 billion, but the gap between income and expenditure amounted to US$ 10.5 billion. In an attempt at realism the ministries in Riyadh predicted a deficit of US$ 7.4 billion for the financial year of 1993–4 and showed some pride when it only reached US$ 8 billion. A balanced budget was scheduled for 1994–5, the first time this had occurred. This meant only a further reduction of government expenditure. The new budget foresaw a reduction of expenditure for cities and municipalities by 24.5 per cent.[78] These reductions carried one obvious message: the government considered saving essential even in the most sensitive areas.

In a broad-based propaganda campaign it fought back against what were termed insinuations in the international press that the financial power of Saudi Arabia was exhausted. It referred to 260 billion barrels of proven oil reserves in the ground, constituting 25 per cent of the world's oil reserves and making Saudi Arabia one of the richest countries in the world. Riyadh proclaimed that its foreign deposits still amounted to US$ 79 billion in 1992 but did not mention that the majority of these deposits were not liquid.[79]

> If these assets have declined over the years, this was because of a genuine threat that has never been anticipated and by this we mean the Gulf War [although this did not mention the losses before the war]. These assets have also been directed toward serving basic infrastructure projects which themselves are considered precious assets whose value increases by the passage of time.[80]

In addition, propaganda referred to the international normality of budget deficits. The United States deficit had after all reached US$ 334 billion in 1992. Even considering the difference in number of inhabitants, the gap between income and expenditure still seemed to be negligible in Saudi Arabia.[81]

It was undoubtedly convenient for the government that the business community profited from the Second Gulf War. Banks and private industry found additional tasks for themselves as suppliers of goods and services to the allied forces or as lenders to exiled Kuwaiti citizens. *Saudi Arabia* quoted a leading banker from Riyadh with the words: 'The Saudi economy is fundamentally strong, and borrowing simply makes good sense,' referring to Prince Abdallah ibn Faisal, the chairman of the Royal Commission for Jubail and Yanbu, who – according to a prominent witness – said: 'One of the reasons why the government is borrowing is to increase the confidence of the private sector.'[82] But the enthusiasm was definitely dampened by the determination of the government not to allow further budget deficits.

The budget discipline of a government primarily affects the middle and lower strata of society, which in Saudi Arabia also constitutes the majority of the population. Immediately after the war the government distributed 'presents', most likely for the last time. It suspended payment of public housing mortgages for two years, lowered traffic rates and increased the subsidies for grain, a present to the Bedouin. But these cosmetic operations could only barely conceal the radical cutbacks in the Saudi Arabian welfare state. Saudi Arabia undoubtedly continues to be an immensely rich country providing many social services to its population, but its resources are by no means sufficient to continue the chequebook diplomacy of the 1970s. Saudi Arabian foreign policy will obviously be forced to take its reduced financial abilities into account.

A new working relationship
Having returned to normality after the turbulence of the Second Gulf War, it is important to consider whether the new relationship between Iran on the one hand and Saudi Arabia and its partners within the GCC on the other could prevail. There were, as has been said, various reasons for the rapprochement, but a further factor must be mentioned: Iraq's aggression against Kuwait was a kind of moral victory for Tehran over the Gulf Arab states who had encouraged Iraq in its war against Iran and bankrolled its war efforts. Radio Tehran later commented, almost maliciously: 'At any rate the Iran–Iraq war ended; and Iraq, by attacking Kuwait, rewarded Kuwait and Saudi Arabia for their financial support.'[83] After Saddam Husain invaded Kuwait, the Foreign Minister of the Emirate went so far as to express regret for his country's previous support of Iraq.[84] In such an atmosphere it became much easier for Iran to re-establish

satisfactory relations with the Gulf states, to buttress and stabilize oil revenues, and also to try and prevent further American encroachments into the region.[85]

The eleventh summit meeting of the GCC in Qatar, in December 1990, acknowledged the need for new collaborative arrangements for regional security between neighbouring countries including Iran. Naturally still unaware of the doomed 6+2 arrangement, followed by the signing of bilateral defence pacts between the United States and several Gulf Arab states, Iran reacted positively to the Qatar summit. Morteza Sarmadie, spokesman for the Iranian Foreign Ministry, was quoted as saying:

> The Islamic Republic of Iran has always sought to expand regional cooperation with neighbouring Islamic countries, based on mutual respect. This communiqué could be regarded as a welcome beginning for some fundamental collaboration between the countries of the region to end the need for the presence of foreign troops in the region . . . Iran would be ready to collaborate in all aspects of the security plans.[86]

On the other hand, the Iranian leadership was skilful enough to recognize the New World Order envisaged by the American President, George Bush, and the West's undiminished need to secure its access to Gulf oil, demonstrated by the war against Iraq. Frequently attacked by radicals and hardliners inside and outside the regime, Rafsanjani and his closest followers reconciled themselves, at least temporarily, to American hegemony. They intensified their campaign to re-establish Iran's membership in the community of nations, which was probably aimed, *inter alia*, at ensuring recognition of their interests in the Gulf region.[87]

Rafsanjani obviously remembered Bush's inaugural address of January 1989 in which the new American President had stated that goodwill begets goodwill, signalling the new American administration's desire to improve relations with Tehran if, for example, the Iranian government would use its influence in Lebanon to free the American hostages being held by Hizballah and other groups sympathetic to the Islamic Republic. Bush had made it clear that such assistance would be long remembered by his administration, and one of the leading Iranian dailies, *Ettela'at*, published an editorial urging the Iranian leadership to support the United States by helping to obtain the release of the American hostages in Lebanon.[88]

But even at the height of his power, Rafsanjani could not afford to re-establish direct, official contacts with the United States. The foreign policy reformers in Tehran recognized clearly that their opponents' tolerance would definitely be exceeded if they tried to improve the relationship with the United States openly and officially.

Velayati condemned the 'unipolar world order of the presence' while declaring his firm conviction that the arguments between the United States, Europe, Latin America and 'the South' would become so frequent within the next ten years that several power centres would emerge, checking the dominant influence of America and 'providing us with enough air to breathe again.'[89] In such an atmosphere even indirect commercial contacts had to be hidden by the government. Only unavoidable concessions were revealed to the public, such as the payment of US$ 600 million to AMOCO as compensation for nationalized property on the island of Kharq, because until agreement had been reached on this point AMOCO had successfully hindered Iranian oil exports on the world market.[90]

Unfortunately, President Bush's suggestions had never been translated into practical politics. The relationship between Iran and the 'Great Satan', America, remained cool. Largely due to American prevarication, it seems that Iranian–American animosity will continue to be a constant factor in global politics. Shireen Hunter may well be right when she states: 'The basic US attitude toward Iran . . . has boiled down to a single proposition: in the post-cold war era Iran is no longer important and if the United States waits long enough the Iranians will have no choice but to come back on American terms. If recent changes in Tehran have created new opportunities to begin some movement in the direction of ending US–Iranian hostility, Washington has not fashioned a response.'[91]

US government aloofness complicated Rafsanjani's efforts to improve relations with the West without losing face. He therefore sought an intermediary of some stature. For various reasons Saudi Arabia was the perfect choice. Without a doubt, Iran's efforts to improve its relations with Riyadh were also driven by its desire to upgrade at the very least her economic relations with the West, particularly with the United States.[92]

Although they did not really intend acting as an intermediary between Tehran and Washington, the Saudi government nevertheless had many other reasons to reply positively to the offers of normalization. The Al Saud never wanted antagonistic relationships with equal or superior powers. They were therefore, in general, pleased at the prospect of a working relationship with the leadership of the Islamic Republic. The Royal family's grip on power was seriously undermined by the presence of hundreds of thousands of foreign troops in Saudi Arabia during the Kuwait crisis. Radical Muslims from all over the world as well as within the Kingdom questioned the legitimacy of a regime that tolerated the desecration of Islam's holiest places. The disappointment in Saudi Arabia was fed by the frustrations of the numerous young graduates from universities and religious schools who had been unable to find jobs in the Kingdom's deteriorating economic conditions. Separately, but at the same time as the liberals, they campaigned for participation in the political process and for social reforms.[93] Given the sensitivity of the Al Saud to anything affecting the religious basis of their legitimacy, it became clear that they had to react quickly.

On the one hand, they initiated some political proto-reforms, establishing a Consultative Council in March 1992, but on the other hand, they tried to avoid more foreign accusations of behaviour against the precepts of Islam such as Iran had made throughout the 1980s. Silencing Iran's reproaches would mean a major political success for the embattled Royal family. According to the Al Saud, one promising measure could be renewing the prominent involvement of Iran in OIC activities.

Iran's Deputy Foreign Minister for International Affairs, Manuchehr Motaki, was invited to Riyadh on 21 October 1991 to discuss the expansion of bilateral ties with his Saudi counterpart, Abd al-Rahman Mansuri, not only in the fields of economy, commerce, agriculture and oil, but also in shaping a common strategy for the forthcoming OIC summit in Dakar. In order to achieve this objective, both sides agreed to exchange ambassadors before the summit.[94] The atmosphere at the Dakar conference (6–11 December 1991) was thus more affected by inter-Arab resentment arising from the Second Gulf War than by Iranian–Arab antagonism. It was not Iran but Iraq that boycotted the meeting, accusing the Al Saud – as Iran once had – of manipulating the OIC. It could be said that relations between Iran and Saudi Arabia improved in direct proportion to the deterioration of Saudi–Iraqi relations.

The united Iran–Saudi Arabian approach was aimed against Iraq as the third competitor for power in the Persian Gulf. Thus when the Saudi Foreign Minister, Saud al-Faisal, visited Tehran in 1991, he granted an audience to Mohammad Baqr al-Hakim, the exiled Iraqi Shia leader, and indicated the possibility of Saudi Arabian support for the Shia resistance in Iraq.[95]

At present the uncertain future of Iraq makes it difficult to predict when and in what form the country will once again participate in the traditional contest for dominance in the Gulf region. Whether this will take at least a decade, as M. E. Ahrari claims, is doubtful in view of the rapidity of political developments in the region.[96] But in the first half of the 1990s it was the Iran–Saudi relationship that dominated the Gulf.

Without doubt, the OIC proceedings served as a vehicle to advance Iranian–Saudi normalization.[97] The OIC could provide ground for common activities, as the Iranian media later admitted: 'the OIC further reveals the significance of bilateral relations between Iran and Saudi Arabia. This is so because, if the two countries reach a ground for bilateral understanding, their key and effective role in improving the situation of the Muslim umma will become undeniable. Therefore, under the present conditions, when bloody fighting in some Islamic countries has created a difficult situation, the [power] of Muslim umma coordination among the OIC member-states, especially Iran and Saudi Arabia, can be of special significance in following up the problems of Muslim nations.'[98]

Immediately after the Dakar meeting in December 1991, the first summit of the GCC states after the Second Gulf War was held. The heads of state finally abandoned the failed 6+2 arrangement against which Iran had lobbied so vehemently. The final communiqué recognized positive developments between the GCC and Iran, expressing a strong desire to further improve those ties. But, it stopped short of envisaging direct Iranian participation in any collective security scheme for the region. Abdallah Bishara, the first Secretary General of the GCC, had previously supported increased Iranian involvement in Gulf security matters, saying that there would be no security or stability in the Gulf region without the inclusion of the Islamic Republic of Iran and understanding with Tehran.

However, he was careful enough to speak of an Iranian role only in terms of the security of the Gulf waters, not the mainland areas of the Arab states. According to Bishara, Iran's role would be limited to the sea and navigation routes, as Iran was a major partner in securing these routes. According to Iran's leadership, a further limit on Iran's future influence was set when defence contracts were signed between the United States and several GCC states: 'The private security of the regional states has nothing to do with the total security of the area.'[99]

Nevertheless, Iran quickly responded that it had no desire to station troops in any GCC states, nor would it object to any of the GCC states signing security agreements with the West. Tolerating Western involvement in the security of the GCC states indicated that the pragmatists still had the upper hand in Tehran. The Deputy Foreign Minister, Mohammad Besharati, however, reiterated that the security of the Persian Gulf was not an exclusively Arab concern and that Iran and the GCC had a mutual interest in maintaining security in the region.[100]

Despite the continuing competition between Iran and Saudi Arabia over a wide range of issues, including economic affairs, oil, dominance in the Gulf, utilization of Islam, influence in Central Asia and Africa and relations with the West, both countries tried to keep the working relationship established between them during the specific circumstances of the Kuwait crisis alive. Velayati said in an interview in 1993 that the two countries were at the stage of 'confidence building,' and hoped that they would patch up their differences and not be satisfied with the slow pace in this direction. Although no dates had been fixed as yet, he was optimistic about another Iranian–Saudi summit, since both heads of state had expressed their intention to meet each other.[101]

When the Saudi Minister for Higher Education, Abd al-Aziz Khuwaithir, visited Rafsanjani in January 1994, the official Voice of the Islamic Republic of Iran radio station concluded:

> Though Iranian–Saudi Arabian ties have undergone several ups and downs during recent years, the trend of events of recent months speaks for the fact that the two countries' officials, in view of the significance of Iranian–Saudi unity and the need for expanding bilateral cooperation, have opened a new phase of bilateral ties with the intention of reinforcing unity among Islamic countries and overcoming the problems of the Muslim world . . . It is worth noting that during the meeting, President Hashemi Rafsanjani welcomed the strengthening of ties in the areas of mutual interest, stressing the need for the exchange of economic and political delegations between the two countries, so as to bring the viewpoints of Iran and Saudi Arabia closer.[102]

Whilst summits attended by both President Rafsanjani and King Fahd remained an exception, lower level negotiations and consultations continued throughout the first half of the 1990s.

Although Iran never abandoned its firm belief that Gulf security should be maintained through regional cooperation, without any foreign interference, it agreed with its Saudi Arabian partners that the door for negotiations must be kept open and that, at any given time, it should be possible to receive each other's Foreign Ministers in order to resolve any difference.[103] Such moderate political behaviour was sufficient to minimize the danger of a sudden and unpredictable deterioration in the bilateral ties, but due to the deep and lasting differences between both countries confrontation could never be eliminated completely.

From foe to partner, to what?

The history of the Persian Gulf since the Second World War graphically illustrates a permanent trilateral struggle for dominance. Three countries, Iran, Iraq and Saudi Arabia, constitute the corners of a balanced triangle continually trying to stay in equilibrium. If one of them seems to be getting the upper hand, there is an immediate response from the other two. During the 1970s Imperial Iran and Saudi Arabia together withstood radical Iraqi nationalism which was supported by the Warsaw Pact. In the 1980s both Saudi Arabia and Iraq fought the Islamic Republic of Iran and its efforts to export its version of radical Islam. At the beginning of the 1990s, Iran and Saudi Arabia once again came to terms with each other in order to prevent domination by Iraq's Saddam Husain.

By the mid-1990s, however, Iraq seemed to be out of the race for some years to come. This opened up new possibilities for intensified competition between Iran and Saudi Arabia, no longer forced by circumstances to unite against a third party. The leadership of the Islamic Republic seemed intent on reverting to the Gulf politics of the Shah, although denying it vehemently in public. The Shah not only built up his military prowess to become the main protagonist in the Gulf, but he also wanted his country to emerge as the dominant actor in oil issues. Militarily speaking, no Gulf state could have challenged Imperial Iran.[104] Looking at the relevant Gulf strategies of the Islamic Republic, the similarities are obvious. Saudi Arabia, on the contrary, continued to maintain claims to leadership in the Gulf based on its superior oil reserves and its dominant position within OPEC.

But, essentially, Saudi Arabia is in many ways at a disadvantage compared to Iran, including in terms of size, population, diversity of resources, capacity and structure of the economy, and military potential. Iran is still going through a painful recovery from the wounds of the First Gulf War. Its military strength is by no means comparable to that during the Shah's rule, but it has nevertheless been superior to Saudi Arabia's since the mid-1990s. Despite steady imports of sophisticated Western weaponry for decades, Saudi Arabia still suffers the embarrassment of being unable to defend its territory and that of its allies in the GCC without outside help. The record of the Saudi Arabian military does not hold out the prospect of a rapid improvement.

For many years after the Kingdom's foundation, the country simply did not have the financial resources to establish a major army. With the rapid improvement in finances in the 1970s, the government in Riyadh tried to create a small volunteer force but with very limited success. The reasons for this failure include the small population of Saudi Arabia, low unemployment rates during the 1970s and early 1980s resulting in middle and upper class resistance to a military career for their children and resistance to either a reserve army or draft recruitment.

For a long time, therefore, army recruitment was almost exclusively limited to those who had very little or no education. There were some exceptions: the Air Force, the Air Defence Forces and the Engineers Corps were able to attract capable university graduates by offering generous financial inducement and a degree of social status. But these branches of the armed forces do not decisively define the overall military power of a country. However, accompanying the economic slowdown of recent years, recruitment of capable graduates by the armed forces is growing. This has allowed the Saudi government to increase the size of its forces from approximately 66,000 in 1990 to 102,000 in 1994,[105] but these numbers are still far below those of Iran, and there are no details available on the military capabilities, motivation and vigour of the new Saudi recruits.

Well-known Iran experts therefore came to the conclusion that the outcome of the Second Gulf War created favourable conditions for Iran to resume the role of leading power in the Gulf region.[106] Others modified that opinion by asserting that the remarkable détente between Iran and its neighbours only occurred because Iran was in desperate need of time and peaceful conditions to restore its military potential.

By taking control of the public sector during the First Gulf War, the Iranian clergy succeeded in dominating almost the entire Iranian economy. Since 1980, the clergy has become the biggest collective owner of the means of production. They have gradually developed an interest in enlarging their economic power through expansion beyond the national borders, if necessary by military means, as proven by their attempts to conquer parts of Iraq. Ayatollah Khomeini's determination to export the Islamic revolution became for many years the perfect ideological cover for his followers' interest in economic expansion.

The main forces determining Iranian politics since 1988 seem to prefer more peaceful means of achieving their objectives, either for political reasons or from economic and military constraints. It should not be forgotten that one of the consequences of the Iraq–Iran war has been a considerable diminution of Iran's hegemonic ambition. Their military forces are still weak. Although the Iranian government is pursuing a hectic programme of rearmament, it will still take years before the great military potential of the country is restored. Nevertheless, even after the ceasefire with Iraq and the death of Khomeini, the influence of those political forces within the Islamic Republic who took advantage of the war with Iraq to seize power, and who are afraid of losing everything in peace, is still omnipresent.

The supporters of the radical 'line of the Imam' in Iran had been pushed into the background. However, should the policies of the pragmatists have failed, it was very likely they would take hold of power again. The President had to avoid displaying any sign of weakness before his domestic opponents, who continually reproached him for abandoning the ideals and vision of Khomeini. For these adversaries even normalizing the relationship with the Gulf Arab states meant a danger 'of becoming a hostage of the United States again'.[107] Khomeini's son, Ahmad, had emphasized that nobody was authorized to publish personal interpretations of the Imam's opinions on a correct foreign policy, let alone express doubts about them.[108] The influential Representative for Mashhad in the Majlis, Qorbanali Salehabadi, elaborated further in an editorial in the daily paper *Resalat* that re-establishing diplomatic relations with Great Britain and Saudi Arabia 'smells of a surrender to the enemies of Islam, of intolerable passivity regarding the demands of the Imam'.[109]

Such allegations can herald the end of a political career in the Islamic Republic. Semi-official newspapers were therefore quick to justify the normalization of ties with Saudi Arabia, trying to make it appear an overwhelming victory for Iranian steadfastness:

Iran's conditions for the resumption of ties were that Riyadh accept a previous quota of between 110,000 and 150,000 Iranian pilgrims annually and allow the holding of 'antipathy towards infidels' rallies (at least) in certain squares in Mecca and Madina during the annual hajj ceremonies . . . the 'US-dependent policy' of the Saudis is to be blamed for the unstable Tehran–Riyadh diplomatic ties in the years after the 1979 revolution . . . and a careful assessment of the Saudi government's efforts to re-establish ties with Iran after 12 years of 'suspicious attitudes' towards the Islamic Revolution is therefore necessary. There is no doubt that such willingness (on the part of Saudi Arabia) cannot be unrelated to the Persian Gulf war and the role of the Saudi clan hosting 500,000 'capricious American soldiers in the holiest Islamic lands'. Because of this policy, the Saudis were detested by regional and world Muslims, and now, to get out of the quagmire, they have to improve ties with the Islamic Republic . . . the Saudis' insistence that Iran should forget the past is a clear proof of their unfounded hostility towards the Islamic Republic during recent years . . . but its attitude towards the Islamic Revolution and its extensive support for the Iraqi Ba'thist regime during the 1980–8 bloody war against Iran cannot be forgotten . . . Iran attaches great importance to the two holiest Islamic sites and the holy land of Hijaz. The same respect and interest for the holy lands makes Tehran establish relations with the government who takes care of them . . . the attitude of the Saudi government towards the issue of the hajj will be decisive in the two countries' ties in future.[110]

But even such strongly worded commentaries were not enough to allay the suspicions of the government's Islamic opponents.

On the contrary, the Anjoman-e Ruhaniyun, the organization of the radical supporters of the line of the Imam, insisted on the the principles of foreign policy that originated from the revolution:

- independence from both the East and the West,
- the United States is the main enemy,
- struggle against the superpowers and against Zionism,
- support for all 'oppressed' peoples,
- liberation of Jerusalem.[111]

The organization tried in vain to get a statement from the one whose line it claimed to defend after the end of the war with Iraq. At that time Khomeini was primarily interested in an extensive strengthening of the circles around Rafsanjani. In his last Will and Testament the chapters regarding foreign policy were therefore deliberately ambiguous.[112] But even when the Imam refused to support them, the opponents of Rafsanjani never doubted the general continuation of the principle of Towhid in foreign policy.[113]

According to this principle, sovereignty is exclusively a matter of divine power and the permanent struggle between good and evil does not leave any room for compromise.[114] The fulfilment of God's will is much more important than the recognition of international laws which moreover are formulated or even dictated by the West.[115] The former Interior Minister Mohtashemi, the personal representative of Khomeini for hajj affairs, Kho'eniha, Ahmad Khomeini, the Speaker of the Majlis until 1992, Karrubi, and others, therefore, did not abandon their uncompromising stance.

Karrubi harboured a special hatred against Saudi Arabia, partly because he had been the leader of the Iranian pilgrims during the disastrous 1987 hajj. He repeatedly said that

the dispute between the Islamic Republic and Saudi Arabia is a deep-rooted and fundamental quarrel between American-style Islam and the genuine Islam of Prophet Muhammad . . . there is no compromise in this dispute (because it) stems from the fact that according to the Holy Koran and traditions [of the Prophet], we believe hajj is a religio-political issue, while Saudi rulers say it is a mere set of religious rites . . . Saudi rulers are wrong to interpret 'Deliverance from Pagans' as if it concerned only the era of the Prophet when there were pagans in Mecca, and does not apply any more even though they are present elsewhere in the world . . . the Saudi reasoning is 'purely political' . . . [because] it is dictated by America and is a policy against the oppressed aimed at covering up the oppressions of imperialist powers . . . Zionists are allowed to commit whatever crime they want: destroy houses of Muslims and make them homeless, and settle Jews from all over the world in the occupied land. But, Muslims are not allowed even to raise a [voice of] protest? . . . Thinkers of the Islamic world should administer these holy cities and discuss issues of the Muslim world there including Palestine, Afghanistan and Kashmir, and also plots against Muslims such as the apostate Salman Rushdie's case . . . we have resorted to all means to reach a conclusion, but the Saudi rulers, in order to prevent Iranians from performing the (divinely decreed) hajj, have put up obstacles upon America's orders. The great annual hajj assembly is highly significant but would be much more important for Muslims when political stands of the Islamic world are reflected in it.[116]

Other opponents of Rafsanjani's foreign policy had temporarily served the Islamic Republic as ambassadors or envoys and felt themselves therefore qualified to influence foreign policy in the period after the cease-fire with Iraq. They maintained excellent contacts with Islamic movements abroad.[117] One of their favourite means of publicity in Iran and abroad was to organize international meetings for radical Muslim laymen and clerics from all over the world.

In the spring of 1990 alone there was news of such meetings in Dacca, Bangladesh and Cape Town, South Africa. An eight point resolution was issued by the 500 religious scholars and personalities that met in Dacca. The resolution called, for example, for the establishment of a committee to safeguard the Holy shrines in the Hijaz, the organization of a march to denounce pagans during the hajj ceremonies and a discontinuation of quotas for pilgrims. The resolution furthermore emphasized the need to hold an international Islamic trial in connection with the killings in Mecca in 1987.

The participants bluntly described the Al Saud as imperialist puppets, not worthy of administering the Holy shrines. According to them, the House of God was in the hands of the enemies of Islam who had taken it upon themselves to introduce laws for all Muslims. The Saudi family had transformed the genuine hajj into a US-style hajj.[118] Similarly, the meeting in Cape Town emphasized the need for decisive action by world Muslims to reveal the 'US and Zionist plots aimed at transforming the nature of the hajj.'[119] The Iranian delegates were proud when the Imam of the Cape Town mosque stated that the Saudi rulers were constantly trying to present an empty hajj as the true hajj to the Islamic world. These meetings represented a new form of exporting the revolution under changed circumstances.

Giving up the ideal of exporting the revolution was unacceptable to the Iranian hardliners and was seen as a sensational betrayal of the 'line of the Imam'. Opponents of Rafsanjani frequently demanded government support for Islamic movements in Egypt, Sudan, Afghanistan and Central Asia. This was seen by them as normal whereas the influence of the United States in the Middle East was not.

For the clerics of the Anjoman-e Ruhaniyun there was a direct link leading from the cooperation between the United States and the Shah via American support for Israel, the assistance given to Iraq in the First Gulf War, the American influence in the Arabian Peninsula to the diplomatic and economic suppression of Egypt.

The Second Gulf War became the backdrop to an open struggle between the two branches of Iranian foreign policy. In the summer of 1990, Karrubi, Ahmad Khomeini, Kho'eniha, Khalkhali and others vehemently opposed the stationing of foreign troops on the Arabian Peninsula and called for the 'Islamic brother-peoples' to rise against the foreign invaders. But their demands were hypocritical. For example, Khalkhali and Mohtashemi emphatically asked President Rafsanjani to immediately dispatch Iranian troops across the Iraqi border after the Iraqi invasion in Kuwait, since it was now inadequately guarded by Iraqi forces. Their pressure was strong enough to cause the new ruling Faqih, Khamenei, to call for a jihad against Western troops on 13 October 1990, despite official Iranian neutrality. More than 160 Representatives in the Majlis welcomed the call with a standing ovation.[120] Fortunately, Rafsanjani was able to paralyse their effectiveness by inviting famous leaders of Islamic opposition groups from all over the world to Tehran to discuss with the 'future political leaders of their respective countries' ways to use the Kuwait crisis to strengthen Islam worldwide.[121] For the same reason he also organized lavish celebrations of the third anniversary of the Palestinian Intifada in the Iranian capital.

This policy also had another, incidental, consequence. Rafsanjani successfully undermined the claim of the Iraqi President to have undisputed rights over the expression of Islamic and anti-Western, nationalist sentiments. Indeed, there were some conditions in favour of Saddam Husain. For example, the Iraq–Iran war had been characterized by a certain interweaving of religious and nationalist motivations. It did not proceed within the context of previous Sunni–Shia conflicts because Iraq's Shia majority by and large refused to be made the instrument of Tehran's ambitions. The religious factor was simply played off against the nationalist one and vice versa. The Second Gulf War deepened this interweaving. In their rejection of the Western presence in Dar al-Islam and the heart of the Arab nation, both the nationalists and the Islamists soon found a common cause and it was therefore imperative that Rafsanjani prevent the idolization of the Iraqi President.

But with the beginning of the allied ground offensive against Iraq, the opponents of Rafsanjani once again tried to regain the initiative. During parliamentary debates both Khalkhali and Karrubi demanded that Iran give military help to the Iraqi people against the 'much more evil America'.[122] They called for mass demonstrations on 21 January 1991 but only 3,000 people participated,[123] making the failure of the initiative obvious. It was clear that most Iranians did not want any new military adventures.

Thus the genuine opportunities for Rafsanjani's opponents to influence foreign policy remained few and far between. Whilst the government further distinguished itself as a source of stability in a turbulent region, the local field of play for the exporters of revolution was restricted and so their attention was directed to more remote areas. Yet one can only speculate whether and to what degree the dramatic economic decline of Iran left the government with sufficient room to pursue a pragmatic foreign policy.

Iranian industry, still suffering from the destruction of the First Gulf War, worked with a capacity utilization rate of 20–40 per cent. In addition, four million men were unemployed. The inflation rate fluctuated between 30 per cent and 40 per cent, which meant the government had to spend US$ 2 billion annually on food imports alone.[124] Due to the uncertainty of the international oil market and the increasing competition within that market, only vague predictions of future profits were possible. Even very optimistic prognoses by the Iranian Oil Ministry were certain that financial requirements would exceed profits from the export of oil by some US$ 200 billion during the next decade.[125] This was the main reason for government attempts to revitalize the oil economy. As early as 1 April 1989 the reconstructed refinery at Abadan began operating, the terminals of Kharq, Sirri, Lavan and Larrak were quickly extended and destroyed pipelines repaired.

A rapid economic recovery presupposes safe transit routes through the Persian Gulf and the readiness of regional and international governments to accept Iran as a partner again, if only to secure the additional financial needs of Iran. So far, the constant debate over the right strategy for the Islamic Republic's foreign policy has led to a fragile compromise. Diplomatic relations are, or were, temporarily cut with nations allegedly hostile to revolutionary Iran; these have included at one time or another: the United States, Britain, Chile, Apartheid South Africa, the Philippines,

Egypt, Iraq, Morocco and Jordan. In this regard the hardliners succeeded. Tehran also looks for cordial if not warm relations with countries and movements presumed sympathetic to the Islamic Republic: Syria, Libya, Algeria, Lebanon, the Democratic Arab Republic of the Sahara, and the PLO. As for the rest of the world, it is subject to a charm-offensive. How foreign countries are handled by the Iranian government, which in general seeks to end its international isolation, depends ultimately on how close they seem to be to the US at any given time or on their attitude towards Iran.[126] This approach, however, will remain ambiguous as long as the domestic opponents of the government can collect enough ammunition to discredit the overall direction of official policy.

As a result of this uncertainty the Gulf Arab states, and particularly Saudi Arabia, were interested in a domestic victory for Rafsanjani's camp, since they would otherwise have to face the return of the fundamentalists. They knew that Iranian inclusion in the future security system of the Gulf would vastly improve the climate for pragmatism in Iran. But nobody within the GCC is in fact ready to go that far. No Arab state wants to see Iranian soldiers on Arab soil as, for example, part of a peacekeeping force. Wavering between strengthening Rafsanjani and avoiding an Iranian say in Arab security matters, the GCC voted for the latter, even though this position gave ammunition to the Iranian hardliners.

It is a matter of speculation whether or not this rejection of Iranian desires to be included in a Gulf security framework encouraged the radicals to outmanoeuvre Rafsanjani by inciting renewed conflict over the islands of Abu Musa, Tumb al-Sughra and Tumb al-Kubra in 1992. The Iranian leadership ordered the expulsion of UAE citizens from Abu Musa, causing a storm of protest on the other side of the Gulf. Ali Akhbar Velayati, and Iran's UN representative, Kamal Kharrazi, hurried to declare that the expulsion referred only to individuals who, according to the still valid bilateral agreements, were not citizens of Sharjah, in particular to Indian contract-workers who were illegal immigrants. After a visit to the province of Hormuzgan to which Abu Musa is administratively attached on the Iranian side, President Rafsanjani also emphasized that Iran would proceed strictly in accordance with the agreement signed with Sharjah in 1971, and the accusations from the UAE were stopped temporarily. After all, since the Second Gulf War there were several US$ billion of profits at risk for the UAE, arising from re-exports to Iran.[127] But their silence proved to be deceptive.

In August 1992 Iranian Marines occupied Abu Musa for the second time since 1971, this time deporting all Arabian residents regardless of citizenship. After the deportation the occupiers stopped all ferry traffic to Sharjah. The leadership in Tehran made an 'historical claim on Abu Musa which could be proved by innumerable documents'.[128] Intensive mediation by Iran's main Arab ally, Syria, failed.

The Abu Dhabi daily paper *al-Ittihad* asked rhetorically: 'Does Tehran want to take over the leadership of the Gulf after the collapse of Iraq?' At any rate, all the GCC governments were more or less convinced that Iran was indeed trying to do just that. Up to this point it had been a generally held opinion that the Islamic Republic would pursue her foreign policy primarily by economic and political means. The occupation of Abu Musa stood in such sensational contradiction to the policies of Rafsanjani after the Second Gulf War that no one was astonished when they learnt that it was Ayatollah Khamenei, the supreme religious leader of Iran, who had ordered the attack, bypassing the President. Once again Iran's body politic had been subject to sudden convulsions, caused by an unresolved struggle for power. Sceptics within the GCC, however, now could feel justified in doubting Iran's claim that it wanted better relations with its neighbours, since it continued to occupy the sovereign territory of a GCC state and showed little sign of altering its general position on all three islands. Those within the GCC who supported defence agreements with the West felt their arguments had been strengthened by the Iranian action.[129]

Regardless of who is to blame for this deterioration in relations, which has continued since 1992, it should be noted that Iranian ideas on maintaining security in the Persian Gulf are still considerably different from those of its GCC neighbours. It starts with an Iranian demand for 'real independence,' that is to say rejection of the influence of any extra-regional powers, primarily the United States. The ever-closer alignment of the security interests of Kuwait, Bahrain, the UAE and Saudi Arabia with those of the US and other Western states directly opposed these efforts. The signing of security agreements between several GCC states and the United States was considered by the Iranian leadership, despite Rafsanjani's verbal acquiescence, to be a slap in the face, since it underscored Arab distrust of Iran's offer of protection and friendship.[130]

After all, Iran had proposed taking over responsibility for shaping a security umbrella for the Gulf area. When Saud al-Faisal visited Iran for the first time after the Second Gulf War in June 1991, the Iranian government spoke out very frankly: 'On the issues of the Persian Gulf security, Iran is strongly opposed to the presence of foreign forces in this region and criticizes the hospitality that the Saudi Arabian government offers to Western forces in its territory. In the opinion of the Islamic Republic, the region's security should be maintained by the region's countries. The Persian Gulf Cooperation Council has been in contact with Iran for some time now in order to create the necessary security provisions in the region.'[131]

Later on, Iranian propaganda was periodically directed against Saudi Arabia on this topic. King Fahd was labelled a puppet of the West for his 'capitulation to the United States' and for overproducing oil during the Kuwait crisis, thus compensating for the deficit in Kuwaiti and Iraqi exports and keeping prices stable, aiding Western consumers.[132] Iran felt threatened by the possibility of US–Saudi hegemony in the Gulf which would restrict its own options for an independent foreign policy to almost nothing. Furthermore, the Iranian leadership still believes that Washington has not yet come to terms with the revolution and, if it was possible, would encourage a change of regime in Iran. This is the reason why Iran so vehemently rejected the statement by the American Secretary of State, James Baker, on the subject of creating a security framework for the Persian Gulf modelled on NATO.[133]

To be isolated in the Persian Gulf would be a nightmare for any Iranian government because of the deep-rooted Iranian belief that the Gulf is Persian regardless of what the Arabs, or even worse, outsiders may say or do. Thus, the Iranian naval and military build-up in the Gulf is not only designed to protect national interests but to show the flag and impress upon the Arabs that the presence of Iran in the Gulf is a fact.[134] Ali Velayati stated at one point:

> Our most important and strategic border is our southern coastline, the Persian Gulf region, the Straits of Hormuz and the Sea of Oman. This region is vital to us . . . We cannot remain indifferent to the fate of this region.[135]

But, fortunately for Saudi Arabia, Riyadh was aware that Iran was, as a result of its limited military capacity, unable to keep its promise to create a security umbrella in the first half of the 1990s, thus providing the Saudi Arabian government with an excuse for refusing, as in the 1970s, to grant its neighbour a blank cheque as it were for leadership of the region. Even less acceptable to Saudi Arabia is a further aspect of the Iranian security scheme, temporarily put on the back burner, which insists that 'only true Islamic governments in the littoral states would have the capacity to secure a safe and peaceful relationship amongst each other'. According to the Gulf monarchs, Iran is no more competent to determine the standards of true Islamic government in the 1990s, than it was during and after the revolution of 1978–9.[136] In this respect the propaganda war between Iran and Saudi Arabia has never ceased.

Publications produced by the Anjoman-e Ruhaniyun, for example, have never ceased attacking the Al Saud for their unIslamic behaviour. From time to time the official Iranian media added fuel to the fire. In August 1993 for instance Radio Tehran attacked Saudi Arabia for its failure to pursue a true Islamic policy regarding human rights. The Saudi Arabian response was very outspoken. The editor of the Saudi Press Agency (SPA) replied:

> It is strange that the Iranian media adopt this unpleasant method against the Kingdom while the Iranian authorities declare their continuing eagerness to improve relations with the Kingdom of Saudi Arabia. If the Iranian intentions are sincere in this eagerness, we do not believe that this media line is the correct way to achieve it. On the basis of its firm policy, the Kingdom refuses interference in its internal affairs just as it does not resolve on its part to interfere in the affairs of others . . . the Kingdom – which has, since it came into existence, established its rule on the teachings of the Islamic faith and has adhered to them in text and in spirit, in a way guaranteed to protect human rights in all matters of human life – does not attach any importance to anyone who attempts to make insinuations from this channel [radio], as the Kingdom knows the aims behind those attempts.[137]

However Saudi Arabia does not have a better record than Iran. Given the fact that there is no free press in Saudi Arabia, the regime must be suspected of being behind attacks such as the following:

> The Iranian catastrophe resulting from the revolution was the biggest ever. The Iranians discovered that the new emperors of the revolution

did not have any administrative programmes other than trouble-making, chaos, deceit, trading in slogans and forming gangster-like organizations, such as the Revolutionary Guards, whose aim basically is to protect the regime from the army . . . The Tehran regime goes on to implement a dangerous task – to build a wall of hatred between the Iranians and the Muslim and other nations, and at the same time continues to amass weapons. Iran is now like a vast prison and a huge arsenal. This is a major catastrophe in the life of any nation.[138]

But such vitriolic tones remained the exception in Saudi Arabian intercourse with Iran, a last resort for feelings provoked beyond bearing by the Iranian radicals. According to Gert Nonneman, Saudi Arabian foreign policy is generally:

liable to waver, to be unclear, sometimes of course intentionally so . . . The decision-making process is diffuse; there is a continual seeking for compromise within the royal family; and there are greatly varying personalities among the senior princes, each with their own backgrounds . . . this results in a predisposition against any strong long-term commitments to alliances or enmities. The normal policy output will, rather, be one of careful manoeuvring, staying in the safer channels of the stream; it will be a policy dictated by pragmatic concern for domestic consensus and political stability, as well as regional security.[139]

Nevertheless, a small number of experts did predict a dominant regional role for Saudi Arabia, rather than Iran, during the 1990s. For example, M.H. Sours emphasized that though Iran may once again become the most powerful country in the region, it cannot change its fundamental character as a non-Arab state. Moreover, Sours contends, Iran is a continental state and 'thus unable to interact well with the outside world',[140] whatever this sibylline sentence might imply. In the overall framework of the Middle East, Iran has only a marginal position, preventing it from taking on a permanent leading role. The disastrous defeat of Iraq, Sours argues, has weakened the only other continental state that had the ability to impair Saudi Arabian hegemony: 'Thus a Saudi Arabian system anchored in the Gulf region through the Gulf Cooperation Council (GCC) represents the best hope for future peace and stability in the region.'[141] Sours, like some other experts, underestimates the range of serious disadvantages, which have been discussed above, that weaken the Kingdom and prevent it regaining a dominant position after the Second Gulf War.

In conclusion, despite a considerable improvement, Iranian–Saudi relations in the period since the Second Gulf War continue to be hampered by a complex range of factors including fundamental ideological differences, rivalry over religious legitimacy, traditional sources of tension between Iranians and Arabs, political imputation, the struggle for leadership within OPEC, rivalry over military supremacy in the Gulf, and the US factor in Iranian–Arab tension.[142] Some of these factors might beome temporarily irrelevant, but then others, such as the extension of rivalry to regions beyond the Gulf, have already been added to the balance. The relationship between the two Gulf giants still swings between hostility and partnership.

NOTES

1 *Far Eastern Economic Review*, London, 8 September 1988.
2 *The Economist*, London, 20 August 1988, p. 56.
3 R.W. Cottam, 'Charting Iran's New Course', *Current History*, 90:1 (1991), p. 37.
4 Quoted in D. Menashri, 'Khomeini's Vision: Nationalism or World Order?' in D. Menashri (ed.), *The Iranian Revolution and the Muslim World* (Boulder: Westview Press, 1990), p. 52.
5 Ibid.
6 M. Sariolghalam, 'Arab-Iranian Rapprochement: The Regional and International Impediments', *Paper presented at the conference on Arab-Iranian Relations: Contemporary Trends and Prospects for the Future*, Qatar, 11–14 September 1995, p. 4.
7 U. Steinbach, 'Die "Zweite Islamische Republik"; Der Gottesstaat auf dem Weg in die Normalität', *Aussenpolitik*, 40:1 (1990), p. 88.
8 A.A. Velayati, 'Ravabet-e beyn al-melal', *Majallat-e siyasat-e khariji*, 1:2 (1988), p. 275–85.
9 L. Lamote, 'Iran's Foreign Policy and Internal Crisis' in P. Clawson (ed.), *Iran's Strategic Intentions and Capabilities* (Washington DC, Institute for National Strategic Studies, 1994), p. 18.
10 M.A. Conant and R. King, *Consequences of 'Peace': The Iranian Situation and Outlook* (Washington DC: Conant and Associates, 1988), p. 61.
11 A. Hashim, *The Crisis of the Iranian State* (Oxford: Oxford University Press, 1995), p. 33.
12 Quoted in M.H. Malek, 'Iran after Khomeini: Perpetual Crisis or Opportunity?' *Conflict Studies*, 237:1 (1991), p. 13.
13 Ibid.
14 A. Hashim, *The Crisis*, pp. 33–4.

15 H. Amirahmadi, 'Iranian–Saudi Arabian Relations since the Revolution' in H. Amirahmadi and N. Entessar (eds.), *Iran and the Arab World* (Basingstoke: Macmillan, 1993), pp. 154–5.

16 G. Nonneman, 'Iraqi–GCC Relations: Roots of Change and Future Prospects' in C. Davies (ed.), *After the War: Iran, Iraq, and the Arab Gulf* (Chichester: Carden Publications, 1990), p. 53.

17 *Middle East International*, London, 13 September 1991, pp. 9–10.

18 Ibid., 27 September 1991, p.13.

19 *BBC Summary of World Broadcasts*, ME/1264/A6, 28 December 1991.

20 *BBC Summary of World Broadcasts*, ME/1226/A21, 11 November 1991.

21 N. Jaber, 'Conflicting Visions', *Middle East International*, London, 22 November 1991, p. 13.

22 G. Nonneman, 'The GCC and the Islamic Republic: Toward a Restoration of the Pattern' in A. Ehteshami and M. Varasteh (eds.), *Iran & the International Community* (London, New York: Routledge, 1991), p. 115.

23 *Yearbook Iran 1989/90* (Bonn: Edition Ausland, 1990), p. 15.

24 S.T. Hunter, *Iran after Khomeini* (New York, Westport and London: Praeger, 1992), p. 130.

25 G. Nonneman, The GCC, p. 115.

26 Quoted in D. Menashri, Khomeini's Vision, pp. 52–3.

27 S.T. Hunter, *Iran and the World: Continuity in a Revolutionary Decade* (Bloomington, Indiana University Press, 1990), p. 121.

28 *Soroush*, Tehran, 22 May 1991.

29 *Foreign Broadcast Information Service – Near East Series*, Washington DC, 4 January 1988, p. 75.

30 A. Ehteshami, *After Khomeini: The Iranian Second Republic* (London, New York, Routledge, 1995), p. 152.

31 Ibid.

32 R.W. Cottam, Charting, p. 36.

33 D.C. Barr, *Rafsanjani's Iran* (3 vols., London, Gulf Centre for Strategic Studies, 1991) vol. 2, p. 4.

34 M.H. Malek, Iran, pp. 13–14.

35 A. Ehteshami, *After Khomeini*, pp. 153–4.

36 *BBC Summary of World Broadcasts*, ME/0341, 22 December 1988.

37 *Saudi Arabian Bulletin*, London, July 1991, p. 5.

38 *BBC Summary of World Broadcasts*, ME/1057, 27 April 1991 and ME/1058, 29 April 1991.

39 M. Massie, *Rafsanjani's Iran* (3 vols., London, Gulf Centre for Strategic Studies, 1991) vol. 3, p. 38.

40 *BBC Summary of World Broadcasts*, ME/1083, 28 May 1991.

41 Ibid., ME/1103–05, 20–22 June 1991.

42 Ibid., ME/1082, 27 May 1991.

43 M. Abir, *Saudi Arabia: Government, Society and the Gulf Crisis* (London and New York: Routledge, 1993), pp. 210–11.

44 H. Amirahmadi, Iranian–Saudi Arabian Relations, p. 152.

45 *BBC Summary of World Broadcasts*, ME/1093, 8 June 1991.

46 *Saudi Arabia*, Washington DC, July 1991, p. 4.

47 *Mideast Mirror*, London, 7 June 1991, p. 4.

48 *Al-Sharq al-Awsat*, London, 5 June 1991.
49 M.H. Malek, Iran, p. 15.
50 M. Abir, *Saudi Arabia*, p. 211.
51 S.T. Hunter, *Iran*, p. 133.
52 *BBC Summary of World Broadcasts*, ME/1224 A/12.
53 M.E. Ahrari, 'Conflict Management of OPEC States', *Mediterranean Quarterly*, 2:3 (1991), p. 104.
54 M.H. Malek, Iran, p. 15.
55 *BBC Summary of World Broadcasts*, ME/1155, 20 August 1991.
56 A. Ehteshami, *After Khomeini*, p. 146.
57 H. Amirahmadi, 'Iran and the Persian Gulf: Strategic Issues and Outlook' in H. Zanganeh (ed.), *Islam, Iran, & World Stability* (New York: St. Martin's Press, 1994), p. 123.
58 A. Ehteshami, *After Khomeini*, p. 147.
59 Ibid., p. 154.
60 H. Amirahmadi and N. Entessar, 'Iranian–Arab Relations in Transition' in H. Amirahmadi and N. Entessar (eds.), *Iran and the Arab World* (Basingstoke: Macmillan, 1993) p. 6.
61 A. Ehteshami, *After Khomeini*, p. 155.
62 L. Lamote, Iran's Foreign Policy, pp. 20–1.
63 H.H. Albers, *Saudi Arabia: Technocrats in a Traditional Society* (New York: P. Lang, 1989), p. 184.
64 A.H. Cordesman, *Western Strategic Interests in the Southern Gulf: Strategic Relations and Military Realities* (Boulder: Westview Press, 1987), p. 17, Table 2.1.
65 N. Safran, *Saudi Arabia: The Ceaseless Quest for Security* (Cambridge MA: Harvard University Press, 1988), p. 457.
66 D.E. Long, 'Stability in Saudi Arabia', *Current History*, 90:1 (1991), p. 12.
67 N. Safran, *Saudi Arabia*, p. 457.
68 E. Thiemann, 'Wirtschaftliche und soziale Transformationsprozesse in den arabischen Golfmonarchien unter den Bedingungen von Erdölwirtschaft und Weltmarktintegration – Eine Bestandsaufnahme nach Beendigung des Golfkrieges', *asien, afrika, lateinamerika (aala)*, 21:4 (1993), pp. 670–1.
69 N. Safran, *Saudi Arabia*, p. 458.
70 A.H. Cordesman, *Western Strategic Interests*, p. 17.
71 K. McLachlan, 'Saudi Arabia: Political and Social Evolution' in I.R. Netton (ed.), *Arabia and the Gulf: From Traditional Society to Modern States* (London: Croom Helm, 1986), p. 103.
72 As an example for such prognoses see A. Krommer, *Entwicklungsstrategien der arabischen Golfstaaten* (New York: P. Lang, 1986), p. 60.
73 D.E. Long, Stability, p. 11.
74 R. Abu-Namay, 'Constitutional Reform: A Systematisation of Saudi Politics', *Journal of South Asian and Middle Eastern Studies*, 17:2 (1993), p. 49.
75 *The Middle East*, London, 230 (1994), p. 23.
76 *Saudi Arabia*, Washington DC, March 1991, p. 9.
77 E. O'Sullivan, 'Saudi Arabia: Special Report', *Middle East Economic Digest (MEED)*, London, 10 (1994), p. 28.
78 *The Middle East*, London, 231 (1994), pp. 24–5.

79 Ibid., 230 (1994), p. 23.
80 *Arab News*, Jedda, 12 October 1993.
81 Ibid.
82 *Saudi Arabia*, Washington DC, March 1991, p. 10.
83 *BBC Summary of World Broadcasts*, ME/1093, 8 June 1991.
84 S.T. Hunter, *Iran*, p. 130.
85 S. Chubin, 'Iran's Strategic Aims and Constraints' in P. Clawson (ed.), *Iran's Strategic Intentions and Capabilities* (Washington DC, Institute for National Strategic Studies, 1994), p. 69.
86 *Kayhan*, Tehran, 27 December 1990.
87 M. Abir, *Saudi Arabia*, p. 211.
88 N. Entessar, 'Realpolitik and Transformation of Iran's Foreign Policy: Coping with the "Iran Syndrome"' in H. Zanganeh (ed.), *Islam, Iran, & World Stability* (New York: St. Martin's Press, 1994), p. 145.
89 *BBC Summary of World Broadcasts*, ME/1195, 5 October 1991.
90 *Frankfurter Allgemeine Zeitung*, Frankfurt (Main), 1 February 1993.
91 S.T. Hunter, 'Post-Khomeini Iran', *Foreign Affairs*, 68:5 (1989/90), p. 147.
92 S. Schoenherr und A. J. Halbach, *Der Golf nach dem Krieg: Wirtschaft, Politik, Rüstung* (Munich: Cologne, London, Weltforum–Verlag, 1991), p. 73.
93 C. Bina, 'Farewell to the Pax Americana: Iran, Political Islam and the Passing of the Old Order' in H. Zanganeh (ed.), *Islam*, pp. 56–7.
94 *BBC Summary of World Broadcasts*, ME/1214, 28 October 1991.
95 *Mideast Mirror*, London, 6 June 1991, p. 3.
96 M.E. Ahrari, 'Conflict Management of OPEC States', *Mediterranean Quarterly*, 2:3 (1991), p. 87.
97 J. Calabrese, *Revolutionary Horizons: Regional Foreign Policy in Post-Revolutionary Iran* (New York: St. Martin's Press, 1994), p. 64.
98 *BBC Summary of World Broadcasts*, ME/1898, 18 January 1994.
99 Ibid., ME/1243, 30 November 1991.
100 N. Entessar, Realpolitik, p. 158.
101 *Tehran Times*, Tehran, 17 March 1993.
102 *BBC Summary of World Broadcasts*, ME/1898, 18 January 1994.
103 *Middle East International*, London, 16 February 1996, p. 18.
104 M.E. Ahrari, 'Iran, GCC and the security dimensions in the Persian Gulf' in H. Amirahmadi and N. Entessar (eds.), *Reconstruction and Regional Diplomacy in the Persian Gulf* (London, New York, Routledge, 1992), p. 205.
105 S. al-Mani, 'Of Security and Threat: Saudi Arabia's Perception', *Journal of South Asian and Middle Eastern Studies*, 20:1 (1996), p. 76.
106 N. Alaolmolki, *Struggle for Dominance in the Persian Gulf: Past, Presence and Future Prospects* (New York, P. Lang, 1991), Foreword.
107 *Kayhan*, Tehran, 7 November 1990; *Jumhuriye Islami*, Tehran, 15 November 1990.
108 *Mideast Mirror*, London, 22 May 1991.
109 *Resalat*, Tehran, 16 May 1991.
110 *Jumhuriye Islami*, Tehran, 26 March 1991.
111 R.K. Ramazani, 'Khumayni's Islam and Iran's Foreign Policy' in A. Dawisha, (ed.), *Islam in Foreign Policy* (Cambridge, Cambridge University Press, 1983), p. 21.

112 *The Iranian Journal of International Affairs*, 1:2/3 (1989), pp. 309–62; *Foreign Broadcast Information Service – Near East Series*, Washington DC, 6 October 1988, p. 53.

113 M. al-Hajj Ali, 'al-Imam Khumaini wa mushkilat al-tab'iya' in *Al-Imam al-Khumaini: al-fikr wa al-thawra* (Beirut, Dar al-Hadatha, 1990), pp. 64–75.

114 R.M. Savory, 'Religious Dogma and the Economic and Political Imperatives of Iranian Foreign Policy' in M. Rezun (ed.), *Iran at the Crossroads: Global Relations in a Turbulent Decade* (Boulder: Westview Press, 1990), p. 56.

115 J.D. Green, 'Ideology and Pragmatism in Iranian Foreign Policy', *Journal of South Asian and Middle Eastern Studies*, 17:1 (1993), pp. 64–6.

116 *BBC Summary of World Broadcasts*, ME/0802, 28 June 1990.

117 A. Faris, *al-Jumhuriya al-Islamiya* (Beirut, Sharikat al-matbu'at li'l-tauzi' wa'l-nashr, 1987). He analyses the different measures and methods of the Iranian efforts to export the revolution, especially in Lebanon (pp. 77–86), he examines the roles of Ayatollah Montazeri (temporarily the designated successor of Khomeini) and other leading clerics (pp. 96–103).

118 *BBC Summary of World Broadcasts*, ME/0770, 22 May 1990.

119 Ibid.

120 S.A. Arjomand, 'A Victory for the Pragmatists: The Islamic Fundamentalists' Reaction in Iran' in J. Piscatori (ed.), *Islamic Fundamentalism and the Gulf Crisis* (Chicago, American Academy of Arts and Sciences, 1991), p. 57.

121 R.W. Cottam, Charting, p. 36.

122 *Kayhan*, Tehran, 20 January 1991.

123 S.A. Arjomand, A Victory, p. 61.

124 R.K. Ramazani, 'Peace and Security in the Persian Gulf: A Proposal' in C.C. Joyner (ed.), *The Persian Gulf War: Lessons for Strategy, Law and Diplomacy* (New York, Watford, London: Greenwood Press, 1990), pp. 226–7.

125 Ibid.

126 W.G. Millward, 'The Principles of Foreign Policy and the Vision of World Order expounded by Imam Khomeini and the Islamic Republic of Iran' in N.R. Keddie and E. Hooglund (eds.), *The Iranian Revolution and the Islamic Republic* (Syracuse Ill: Syracuse University Press, 1986), p. 201.

127 *Süddeutsche Zeitung*, Munich, 21 April 1992.

128 *Kayhan*, Tehran, 28 August 1992.

129 *Iranian Links with Radical Organizations* (London, Gulf Centre for Strategic Studies, 1994), pp. 17–18.

130 H. Amirahmadi, Iranian–Saudi Arabian Relations, p. 157.

131 *BBC Summary of World Broadcasts*, ME/1093, 8 June 1991.

132 D.C. Barr, *Rafsanjani's Iran*, vol. 2, pp. 4–5.

133 S.T. Hunter, *Iran after Khomeini*, p. 130.

134 A. Hashim, 'Iran's Military Situation' in P. Clawson (ed.), *Iran's Strategic Intentions and Capabilities* (Washington DC, Institute for National Strategic Studies, 1994), p. 169.

135 *Middle East International*, London, 3 April 1992, p. 18.

136 R.K. Ramazani, *Revolutionary Iran: Challenge and Response in the Middle East* (Baltimore, Johns Hopkins University Press, 1986), pp. 27–31.

137 *BBC Summary of World Broadcasts*, ME/1769, 17 August 1993.

138 *Al-Yawm*, Riyadh, 6 October 1994.

139 G. Nonneman, 'The GCC and the Islamic Republic: Toward a Restoration of the Pattern' in A. Ehteshami and M. Varasteh (eds.), *Iran and the International Community* (London, New York: Routledge, 1991), p. 103.
140 M.H. Sours, 'Saudi Arabia's Role in the Middle East: Regional Stability within the New World Order', *Asian Affairs: An American Review*, 17:1 (1991), p. 47.
141 Ibid. p. 50.
142 H. Amirahmadi, H., Iranian–Saudi Arabian Relations, p. 157.

PART II

MAIN AREAS OF RIVALRY

4

Centres of Rivalry

The Persian Gulf

Any analysis of the competition between Iran and Saudi Arabia has to consider the geography of the Gulf region. The Gulf is a major lifeline for both countries, since both their economies are almost completely based on oil and the free flow of their oil exports demands safe transit routes through the Gulf and the Straits of Hormuz.

Apart from Iraq, whose access to the Gulf waters is extremely narrow, being limited to Basra, Iran has the most delicate and difficult situation because, unlike the other oil producers with access to overland routes, all Iran's oil exports go through the waterway. These exports account for more than ninety per cent of its foreign exchange revenue, with which it imports additional food (Iranian agriculture is not able to feed the exploding population) and is able to reconstruct the country's economy after the disruption of the revolution and the two Gulf wars. Freedom of navigation is a question of survival for Iran.[1]

Throughout history the region has witnessed many conflicts and even all-out wars waged by local and foreign protagonists, but its unique oil reserves have enhanced its value in modern times. The importance of the Gulf region for the oil-consuming industries of the West cannot be underestimated, making it an attractive target both during and after the colonial period. As the states and peoples of the region gradually gained control over their own oil reserves in the decades after the Second World War, they became increasingly important political and economic actors in global politics. But in the end both factors, i.e. foreign interests and national emancipation, led to a situation in which previously latent or less important conflicts could take on new and more virulent forms.

> Thus, the sectarian conflicts in the Gulf area between extremists and moderates and between Shiites and Sunnis, as well as the ethnic conflict between Persian and Arab, have both been seriously exacerbated.[2]

Dominating the Persian Gulf not only became a matter of regional prestige but an issue of global importance. This is also the reason for the many similarities between Iran's Gulf policy before and after the revolution, because the basic *national* interests of the country have remained constant in spite of fundamental change in its political and social outlook. Tehran's current policy in the Gulf is dictated by nationalism and economic, political and strategic interests. These were also the constants of Iran's Gulf policy for the previous thirty years at least.[3]

Iran's post-Second Gulf War suggestion for a regional system of collective security sounds familiar because it recalls when the Shah, anticipating the prospect of becoming the pre-eminent guardian of the Persian Gulf after British withdrawal, proposed the creation of a defensive alliance consisting of all the Gulf states including Iraq.[4] The strategic objective of Iran in the Persian Gulf has never fundamentally changed: to establish itself as a major regional force. Equally, it seeks to ensure both local and international recognition of its pre-eminence in the area and to contain any development that it perceives as contrary to its interests and political outlook.[5]

Mohammad Javad Larijani, previously Iranian Deputy Foreign Minister, and later Deputy Chairman of the Majlis Foreign Relations Committee, summarized the Iranian objectives for the Gulf in this way:

> In the Persian Gulf, we enjoy a geostrategic omnipresence and our interests in it are not difficult to list:
> - To exploit its natural resources, that is, oil, gas and marine resources;
> - To ensure the waterway as a safe route of passage;
> - To live in peace and tranquillity with others in the region.[6]

This approach was more or less shared by both Rafsanjani's camp and its more radical opponents. They both wanted, and indeed still want, Iran's dominant geographical, economic, military and demographic position in the Gulf to be reflected in a dominant geostrategic role. They wanted the Islamic Republic both to lead a surge of protest against American influence and be omnipresent in the Islamic world.[7] Of course pragmatists will always prefer internationally recognized methods to fulfil their objectives, whereas radicals do not care much about their global reputation. But as the Mykonos trial in Germany in 1997 proved, even the official Iranian line will support terrorism if it is politically expedient.

Of course Iran is not the only party that matters in Gulf politics. As previously mentioned, there is a triangle of interests in the Persian Gulf whose corners are formed by Iran, Iraq and Saudi Arabia. In 1990, K. Krause summarized the possibilities for a regional balance of power as follows:

- Hegemonic: one actor is so powerful that its full acceptance of regional security arrangements is necessary.
- Bipolar: conflicts possess a rough balance of power in which two actors (or coalitions) pose the greatest threats to each other.
- Multipolar: actors are not grouped in rival coalitions and threats to security are multiple and cross-cutting.[8]

Of these, the third option seems to fit the situation in the Persian Gulf best, although Iran, Iraq and Saudi Arabia are all competing for the role of dominant power as in the first option. But the multipolar variant has definitely been fostered by relations between Iran, Iraq and Saudi Arabia during the last twenty years.

As a result of the Second Gulf War, Iraq was forced out of the race for the time being and the competition for hegemony in the region became almost exclusively a matter between Iran and Saudi Arabia in the 1990s. Whereas Iran tried after the revolution and after each of the Gulf wars to prevent an overall Arab alliance against it and to gain acceptance for its claim that the Persian Gulf is de facto an inland water (as the name suggests), Saudi Arabia was interested primarily in dominating the Arabian Peninsula and the oil-rich sea shelf. Challenging Saudi Arabia on the Peninsula was only a tactic to help Iran gain the upper hand in the Gulf itself. But as stressed in previous chapters, the conditions in which either country might win the contest are extremely different.

The political and strategic relations between the two states are primarily characterized by certain geographical, demographic, economic and military factors. Saudi Arabia is by far the largest state on the Arabian Peninsula and is the greatest economic power there. It possesses about 66 billion barrels of proven oil reserves, a source of economic influence which it has used to dominate regional politics since the sellers' market in the 1970s. Although the political power of its oil wealth decreased in the 1980s buyers' market,[9] it was able to limit the consequences of that change as a result of increased oil demand during the First Gulf War. Nevertheless, Saudi Arabia has much higher oil reserves than Iran, which will never be able to challenge the Kingdom in the oil sector.

However, though Saudi Arabia is 1.3 times larger than Iran, it contains a far smaller population. Saudi Arabia's Gulf coastline is smaller than Iran's, although it does have alternative access to the oceans via the Red Sea. What is more, Iran owns many islands in the Gulf, including Qeshm, the largest, and together with Oman controls the Straits of Hormuz, the Gulf's most strategically sensitive point and also the Saudis' main oil export outlet.

Saudi vulnerability is increased because the gigantic excavation, loading and processing installations for Saudi Arabian oil are situated, almost without exception, in the Gulf coastal regions, and are thus within range of Iranian firepower. But because eighty per cent of Iranian oil is produced in the province of Khuzestan, which borders the Shatt al-Arab to the east and the northeast shoreline of the Gulf, a fragile stalemate containing a potential mutual threat has arisen.

The Al Saud worry about the serious demographic imbalance. At the beginning of the 1990s there were about 60 million Iranians in contrast to a Saudi Arabia with not more than 13 million inhabitants. Although the 60 million citizens of Iran are made up of a variety of ethnic groups, Saudi Arabia has never been able to turn this to its advantage. Although at least 2 million Arabs live in Iran today, they are almost without exception Shia and thus immune to Wahhabi and Saudi influence. Due to the fact that the population of Saudi Arabia is also divided into many different nationalities and only a minority possesses full Saudi Arabian citizenship, Riyadh dare not attempt to play the ethnicity card in its political game with Iran.

Of course, the demographic imbalance between both states influences their respective military strengths. Although the Saudi Arabian government has always tried to compensate for low manpower levels by purchasing the most sophisticated military hardware available, this was not sufficient to outmanoeuvre the Iranians, who were of course supplied by the same sources until the end of the 1970s and the quantitative discrepancy has remained to the present.

Fortunately for Saudi Arabia, the discrepancy in the quality of military capability decreased significantly after the Iranian revolution. Iran was cut off from its traditional suppliers of military hardware in the West, most importantly the United States. New armament agreements with the Soviet Union, later Russia and other CIS members, China, North Korea and other developing countries could not compensate for that loss. The rank and file of the Iranian military, in the regular army as well as among the Pasdaran, was not accustomed to the new armaments, a fact which decisively influenced performance during the First Gulf War. The vigilance and motivation of largely Western-trained Iranian officers produced some breathtaking gains on the battlefield, but were not sufficient to win a victory over Iraq, as the troops were forced to use unfamiliar weapon systems. This factor, coupled with the tremendous material and human losses Iran suffered during the First Gulf War, resulted in relative military weakness by the beginning of the 1990s.

For Iran, therefore, the growing military capabilities of Saudi Arabia were a source of concern. After the Second Gulf War in particular, the Iranian leadership was convinced that Saudi Arabia had been allowed by its American mentors to obtain the most advanced Western military technology, what is more purchased for it by the United States, in order to secure the long-term political survival of the Al Saud and to assist the US in containing the Iranian revolution. Iran was, in fact, unable to compete with the size and quality of the Saudi Arabian rearmament.[10]

This sense of being militarily outmanoeuvred by both Saudi Arabia and the United States was the cause of frequent Iranian media attacks on their governments. The daily *Jumhuriye Islami* deplored, for example, the fact that Saudi arms purchases and the US–Saudi military agreement had turned the country into an arsenal of the US:

> The incompetence in utilizing the arms makes the recipient countries give in to the military presence of the arms manufacturers and put all their resources, including military bases, at the disposal of foreigners in a bid to preserve their security . . . If these weapons could be used by the Saudi nation based on rational policies there would be no objection, but they only serve the illegal interests of the Arrogance.[11]

Observing Iranian reactions to the Saudi rearmament programme makes it more and more obvious that the permanent American military presence in the region is the real point of contention. Mohammad Javad Larijani, the then Deputy Chairman of the Majles' Foreign Policy Committee, estimated that around 20,000 American military personnel and more than 20 ships together with scores of land-based aircraft and other units were present in the Persian Gulf at any one time:

> A robust exercise program puts significant ground combat power into the Persian Gulf on a regular basis, while measures taken both alone, such as procurement of additional strategic lift capability, and in concert with regional friends and supporters, such as the propositioning of equipment, have given the US overwhelming ability to deploy forces in a perceived crisis situation . . . Billions of regional resources are spent to maintain such a massive military presence . . . Even our Arab neighbours in the Persian Gulf know that it is becoming increasingly costly and socially intolerable to host arrogant guests such as the US forces for a long period of time.[12]

Given Saudia Arabia's small and heterogeneous population and its long-standing abstinence from military force, the Islamic Republic's leadership does not really fear it will present a military challenge to Iran's own ambitions to dominate the Gulf and its contiguous areas, despite Iran's speedy rearmament. It is America that counts. But however it may be, Iran feels that it cannot afford to relax but must rebuild its own military power rapidly – the arms race between Tehran and Riyadh is on again. However, 'this is only a side show. The real game is about which country will emerge as a dominant actor.'[13]

Notwithstanding this background, Saudi Arabia in its turn had reason to condemn Iranian rearmament. Military planners in Riyadh were deeply concerned about Iran's swift military recovery, in particular the purchase and manufacture of sophisticated weapons, missiles and a presumed nuclear programme. As far as they are concerned it is a fact of history that Tehran has always sought to exploit regional squabbles in order to increase its influence. And even if there is no immediate danger of an Iranian attack, it has a proven record of military intervention in regional affairs.[14] Therefore, pro-Saudi writers and official Saudi institutions alike never tire of accusing Iran of aggressive behaviour.

Mazher Hameed stated, for example:

> Beyond territorial ambitions . . . it is quite clear that the fanatic leadership of the Islamic Republic is bent upon creating a new, revolutionary, anti-western, and Iranian-dominated regime throughout the Gulf. Saudi Arabia's leadership of the Arab Gulf outside Iraq has made the kingdom an especially attractive target. Its close co-operation with the United States on security issues has only served to increase this attraction. Symbolically, any attack on Saudi Arabia serves several purposes. It is an attack on the United States.

It is therefore an attack on the 'tilt' of the conservative Gulf states toward the West. It is an attack on moderation. It is an attack on the remaining pillar and clear leader of the lower Gulf. It is an attack on political legitimacy, because the support and roots of the Saudi government are greater than those of most of the other Gulf states. Thus, a high priority has been placed on undermining the security of Saudi Arabia.[15]

The Saudi newspaper *Ukaz* was sure that the ruling regime in Tehran did not know where its main problem lay. At a time when the Iranian people could expect an amelioration of the socio-economic situation, the Iranian regime still voiced empty slogans regarding the pace of change:

The Iranian regime interferes in the affairs of its neighbours by way of sedition and planting the seeds of discord and conflicts, thus repeating its old mistakes and concentrating its aggressive intentions in an attempt to cover up the acute internal crisis and problems. This regime has not realised that anger was lying in wait for it from within: poverty, need and the formidable inflation which is taking the country by storm, as well as the economic instability and the lack of hope among most Iranian people, are the real enemies of the Tehran regime . . . instead of devoting the resources to construction and making available new employment and economic expansion opportunities to meet the needs of 60 million people, the regime spends the people's money on armament, spreading sedition, interfering in the internal affairs of others and supporting terrorism.[16]

Nevertheless, it is the general conviction of the Al Saud that their trust in the American security shield can only be a last resort. In an emergency, for example an immediate threat to their political survival, they would not hesitate to call on it, but its very use would diminish their regional standing dramatically. As long as the competition between Iran and Saudi Arabia is influenced by a mutual perception of each other's means of power, rather than actually fought out on the battlefield, Saudi Arabia must present an image of being able to stand on its own. But because conditions, geographic, demographic, military, economic and political, in general favour Iran, Saudi Arabia has to find other means to create the image of an equal competitor.

At this point the GCC comes into play. The motives of the Al Saud in establishing a close network among the littoral states included not only protection against the various threats stemming from the Iranian revolution and the Iraq–Iran war, but also a desire to increase their power in the future. Thus any probable future confrontation among the Gulf states would no longer follow in the pattern of Iran vs. Iraq vs. Saudi Arabia, but rather Iran vs. Iraq vs. the GCC.

Despite the numerous contradictions and unresolved conflicts between the GCC members, Saudi Arabia has presented the other members of the Council as de facto no more than Saudi clients. The enormous demographic, political, economic, financial and military discrepancies between each individual member of the Council on the one hand, and Iran or Iraq on the other, have worked in favour of the Saudi strategy because the smaller Gulf states have had no choice but to concentrate their potential in the GCC.

Saudi Arabia faces similar discrepancies in its position towards Iran and Iraq, with the exception of its geographic and financial dimensions. Quite apart from other common interests, it was these factors which particularly motivated the smaller Gulf Arab states to seek a coalition with Saudi Arabia and not, although it was theoretically possible, with Iraq or Iran.[17]

According to the main factors (geographic size, number of inhabitants, economic and financial resources, military weight etc.) that determine a regional balance of power, the centre of the political and strategic system of the Persian Gulf does not consist of three, but, at best, of two and three-quarter states. Even the involvement of Saudi Arabia in the new security structures of the Arabian Peninsula, in the form of the GCC, could not remove this disparity completely.

When considering the above-mentioned main factors determining the regional balance of power, it becomes obvious that Saudi Arabia alone cannot really compete with Iran or Iraq. To overcome its somehow 'hermaphrodite' position between centre and periphery, the Kingdom had to add the combined capacity of the other five GCC members behind it.

Thus it was a political success for the Al Saud that the current balance of power in the Gulf area consists of Iran, Iraq and the GCC instead of Saudi Arabia alone.

The asymmetries in the Persian Gulf, however, are not exceptional. Indeed, there is hardly any case of a symmetrically balanced political system in the world. The reactions to asymmetry are also fairly standard.

Weaker states in a given region either try to secure the help of an extra-regional state (elements of this are contained in the defence contracts that several GCC states signed with the United States and Britain after the Second Gulf War), normally adding new tensions to those already existing, or they combine their arsenals in a collective alliance in an endeavour to create symmetrical conditions.[18] A possible, though not necessary, modification to the last-mentioned variation would be a partnership between the alliance of peripheral states and one or more central states to compensate for the dominant position of other central protagonists in the regional system, whose superior strength is seen as overwhelming. The peripheral states of the Gulf region chose this path, tolerating the unusual feature that the chosen central partner was in fact already involved in the process of establishing the alliance.

However, the reasons for this peculiarity can be found in the already indicated specific circumstances of the GCC's foundation. Some authors nevertheless continue to claim that Saudi Arabia not only controls the GCC, but that it uses the Council as a vehicle in its fight for dominance of the overall regional system.[19] This point of view, however, ignores the other side of the coin, as elaborated in the previous chapters, without being completely wrong. Saudi Arabia certainly needs the GCC just as the Council needs the Kingdom.

But what about the role of the GCC in the competition between Iran and Saudi Arabia? Fortunately for the latter, the smaller Gulf Arab states know how vulnerable they are to subversion and terrorism, their expensive police and intelligence systems notwithstanding, and how inferior they are in almost all the requirements for strategic power in contrast to Iran. Therefore it comes as no surprise that they try to speak to Iran with one voice on interstate issues such as territorial disputes (Abu Musa, the Tumb islands), fishing rights, hajj quotas and oil policies. Iran's opposition to any external influence in Gulf security (Western or Arab) concerns all of them, as does Iran's radical Islamic profile, its support for radical Islamic movements, its potential for fomenting Sunni–Shia conflict and its perceived hegemonic ambitions in general.[20] These are also the reasons for the frequent rejection of Iranian demands for collective security arrangements with the GCC, which the small Gulf states do not see as a credible alternative to their defence agreements with the West.

But it is the entire GCC, too, that tries to maintain close contact with Iran, to reassure it of the defensive nature of its mid-1990s security arrangements and thus to minimize Iranian threat perceptions. Gulf Arab fears of Iranian hegemony are offset by Iran's economic difficulties, its military constraints and its broader insecure environment. Thus, in the short to medium term, a viable GCC policy towards Iran will also contain certain elements of appeasement in order to discourage Iran's tendency to interfere in affairs the GCC regard as internal. But the GCC cannot afford either to ignore or to actively provoke Iran, nor can it escape the geo-strategic reality of Iran's presence in the Gulf, the Islamic Republic's demographic weight and its military potential.[21] On these issues, an accord between Saudi Arabia and its GCC allies is near completion.

When the Iranian government reacts to GCC politics en bloc, it does so mostly in response to Saudi Arabian interests. Fortunately for the Al Saud, Iranian propaganda often does them a favour. The following radio commentary serves as an example of counter-productive propaganda:

> Why during the 14-year life of the Cooperation Council has the process of greater convergence and unity among the members of the Cooperation Council not met much success, and why do the border problems between the members of this Council still exist with the same intensity as before? What increases the answer to this question is the fact that the members of the Cooperation Council, as far as political and social structures are concerned, are very close to one another. Such a positive point could have speeded up the process of greater convergence and unity among the countries. However, such a process has never materialised, and as far as the trend of greater unity is concerned, these countries are still where they started 14 years ago . . . In reality, the fact that the arrogant powers have created an adverse atmosphere against the Islamic revolution, as well as the passage of time and various developments in the region, in particular the attack by Iraq – who used to be considered as a friend of that Council – against Kuwait, have transformed the viewpoints and security concerns of each of the shaykdoms on the southern shores of the Persian Gulf. These factors, moreover, brought about some changes in the stances of these states. Additionally, the refusal of the southern Persian Gulf littoral states to establish joint armed forces which would be able to defend them against any foreign attacks – especially after the oil war – and their decision to sign bilateral military pacts with Western countries demonstrate that the small GCC countries are worried about the disparity in

the level of strength among GCC member states. Consequently, they are not prepared to invest only in that Council in security areas.[22]

These last remarks in particular should alert the reader to a more sophisticated Iranian policy regarding the GCC. On the one hand President Rafsanjani and his government tried to permanently diffuse any fears the Sheikhs and Emirs might have of an Iranian threat. Rafsanjani stated in an interview on February 1 1993 that

> World propaganda contains some elements of mischief aimed at diverting public opinion in the regional Islamic countries from the problem of Israel . . . depicting Iran as a threat, even though our nation proved during the Iran–Iraq war and its self-defence that it is very serious about safeguarding its defence and its interests and that it will not give way to any power. But that does not mean interference in the affairs of others or aggression against neighbouring countries. No country should be concerned about Iran's power.[23]

Iran's President was equally firm when he answered the questions of a Kuwaiti journalist during the same interview. The interviewer raised just about all the misunderstandings between the GCC and Iran, referred to the apprehension in the Gulf regarding Iran and Arab fears of its quest for power and hegemony, its attempts at exporting the revolution, the rearmament of Iran and its stance towards the Arab–Israeli settlement, only to be answered by Rafsanjani on 1 February 1993:

> we do not know in which language we should state that we do not have any unfriendly attitude towards any of our neighbours. We proved this during the Iran–Iraq war. Many Arab countries in the south acted badly towards us during the war. They gave money to Iraq, they provided her with assistance, but we overlooked all these issues. We have extended a hand of friendship towards them.[24]

Although insisting on rejecting any interference by extra-regional powers in the security of the Gulf, the Iranian government presented a number of suggestions it thought the GCC could not ignore. It tried to convince GCC members that only security arrangements based on peaceful interaction and cooperation between neighbouring states could ensure that the price of oil would not fluctuate, thus bringing hardship and even bankruptcy to oil-exporting countries. On 26 June 1993 the Foreign Minister, Ali Velayati, put it this way: 'if aliens control our oil prices, events similar to the Kuwaiti crisis will unfold and endanger international peace and security.'[25]

On the other hand, the Iranian leadership as a whole sought opportunities to create, and if already in existence, to widen gaps between Saudi Arabia and its GCC allies. Tehran was well aware that it could seriously harm the Saudi strategy by spreading discord amongst GCC members, particularly between Saudi Arabia and the other GCC states. One way to do this was to exploit the various, mainly territorial, disputes which continued unresolved between Saudi Arabia and certain of its Arab neighbours.

Qatar for example has been exploited masterfully by the Iranians. The attack by Saudi military forces on Qatar's Khufus border post as well as the shooting at Qatari ships by Saudi border guards were used by the Iranian media to convince the government in Doha that Saudi Arabia posed a threat to their national security, thus ensuring it maintained its obstreperous attitude within the GCC.

Apart from Qatar, the traditions of fruitful cooperation between Iran and other southern members of the GCC, especially the UAE and Oman, were helpful to Tehran. Even the renewed clashes over the islands of Tumb and Abu Musa in 1992 were not entirely in Saudi Arabia's interest. As could be expected, Tehran was quick to justify its action. There were the usual different explanations from the different political camps within the leadership.

For Ayatollah Jannati, the conservative member of the Council of Guardians (Shura-ye Negahban) and leader of the Friday prayers (Imam Jom'e) in Tehran (Friday prayers take place regularly all over Iran, serving as one of the main links between the Islamic leadership and the population) the incident merely raised a few questions:

> What has happened that suddenly – after many years that the islands were in Iran's hands and nobody uttered a word – now, at this juncture, they are making a lot of noise . . . What has happened? What is new? What has happened is that they wish to turn that issue into another tool as well, with which to inflict blows upon us and create bad feelings in the UAE towards us; either provoke them against us or sell arms to them. They say to them: Go on, you must take the islands by force.[26]

Rafsanjani put it more politely:

Unfortunately we see some provocation in the region, and the old issue of the three islands is raised again with vague excuses. We hope this problem will be solved amicably, thanks to the aptitude of our neighbouring countries. Iran thinks that the solution lies in bilateral talks. For this same reason we dispatched a delegation to the UAE. They held talks and we are ready to resume the second round of talks. We hope our brothers in the Persian Gulf region would appreciate that it will not be in the interest of the region to see tension.[27]

But what made Rafsanjani so sure of the moderate UAE reaction? It seems as if President Nahayan and the other rulers of the UAE considered they could gain much less from a military confrontation with Iran if they tried to regain the three islands by force than from continuing profitable commercial relations with their neighbour on the other side of the Gulf.

In addition, the UAE leadership was not sure of the reactions of other GCC members, including Saudi Arabia, in a worst case scenario, that is to say a military confrontation with Iran. They did not want to become a spearhead for, or rather a puppet of, either Saudi Arabia or the United States in their dispute with Iran. The constant Iranian warning of a 'US-provoked military clash' made them nervous and anxious to reduce tension. They understood the military and economic damage that the UAE could suffer in a clash with Iran. The latter's warning thus pandered directly to their fears of an impetuous and aggressive America lashing out and a determined and bloody-minded Iran taking revenge on America's vulnerable regional allies. Leading UAE newspapers even warned that America's new sanctions against Iran might end up only hurting the GCC states.[28] It is instructive that concerns over Iranian aggressiveness in the Gulf region are very often voiced by the United States rather than by the UAE, Qatar or Oman, which perhaps do not regard the Iranian regime as such an immediate threat as Washington believes it to be.

Oman, for example, was proud of its stable relationship with Iran that has lasted for decades. Sultan Qabus would allow neither the United States nor Saudi Arabia to spoil this relationship for their specific interests. Omani officials have repeatedly stated their accordance with major elements of Iranian politics. When the Speaker of the Omani Parliament met Velayati in Tehran, he emphasized that regional problems had to be solved by the countries of the region. He also mentioned that common interests, and above all Islam, are considered important factors for the realization of unity among the regional states. He pointed furthermore to the brotherly ties between the two countries and sought an expansion of bilateral relations 'in all fields'.[29] Moreover, whilst GCC states, such as the UAE, have invested in maritime military equipment, which might indicate nervousness concerning Iran, they have also invested substantial sums in conventional defence armaments, indicating possible concerns over the security of their western borders.[30]

It is the transience of political relations and alliances in the Gulf region that makes certain GCC states really nervous. To what extent can they really trust Saudi Arabia? Remembering the rapid changes in partnerships and enmities between the big three during the last three decades, they have to be careful not to get crushed between Iran, Iraq and Saudi Arabia.

The island incident of 1992 not only served Iranian domestic purposes in rallying the nation behind a patriotic cause, it also served to remind the GCC states not to ignore Iran when deliberating the security of the Persian Gulf. What if the lack of any significant advance in confidence building between Iran and the GCC meant that Tehran might retaliate in the future by forming an anti-GCC alliance with Iraq? 'A perceptible gesture of Iran towards an alignment with Iraq served the "bandwagoning" purposes of Iran; it could create just the kind of fears on the part of the Southern Gulf States that would move them in the direction of a pre-emptory alliance with Iran; what made this a viable scenario was Iran's crisis-related penchant for a system of collective security in the Persian Gulf.'[31]

Even though this scenario might seem very futuristic, it is already certain that some GCC members do want Iran to be a vital counterweight to Saudi Arabia – not within the GCC but outside it.

As demonstrated during the First Gulf War, Saudi Arabia can rely far more on the northern members of the GCC. Bahrain, for example, has increasingly moved further into the Saudi orbit. Whilst Manamah looks to the United States as well for support, it knows that the Fifth Fleet cannot protect it against an intensification of subversive activity by Iran. However, the leadership of Bahrain believes Saudi Arabia can compensate for this. But unlike the other GCC members, Bahrain has also became financially dependent on Saudi Arabia. Its oil wells dried up long ago and the country derives the major part of its revenue from the provision of various services to the Saudi Arabian economy. Manamah takes practically every opportunity it can to prove its usefulness to the Al Saud in their rivalry with Iran. It repeatedly warned that Iran's build-up of armaments posed a regional threat and far exceeded its defence needs.[32]

Common interests also emerged with regard to Qatar. Bahrain has similar border disagreements with Doha as Saudi Arabia has, and therefore tries to alleviate its security worries by harmonizing its anti-Qatar policies with Saudi Arabia. Of course, Saudi Arabia cultivates this special relationship. Leading members of the Al Saud such as Crown Prince Abdallah have more than once reiterated that 'the Kingdom of Saudi Arabia stood by Bahrain in everything that preserved its security and safeguarded its stability and territorial integrity'.[33]

When considering the internal difficulties of the GCC, what future prospects can be envisaged? What has been the result of other regions' security arrangements? In some other regional systems an additional variant has developed. Its nature consists of a security alliance, initially concluded to fight obvious asymmetries, but which has developed into a regional security system including both the centre and the periphery of the system. The experience of the ASEAN states is a good example of this particular process, since it proves the possibility of harmonizing interests between such giants as Indonesia or the Philippines and small states such as Singapore or Brunei.

However it would seem that the GCC is not taking that path. Its exclusivity and the peculiarities of its member countries limit the number of probable developments. Contrary to Iraq and Iran, the GCC states represent a historical period 'in which the ruling family is the owner of the state. The state is essentially a family estate, which, with its membership in the UN system, has gained the trappings of international authority and legitimacy.'[34]

Concepts such as 'citizen' or 'nation' still carry less weight than tribal membership and tribal loyalties. Traditional inter-tribal relations, ties and feuds, still determine the nature of life on the Arabian Peninsula far more than the relations between governments.[35] The sense of exclusivity among GCC members was even fostered by the outcome of the Second

Gulf War. In November 1990, Secretary General Bishara stated in an interview: '(We) learned two things from this crisis. First, we never trust anybody. No matter how much his intimacy with us is. And second . . . we have to rely on ourselves.'[36]

There are, however, additional reasons which prevent the GCC from fulfilling the generally recognized functions of a regional security system. It begins with the geographical dimension. Sheer distance hinders the cohesion between Kuwait situated at the north and Oman at the far south of the alliance. As mentioned in previous chapters, these widely different geographic positions lead inevitably to different points of view and thus to different opinions about the importance of certain problems.

On the other hand, the peripheral states do not see any absolute need, for the time being, to accept additional states from the centre into the GCC. Full of pride over their successful containment of Saudi Arabia, they refuse to allow another great power to join the Council to form a counterbalance to Saudi Arabia. The risk of integrating a socio-economically and politically related state, like Saudi Arabia, into an alliance seemed feasible. Giving GCC membership to Iran or Iraq would, however, change the nature of the Council irreversibly without making gains in collective security. For an effective Subregional Security Organization (SRSO) W.T. Tow listed the following criteria:

- How successful the SRSOs are in enabling their members to overcome their sense of strategic and economic vulnerability to the outside world;
- The extent to which they allow members to overcome their suspicions of each other's intraregional ambitions and policies; and
- The levels of military, economic, and diplomatic competitiveness SRSO members achieve, individually and collectively.[37]

At present, the GCC does not fulfil these criteria either in its form, its preferred plans or its objectives. An expansion of its function turning it into the basic structure of a security arrangement for the whole region would overtax it completely.

Due to the evident inability of the most important states of the Gulf region, Iran, Iraq and Saudi Arabia, to establish a security partnership, some observers have reached the conclusion that only the West could take on the role of an – external – security guarantor, at least for the time being.[38] The West should be made responsible for creating a strategic balance between the three main regional opponents. Obviously this means increasing the military power of the GCC members gathered around Saudi Arabia.

But there is only a remote possibility that the GCC will develop into a security organization that will, like the Conference for Security and Cooperation in Europe (CSCE), be able to decrease tension through enhancing communication and creating common interests. The GCC is still primarily a traditional pact directed against third parties. Future concentration on military aspects is therefore exceptionally doubtful, because the absolute dependence of the GCC on the United States would inevitably lead to a new polarization within the region.

Then, even the currently unthinkable alliance between the anti-Western states of Iran and Iraq against Saudi Arabia and the GCC would come as no surprise. 'Essentially, the root causes of political instability in the Gulf are just as strong as they have been for the last three decades. Iran and Iraq have antagonistic, anti-western regimes, and the Gulf states are weak and unpopular in the rest of the Middle East. There is the consolation that the Gulf War has diminished the Iraqi threat for the foreseeable future, and has acted to deter similar acts of aggression against the Gulf states. The war has bought time but, in the long-term, the pattern of destabilizing political upheavals will be likely to continue.'[39]

The political wisdom of not taking the second step before the first one, when applied to the system of the Persian Gulf, means nothing more than to first strengthen confidence between the protagonists before the creation of institutionalized security structures can be carried out in the second phase.

Afghanistan

A decade of Afghan resistance to Soviet occupation, followed by a factional war between different mujaheddin groups seeking power in Kabul, made the country extremely vulnerable to external influences. Not only the Soviets and later Russia, but the West, in particular the United States, and Pakistan were competing for the utmost influence in the future development of Afghanistan. Two other countries geographically close to Afghanistan but harbouring different views about the best solution to the conflicts in that country – Iran and Saudi Arabia – were also interested in the fate of Kabul.

Iran shares a border of more than 600 kilometres with Afghanistan. Geographical proximity to the Afghan conflict has naturally been important to Iran, though in different ways and not to the same degree as it has been for Pakistan. Unlike the border between Pakistan and Afghanistan, the Iran–Afghan frontier is sparsely populated. Yet, despite its ruggedness and impenetrability, for Iran Afghanistan represents a vast strategic land bridge to the East.

The Iranian revolution and the Soviet invasion of Afghanistan happened within months of each other. The launching of the Afghan guerrilla war against the Soviet occupying forces and the victory of Iran's revolutionaries against the Shah's regime thus virtually coincided with each other. For most of the 1980s, Iranian–Afghan relations reflected the interplay between the course of the Iranian revolution and the Afghan guerrilla campaign.[40] On 5 March 1979 an uprising broke out in Herat. Between 5 and 16 March the garrison of Herat was besieged by Muslim rebel forces. Eventually the air force, sent in by the central government in Kabul, crushed the rebellion, leaving more than 24,000 combatants and civilians dead. Kabul later accused Tehran of having dispatched Pasdaran camouflaged in civilian clothes to the conflict.[41]

Although the accusation could not be verified, it was obvious that the Iranian leadership was assisting the mujaheddin. Nevertheless, both fear of Soviet retaliation and the ensuing war with Iraq, which consumed most of Iran's attention and resources, resulted in a discrepancy between the rhetoric of the Iranian leadership and the level of material support actually awarded to the Afghan resistance. Iran basically limited its commitments to furnishing the guerrillas with offices in Tehran (Gulbuddin Hekmatyar's Hizb-e Islami and Burhanuddin Rabbani's Jama'at-e Islami opened offices there) and supporting their publications. Stories about guerrilla training camps on Iranian soil remained unconfirmed rumours. In fact, the only mujaheddin who received military training in Iran were Pasdaran. Iran could not be held directly responsible when some of them on their own initiative later participated in the Afghan guerrilla war.

It was within the logic of the Iranian revolution that most of Iran's assistance to the Afghan resistance went to Shia groups more influenced by Iran than by any other country involved. The Shia comprise between 15 per cent and 20 per cent of the Afghan population. Most of them belong to the main Hazara, Qizilbash and Farsiwan groups.[42] The Hazaris were initially the group who seemed most promising to, and were most favoured by, Iran. They are a relatively homogeneous segment of Afghan society and have traditionally strong bonds with Iran's Farsi speaking population. As early as 23 June 1979 the Hazara Shia in Kabul revolted.[43] It was already obvious before this revolt was crushed that concentrating only on the Hazara Shia had its shortcomings. This group lives in Afghanistan's central massif, an area which was of only minor strategic importance during the Soviet–Mujaheddin struggle.[44] Therefore Iran also tried to strengthen its ties with non-Hazari Shia. Some of their leading personalities were invited for military training to Iran.

Initially Tehran welcomed the initiative of Sayyid Ali Beheshti to unite the Afghan Shia in September 1979. He founded an organization called Shuraye Etefaq-e Islami (Council of the Islamic Union) to administer the affairs of the Shia after the expulsion of Afghan government troops from the main Shia areas. But Beheshti's organization never came under full Iranian control. He was not an admirer of Khomeini but of Ayatollah al-Uzma (Grand Ayatollah) Kho'i in Najaf, meaning that he was looking for neither religious nor political guidance from Iran.

Among the Afghan Shia there were at least three main ideological components: Islamists, Hazara Nationalists and Socialists,[45] the latter having partially served under different Soviet-backed governments. In the course of the Civil War the Afghan Shia had splintered into numerous parties. In addition, by concentrating their support on the Shia, the Iranians risked their credibility with the Sunni majority, some 80 per cent of the Afghan population, who were the main force fighting the Soviets and their proxies in Kabul. In general, though Iran did have opportunities of increasing its influence in war-torn Afghanistan and exporting its brand of radical Islam, domestic weaknesses and the constraints of the war with Iraq (Iran could not risk, for instance, antagonizing the Soviet Union completely due to its dependence on Soviet armour and Soviet diplomatic assistance) prevented the establishment of a high Iranian profile there.[46]

This state of affairs angered the Iranian leadership because of Saudi Arabian designs to expand the bilateral struggle for dominance in the region into Afghanistan. Riyadh assisted all the mujaheddin groups that were not on Iran's pay roll.[47] Moreover, fully supported by the West, particularly by the United States, and using its Sunni credentials, Saudi Arabia outmanoeuvred Iran in Afghanistan. Saudi funding of the Afghan resistance by far exceeded that of Iran. Riyadh financed its own spearhead in Afghanistan, the Ettehad group, led by Abdul Rasul Sayyaf, but it also successfully influenced other Sunni rebel leaders such as the influential Gulbuddin Hekmatyar.

When the last Soviet soldier had left Afghanistan, the Soviet Union had fallen apart and Pakistan's direct involvement in the conflict had receded temporarily, Iran and Saudi Arabia were left to compete with each other for influence in Afghanistan: 'the "external" component of the battle for Afghanistan passed from the choice between Islam and communism, to a contest for influence between Saudi Wahhabism and Iranian Shiism'.[48]

Struggling to keep up with Saudi Arabia, the post-Khomeini Iranian leadership relied notably on a combination of pressure (provision of material assistance, including arms, to Shia groups) and diplomacy (cooperation with Pakistan and with the UN). Later on Rafsanjani and his government even announced the termination of all arms supplies to their Afghan clients and pressed the pro-Iranian factions to resolve differences through negotiation.[49] This shift in emphasis from armed struggle to diplomacy was immediately criticized by Iranian hardliners.

Although the hardliners attacked Saudi Arabia for 'meddling' in Afghanistan and for the 'suppression' of the Shia there, they even-handedly blamed Rafsanjani for 'sacrificing Iran's allies in Afghanistan on the altar of stability'.[50] The accusations against Rafsanjani lacked a sound basis since he had in fact tried to secure Iran a fair say in any future solution to the Afghan crisis. He maintained his commitment to ending the rule of the pro-Soviet Afghan President, Najibullah, and to ensuring adequate representation in the post-Najibullah government for Iran's Afghan allies.[51] But his demand for a guaranteed 25 per cent Shia representation in every future Afghan government was flatly rejected by Saudi Arabia and its local disciples.[52]

When Najibullah's regime finally collapsed in April 1992, so far from improving, Iran's interests suffered. Without a common enemy uniting the various mujaheddin groups Afghanistan disintegrated into a series of heavily armed, warring, confessional cantons in which there was only minor Shia influence. This development created two major problems for Iran.

First of all, the overwhelming influence of Sunni factions in the post-Najibullah political landscape gave an advantage to Saudi Arabia. Riyadh immediately sought to intensify its dialogue with the Sunni mujaheddin, promising further financial aid and donations for mosques, schools and so on.[53]

Secondly, the continuing bloodshed in Afghanistan meant a delay in the repatriation of some two to three million Afghan refugees living in the Iranian border province of Khorasan. These unassimilated refugees existed side by side with disgruntled ethno-sectarian minorities, thus contributing to a serious lapse in security and stability in Khorasan. It should be added that the breakdown of the Afghan state, the corresponding increase in drug trafficking as a major source of cash income for various mujaheddin outfits, corruption in the law-enforcement agencies in eastern Iran and the proliferation of weapons in the remote border regions had all resulted in a virtually unhindered expansion of drug routes through eastern Iran.[54] Furthermore, taking care of millions of refugees for over a decade had imposed tremendous additional strains on Iran's financial resources and social services.

Iran therefore encouraged the efforts of the Afghan interim President, Rabbani, favouring a peaceful route to power-sharing, seeking to disarm the various mujaheddin groups as 'the only way out of the chaos presently reigning in Afghanistan' and linking the stability of Afghanistan directly to its own national security.[55] Tehran could live with the Jama'at Islami of the ethnic Tajik, Burhanuddin Rabbani, and his allies in the so-called Northern Alliance, including the Tajik, Ahmad Shah Mas'ud, the Ismaili, Naderi, the Hizb-e Wahdat of Abdul Ali Mazari and the Uzbek, General Dostam, who were fighting Pashtuns supported by Pakistan and Saudi Arabia. But after the victory over President Najibullah the Northern Alliance fell apart. Dostam started fighting Mas'ud and both attacked the Shia. Mas'ud even sought the cooperation of the pro-Saudi faction led by Abdul Rasul Sayyaf and presented himself to the West as the most reliable future leader of Afghanistan.[56]

Once again, Iran's influence in Afghanistan declined, and this was carefully noted by other interested neighbours of Afghanistan. For instance, Russia and the secular leaders of the CCARs considered that there was more of an Islamic threat, as it were, from Saudi-backed mujaheddin than from the Iranian-backed Shia mujaheddin.[57] Factional fighting between pro-Iranian and pro-Saudi groups continued in Kabul and other major cities of Afghanistan, but, although further supporting the Shia, Iran also tried to open a dialogue with Sunni and non-Hazari groups.[58]

Riyadh took this as a challenge. Just as the Iranian media had blamed Saudi Arabia for its Gulf policies, whilst Iranian radicals were initiating unrest in the area, the Saudi press now started attacking Iran for its behaviour in Afghanistan, although Saudi Arabia had the upper hand there. *Al-Bilad* for instance remarked: 'It is regrettable and painful that the Afghans – who united in a single trench to resist Soviet occupation and its lackey government in Kabul from the beginning of the 1970s until the liberation of Afghanistan, the evacuation of Soviet troops and the fall of the Marxist regime – have since then become divided and are slaughtering and fighting each other . . . Therefore, we have to ask who is playing havoc in Afghanistan, and who is exploiting the situation in a country which has just emerged from a great jihad, in every sense of the word, against occupying forces to rebuild itself after the destruction caused by years of war. It is no secret that the first to be blamed are the sons of the Afghan people themselves, and then the Tehran regime which kindled the fire in Afghanistan and came between the jihad brothers, divided them and tore them apart.'[59]

With the Taliban coming into the picture, Iranian–Saudi competition for influence in Afghanistan continued to benefit Riyadh. The Taliban's strong Sunni background, accompanied by assistance from Pakistan and the United States, definitely did not play into the hands of Iran. When the Taliban launched a new offensive in the late spring of 1997, conquering nearly all the provinces of Afghanistan, a new alliance emerged binding the pro-Iranian Shia, the units of Ahmad Shah Mas'ud and the Uzbek forces of General Dostam together against them. The Taliban's anti-Iranian stance became clear when they forced the Iranian embassy in Kabul to close. However, their attitude towards Saudi Arabia is ambiguous. Thus, the race is open until the situation in Afghanistan is finally resolved and some lasting power structure emerges.

Pakistan

In sharp contrast to Afghanistan, Pakistan is not a hotspot of Iranian–Saudi Arabian competition, but, like Turkey, is itself a major player in the Middle Eastern political game. Islamabad is not that influential in the Persian Gulf, nor in Central Asia from which it is separated by Afghanistan, but it is definitely a thorn in Iran's side. As mentioned before, funded by Saudi money and accompanied by the best wishes of the United States, Pakistan supports the purist, Sunni Taliban militias. Therefore, the relationship between Islamabad and Tehran is only officially described as brotherly.[60]

However, in general, both countries have a sincere interest in preserving a working relationship. There is the issue of border security in Baluchistan, a concern for the Iranian leadership as well as the Pakistani government. In the 1970s, Imperial Iran and Pakistan cooperated in combating Baluchi separatists. Interrupted in the early years of the Iranian revolution, their cooperation resumed in the late 1980s, but this time both countries also tried to coordinate their struggles against drug trafficking. When Pakistan's President visited Iran in 1994, both countries reiterated their determination to work towards establishing joint security operations along their common border.[61] Three years previously, both governments had agreed on cooperation between their respective Institutes for Strategic Studies. In 1994 the Iranian and Pakistani navies conducted joint exercises for the first time, signalling that relations between both countries had also assumed a strategic, military aspect.

Up to now, Iran has gained more from this military cooperation than Pakistan, since Pakistan has a more formidable military, a more developed arms industry and a nuclear infrastructure. On the other hand, Iran is constrained from developing closer relations with Pakistan because it does not want to alienate India, which it views as a major global power and a potentially important economic partner.[62]

Relations between Iran and Pakistan are also temporarily grounded by Sunni–Shia clashes in Pakistan. The Shia are a minority in Pakistan, and, sensitive to their inferior position, have often articulated pro-Iranian and pro-Khomeini sentiments. There has been among them a growing adherence to Iranian interpretations of religious observance and the hierarchical aspects of Shiism and the Iranian revolution, with Khomeini as its leader, became a source of pride for them. Many of them clearly felt something to the effect that Khomeini 'is a great Shi'i leader who has shaken up and influenced the world'.[63]

Iran, naturally, must have had some interest in nourishing these sympathies, and certainly in cases of anti-Shia incidents in Pakistan it never hesitated to side with its fellow-believers. But, where possible, the Iranian leadership tried to avoid direct criticism of the Pakistani government, focusing instead on other parties. For instance, in one relevant case, the Speaker of the Iranian Majlis, Ayatollah Nateq Nuri, stated: 'Division [among Sunni and Shia in Pakistan . . . is being fed from elsewhere . . . the Pakistani government [should] . . . seriously counter the Wahhabi mercenaries.'[64]

On one hand, the Iranian leadership considered it very unlikely the Shia minority in Pakistan would be able to lead an Islamic revolution or to unite with the Sunni majority to promote a nonsectarian Islamic revolution. On the other hand, it was fearful that increasing sectarian violence in Pakistan might lead to growing instability there, thus depriving Iran of a reliable partner in the yet undecided competition for influence in the Middle East.

Sudan

At first glance, the issue of the struggle between Iran and Saudi Arabia for influence in such a remote country as Sudan comes as a surprise. Since Iran is situated in a sub-region of the Middle East on another continent, distant from Sudan, relations between the two countries have, throughout history, naturally been limited.

But keeping in mind the deep and complex historical roots of Sudan's Islamic revivalist movements, it comes as no surprise that the Iranian Islamic revolution of 1978–9 was broadly welcomed by the Sudanese Muslims and that Iran became a source of inspiration for them. Throughout the 1970s Sudanese Islamic revivalist groups such as the Mahdists and the Muslim Brotherhood had tried in vain to topple the government of President Jafar al-Numayri. Then the Sudanese Head of State felt the heat of the Iranian revolution. He quickly began to develop a quasi-Islamic state ideology and to incorporate his Muslim opponents into the regime and a kind of Islamization was instituted from above. This more congenial environment gave increased opportunities to Sudanese Islamic groups, especially to the Muslim Brotherhood, to develop contacts with Tehran once the revolution there had succeeded.

Shortly after the downfall of the Shah, Hasan al-Turabi, the leader of the Sudanese branch of the Muslim Brotherhood, visited Iran, enthusiastically supporting the new Iranian leadership's goal of Islamization. Yet, there were some marked differences between Turabi's vision of a just Islamic state and its position in international politics and that of the Iranian revolutionaries. Turabi, for instance, advocated power-sharing between committed laymen and clerics in a future Islamic state as well as preserving good relations with Egypt, Saudi Arabia and the United States, a position of which the Iranians were very suspicious.[65]

Suspicion also influenced the politics of Numayri. He felt unable to control the growing contacts between Iran and Sudanese Islamic groups. Continuously enraged by the situation, and knowing that he was not strong enough to risk antagonizing domestic Islamic opposition again, Numayri agreed to participate in a coup to uproot the main source of his anger, the Islamic revolution in Iran. This particular attempt in 1982 was only one of at least half a dozen plans to suppress the Iranian revolution from without. This time, the plan, which aimed at placing the Shah's eldest son on the throne, was organized by the Israeli Defence Minister, Ariel Sharon, and some dubious Israeli arms merchants. It was financed by the Saudi Arabian government to some US$ 800 million, logistically backed by the CIA and – last but not least – based in Numayri's Sudan. The coup was finally called off because of changes in the Israeli cabinet after the massacres at the Sabra and Shatila refugee camps.[66] In the end, Numayri's attempts to integrate Sudan's Muslim revivalists into his power structure could only delay the disintegration of his regime and his overthrow until 1985 when Sadiq al-Mahdi, head of the influential Mahdiyya movement, took power in Khartoum.

At first, the Iranian leadership did not wholeheartedly welcome this shift in power. Of course, for the mullahs in Tehran, al-Mahdi was an improvement on Numayri but they would have preferred Turabi who was better known to them and not as outspoken in his sympathy for Saudi Arabia as Sadiq al-Mahdi. Nonetheless Iran later came to terms with the new Sudanese President when his strong commitment to resolve the civil war in the south of his country by military means had created friction between him and the Western benefactors of Sudan, especially the United States. Washington cancelled its aid commitment, causing an acute worsening of Sudan's economic situation[67] and anti-American feelings began to unite Iran and al-Mahdi's regime, at least partially.

In the meantime, Hasan al-Turabi did not stand idly by. He strengthened the organizational capabilities of the Muslim Brotherhood and established a support base in strategic parts of the population. He helped to build and put in use an extensive network of Islamic banks with the active assistance of Saudi Arabia. This network enabled him to direct money to influential personalities and organizations as well as to individuals from the lower classes, thus securing sympathy and support for the Muslim Brotherhood among large sections of the population. During Numayri's rule he had managed to establish ties with the military because the President had asked him to instruct the officer corps in Islamic theology. He nurtured the careers of his own students and disciples, pressing for their acceptance into the bureaucracy or the military academy. What is more, by founding the National Islamic Front (NIF), he successfully strengthened the political nature of the Muslim Brotherhood, giving it a party-like organizational structure. Thus he was more than prepared when officers, led by Colonel Umar al-Bashir and sympathetic towards the NIF, finally toppled Sadiq al-Mahdi's government in 1990 and took power. By exerting influence over the key centres of power in Sudan, Turabi became the *éminence grise* of the new military regime.[68]

In this situation it was logical that the Iranian government should be highly optimistic about the prospect of a closer cooperation between the Islamic Republic and its friend, Hasan al-Turabi. Good relations with the new Islamic regime in Sudan could help Iran to spread its influence beyond its territorial borders into areas otherwise closed to it. 'Sudan is perfectly situated – opposite the Arabian Peninsula, wedged between the Horn of Africa and Egypt – to serve as a vehicle from which Iran's revolutionary activities can radiate in all directions.'[69]

With the overthrow of traditional power structures in Ethiopia and Somalia, Sudan emerged as a key power in the Horn of Africa and the Red Sea. As such it could also procure Iran's entry into Africa.[70] Alas, it was not only the large Muslim community in Subsaharan Africa that interested the Iranians, but the prospect that they now might be able to increase their leverage on Saudi Arabia and to get Riyadh in a double lock represented by themselves and Sudan.[71] Therefore, not surprisingly, the probable establishment of closer relations between the radical Muslim states of Iran and Sudan created considerable anxiety amongst their neighbours including Saudi Arabia and Egypt, and the West was also concerned with what domino effect this combination might produce.[72] The Red Sea and the Upper Nile regions were regarded by Saudi Arabia and Egypt respectively as their legitimate spheres of influence, and a challenge to that influence must have provoked a strong reaction; indeed, both countries reportedly backed Sadiq al-Mahdi's efforts to regain power in his home country.[73]

Thus the governments and media of both Saudi Arabia and Egypt were particularly critical of the cooperation between Sudan and Iran when the latter started to funnel weapons into Sudan. The first arms deal between the two countries was reported in March 1991. In the summer of that year several substantial weapons shipments, paid for and arranged by Iran, arrived in Sudan. A single delivery in August reportedly included 1000 tons of small arms and ammunition. In September Khartoum received 5 dismantled Chinese F-6 combat aircraft. In November, a third shipment arrived in Port Sudan, consisting of 50,000 automatic rifles. In December a delivery of unspecified Chinese arms landed in Sudan, channelled through Iran.[74]

In the middle of the same month, between 12 and 16 December, the Iranian President Rafsanjani paid an official state visit to Sudan heading a delegation of 157 individuals. It included Iran's defence minister, chief of intelligence and the commander of the Pasdaran who publicly signed a mutual defence pact with Sudan's new Islamic shock troops, the Popular Defence Force (PDF).[75] The talks between the two sides also resulted in a number of commercial and economic deals, which allowed both governments to play down the military aspects of their cooperation.

And indeed, economic cooperation was of equal importance for the new Sudanese regime. Isolated from the West and its local allies as a result of its continued suppression of the Christian and animist secession movement in the South, its militant Islam, its support for Iraq during the Second Gulf War, its initial rejection of the Madrid accord and its alleged harbouring of terrorists, Khartoum was in desperate need of alternative partners. Of primary importance was the securing of an energy base for its economy after access to Iraqi and Libyan sources was cut. An initial Iranian–Sudanese agreement on this issue included the exchange of desperately needed Iranian crude oil for Sudanese cattle-feed products.[76] A later trade agreement, worth US$ 300 million, consisted in part of 3.4 million barrels of oil for Sudan. In April 1992 Tehran offered Khartoum free oil for six months and supplies at easy terms for one year thereafter. The National Iranian Oil Company (NIOC) began to help the Sudan to explore and exploit its own oil reserves. In addition Iran constructed a 'peace road' at its own expense, linking Kusti, al-Rank and Malakal, the capital of the Upper Nile Province.[77]

However, the outside world was far more interested in information on the military cooperation continuing between Iran and Sudan in different forms and at different levels. The talks between Rafsanjani and his Sudanese allies had also focused on military matters. Information leaks revealed further Iranian funding to enable Sudan to acquire sophisticated jet fighters, tanks and armoured vehicles from China. These arms purchases were to include eighteen F-7 and F-8 fighters, 160 tanks, 210 armoured personnel carriers and an undisclosed amount of heavy artillery and multiple-launch missile systems.[78]

In August 1992, reports emerged of an additional Iranian–Sudanese agreement, whereby Iran pledged to supply 100 Chinese tanks, medium-range artillery, five F-5 aircraft, an unspecified number of 108-mm Katyusha mini-rockets and an additional purchase from China of 20 combat aircraft and several dozen T-59 tanks in the near future. In connection with these purchases some reports asserted that Iran, in exchange for military assistance, had gained access to Port Sudan.

The Egyptian news agency MENA claimed that Iran and Sudan had reached agreement in June 1992 on the use of the port facilities for a period of 25 years, thereafter subject to possible renewal for another 15 years. Iran would look after the security of the port facilities by supplying a number of Chinese Silkworm missiles. The construction of a military base was reported to have begun in Trinkitat, south of Port Sudan.[79]

Besides the arms supplies, regular consultations were being held between military officials from both countries, at the highest level. Shortly after Rafsanjani's second visit to Sudan in March 1992, the Sudanese Head of Armed Forces, General Ihsan al-Rahman, visited Tehran for meetings with the Iranian Defence Minister, Hassan Torkan, and the Commander of the Pasdaran, Mohsen Reza'i. The latter became well known for his frequent visits to Sudan to assess its military aid requirements. It was certainly the Pasdaran, and not the regular Iranian army, who took the lead in fostering military cooperation with Sudan. When rumours emerged of the dispatch of Iranian troops to Sudan, only the Pasdaran were involved. Speculation was rife as to the number of troops actually involved. The Saudi-funded newspaper, *al-Hayat*, spoke of an Iranian troop presence of between 4,000 and 12,000, and the Egyptian newspaper *al-Wafd* put the figure at a total of 10,000 Iranian soldiers and military experts. There were even reports linking the Pasdaran to combat operations in the south of Sudan.[80]

Whilst President Rafsanjani flatly denied the presence of any Iranian troops in Sudan, stating that the Western media was lying when it claimed that Iran was interfering in Sudan or elsewhere, because 'Iran is only exporting words and visions and not troops',[81] his Foreign Minister,

Ali Velayati, confirmed the presence of 'several hundred' Pasdaran in Sudan.[82] Their main purpose was said to be training the 85,000 strong PDF. The former Sudanese Labour Minister, George Logokwa, confirmed the establishment of seven training camps operated by the Pasdaran.[83] Western, as well as Israeli, Egyptian, Saudi Arabian, Algerian and other Arab experts suspected a double purpose for these training camps. According to them, the camps and other facilities including weapons were provided for the use of Egyptian, Libyan, Tunisian, Moroccan, Lebanese and Syrian radical Islamic and terrorist organizations[84] to enable them to carry out attacks in their home countries.[85]

Though these allegations lacked the backing of sufficient evidence, there were few doubts as to the presence of certain radical Palestinian and Lebanese groups in Sudan such as the Popular Front for the Liberation of Palestine – General Command, the Abu Nidal group, the Iranian-backed Islamic Jihad for the Liberation of Palestine and various Lebanese Hizballah outfits. The suspicion of an Iranian connection was initially linked to the presence of Majid Kamal, the Iranian chargé d'affaires in Khartoum, who had previously acted as the Iranian emissary to Hizballah in southern Lebanon.[86]

It is no wonder that Western and regional politicians constantly suspected the alliance between Iran and Sudan of being a means to sponsor terrorism and Islamic radicalism. Leading Sudanese officials have been trying in vain to dispel these suspicions. The Foreign Minister, Ali Ahmad Sahlool, for instance, depicted Sudan's relationship with Iran as born of shared Islamic fundamentalist sympathies in a hostile world. Both countries had a commitment to 'stand up to American imperialist intervention' and to 'unify the ranks of all Muslims.' But he denied that his country and Iran were building a 'Khartoum–Tehran axis to the detriment of other countries in the region. No axis exists under such circumstances.'[87] Hasan al-Turabi added: 'We are interested in spreading Islam all over the world . . . and people of course want to read into this forceful expansion . . . But there's no question of that. We're too weak . . . What we are sending forth in terms of radiation is just an idea.'[88]

Sudan's economic weakness is the key to any serious evaluation of the Khartoum–Tehran axis. Its endemic economic crisis, prolonged by the struggle against the Sudan People's Liberation Army (SPLA), diminished Western and regional economic and military assistance and the suspension of Saudi oil supplies in retaliation for its stance during the Second Gulf War – in addition to the already-mentioned loss of Libyan and Iraqi supplies – left the government of Umar al-Bashir almost no other choice but to accept the Iranian offer. The Sudanese regime had much to learn from Iranian experiences of a decade of unrest, a devastating war and international isolation. Tehran's technical, economic and military assistance, estimated at about US$ 20 million per annum,[89] has strengthened the Sudan against the threat of economic disaster, civil war and regional opposition.

But what are the main reasons for Iran to get involved with the Sudan? Abd al-Salam Sidahmed provided a convincing summary:

> There seems to be no place for Iran in [America's] new world order. Iran was deliberately excluded from the Gulf security arrangements after the [Second Gulf] war, first by the "six plus two" Damascus talks, and then by the individual defence pacts signed between some GCC countries and the US. Its failure to persuade France and Germany to rebuild its nuclear installations, which were destroyed by Iraq during the first Gulf war, was followed by the Middle East peace talks which alienated Iran further and distanced it from its closest ally in the region, Syria. These developments seemed to throw Iran, once again, to the brink of isolation. The Tehran–Khartoum joint venture could therefore be interpreted as the coming together of two isolated regimes who happen to share a common ideological orientation.[90]

But given its own considerable economic problems it is obvious that Iran must limit its assistance to the Sudan. The Tehran–Khartoum axis is an alliance of two economically weak and politically embattled regimes. It may give encouragement to a few dubious radical organizations or terrorist groups, but its capacity to pose a military threat to neighbouring countries is definitely limited. Perhaps the Western and regional media have their own political reasons for exaggerating this danger.

Furthermore, it should not be forgotten how many differences still exist between Iran and Sudan. Khartoum, for instance, refused to join Iran's attempts to isolate Iraq from the rest of the Muslim world, and it encouraged the PLO in the US-brokered Middle East peace process, which Iran opposes. And, last but not least, Hasan al-Turabi and his NIF are devoted Sunni Muslims who can, at best, only be political allies of Iran's Shia leadership. Taking into consideration Turabi's previous contacts with Saudi Arabia, it is clear that although under prevailing circumstances Iran has decisive leverage which can prevent the NIF from entering into deals with Saudi Arabia, Egypt or the West, there are no guarantees for the future.

In the Sudan, however, Iran has won in its contest with Saudi Arabia almost as much as it lost in Afghanistan.

Other countries

Since most states in the Arabian Peninsula declared that they are more or less linked to Saudi Arabia within the Gulf Cooperation Council, only Yemen remained as an arena in which Iran could challenge Saudi Arabia directly as it were, on the soil of the Peninsula. During the First Gulf War, South Yemen criticized the Iraqi attack on Iran, declared its sympathy for the besieged revolution in Iran, and offered temporary economic assistance to Tehran by refining a certain amount of Iranian crude oil in Aden after Iran's major refinery at Abadan was destroyed. But Tehran was well aware that South Yemen belonged to the Soviet hemisphere and that it could count on South Yemen's support only within the framework of Soviet interests. And Moscow was certainly not interested in becoming a tool in the Iranian–Saudi contest.

As a result of the battle for the occupation of Asir, which ended with a Saudi victory in 1934, as well as the Saudi–North Yemeni confrontations during the civil war in North Yemen in the 1960s, the relations between these two countries have not been as amicable as those between Saudi Arabia and the Gulf Arab states. Nevertheless, the San'a government could not afford to alienate Saudi Arabia. Hundreds of thousands of Yemeni workers were employed in Saudi Arabia, creating a considerable influx of cash vital to a poverty-stricken country such as North Yemen. As a result of these circumstances, Iran's influence in North Yemen remained limited. But when San'a sided with Saddam Husain during the Second Gulf War, prompting the expulsion of thousands of Yemeni workers from Saudi Arabia, Iran hoped it could take advantage of the souring of Saudi–North Yemeni relations. It became even more optimistic when Saudi Arabia – as a further measure of retaliation for North Yemen's position during the Kuwait crisis – clandestinely supported South Yemen in the civil war of 1994.

Tehran's media sided with North Yemen, only to be immediately criticized for so doing by Saudi Arabia. 'Until now, and after 15 years in power, the mullahs in Iran have attempted to kindle flames of sedition between the Kingdom of Saudi Arabia and its sister, the Republic of Yemen, after the mullahs noticed that a small misunderstanding had arisen . . . This has not achieved the wicked desire to engineer bloody confrontations between the sisterly Arab countries, which Iran was seeking. Iran's mullahs do not understand the language of dialogue. The only language they understand is the language of killing, destruction and bloody terrorism.'[91] But on balance, Iran was not very successful in Yemen.

However there were also the large Muslim populations outside the Arabian Peninsula. Since its emergence, the Islamic Republic of Iran has tried to present itself as a model for all the suppressed and downtrodden peoples of the world to follow. But since the model was a specifically Islamic one, it was clear from the beginning that the main recipients of Iran's revolutionary messages would be Muslim. There were differences in degree of commitment, but generally Iran supported a wide range of Islamic and indeed some non-Islamic liberation movements throughout the world, from the Philippines (MORO Liberation Front) to Saharan (the Sahara Liberation Front) and Subsaharan Africa (SWAPO, ANC) and even Europe (the Bosnian Muslims).[92] However the majority of the organizations supported were active in the Middle East and West Asia. It is true there were hints of Iranian influence among the Indian Shia, who outnumber, for instance, the Lebanese Shia by about 20 times;[93] nevertheless, the number of Muslim opposition groups supported by Iran increased according to their proximity to Iran. Among them were the Council of Islamic Union and the Jama'at Islami in Afghanistan, the Patriotic Union and the Democratic Party of Kurdistan as well as the al-Da'wa Party, the Islamic Action Organization and the High Council of the Islamic Revolution in Iraq, the Hizballah and the Islamic Towhid Movement in Lebanon, the Nahda movement in Tunisia, the Jama'at Islami in Egypt, the FIS in Algeria, but above all groups in the Persian Gulf region such as the Islamic Revolution Organization of the Arabian Peninsula, the Islamic Liberation Front of Bahrain or the Hizballah of Kuwait.[94]

All these groups were used by Iran in its fight against America's Middle East strategy, especially against the Israeli–Palestinian peace process[95] and against traditionalist Arab states with hereditary rulers. Tehran tried to find a common denominator between itself and the various Islamic opposition groups, blaming the existing Arab regimes for being perpetrators of 'American Islam', thus lacking legitimacy, ostensibly because Islam is opposed to the rule of kings. This policy, nevertheless, did not hinder Iran in maintaining pragmatic, and indeed profitable, relations with non-Arab neighbours like Turkey or Pakistan.

With some irony, even Iranian newspapers run by the hardliners noted the extent of that pragmatism. Turkey and Pakistan were each at one time or another governed by women Prime Ministers, unthinkable in the Islamic Republic of Iran. Pakistan claims to be an Islamic state, but it is very different from Iran, whereas Turkey has been a secular state since the 1920s. Turkey has excellent relations with the United States and is a member of NATO, whist Iran is an enemy of both. Both Turkey and Pakistan follow a Western model of pluralist democracy, but Iran's political system is not similar to that of any of its neighbours.[96] Having accepted, or at least tolerated, friendship with these regimes, Iranian radicals were not astonished to see their government develop closer links with even radical secular Arab states such as Syria, South Yemen (until 1990) and, to a lesser extent, Libya. In the course of the Islamic Republic's development Tehran's rulers have recognized that the country's geopolitical imperatives did not permit a complete isolation from the existing web of regional relations,[97] but these relations were filtered through their ideology.

As the main guarantor of traditional, conservative Islam, as well as being economically and militarily bound to the Western hemisphere, Saudi Arabia saw itself as the special target of threats originating from the Iranian revolution. By looking for allies among other challenged Arab regimes and Western countries while strictly adhering to the rules of traditional Sunni Islam, Saudi Arabia has, up to now, been able to meet the wider challenge of Iran's revolutionary offensive in the Muslim world.

NOTES

1 S. Chubin, *Iran's National Security Policy: Capabilities, Intentions & Impact* (Washington DC: Carnegie Endowment for International Peace, 1994), p. 10.

2 M.A. Hameed, *Saudi Arabia, the West and the Security of the Gulf* (London: Croom Helm, 1986), p. 34.

3 A. Hashim, *The Crisis of the Iranian State* (Oxford: Oxford University Press, 1995), p. 43.

4 K.L. Afrasiabi, *After Khomeini: New Directions in Iran's Foreign Policy* (Boulder: Westview Press, 1994), pp. 101–2.

5 F. al-Mazidi, *The Future of the Gulf: The Legacy of the War and the Challenge of the 1990s* (London and New York: Tauris, 1993), pp. 2–3. For more details see also M. Dezfuli, 'Iran va hamshayegan-e arabesh – amniyat-e Khalij-e Fars va nazm-e novin-e mintaqehaye (Iran and its Arab neighbours – the security of the Persian Gulf and the new regional system)', *Ettela'at-e siyasi-eqtesadi*, 8:5/6 (1994) pp. 20–5; H. Amirahmadi, 'Siyasat-e Kharijiye mintaqaye Iran', Ibid., 7:11/12 (1993), pp. 4–13.

6 M.J. Larijani, 'Iran's Foreign Policy: Principles and Objectives', *The Iranian Journal of International Affairs*, 7:4 (1996), p. 759.

7 'Iran's Winning Ways', *Gulf States Newsletter*, 21:543 (1996), p. 8.

8 K. Krause, 'Constructing Regional Security Regimes and the Control of Arms Transfers', *International Journal*, 45:2 (1990), p. 391.

9 H. Amirahmadi, 'Iranian–Saudi Arabian Relations since the Revolution' in H. Amirahmadi and N. Entessar, (eds.), *Iran and the Arab World* (Basingstoke, Macmillan, 1993), p. 149.

10 J. Reissner, 'Der Iran auf dem Weg zu einer Regionalmacht', *Aus Politik und Zeitgeschichte*, Bonn, 26 April 1996, p. 37.

11 *Jumhuriye Islami*, Tehran, 3 November 1991.

12 M.J. Larijani, Iran's Foreign Policy, pp. 759–60.

13 M.E. Ahrari, *The new Great Game in Muslim Central Asia* (Washington DC, Institute for National Strategic Studies, 1996), p. 46.

14 S. al-Mani, 'Of Security and Threat: Saudi Arabia's Perception', *Journal of South Asian and Middle Eastern Studies*, 20:1 (1996), p. 80.

15 M.A. Hameed, *Saudi Arabia*, p. 35.

16 *Ukaz*, Riyadh, 8 October 1994.

17 W.T. Tow, *Subregional Security Cooperation in the Third World* (Boulder, Westview Press, 1990), p. 7.

18 F.O. Hampson, 'Building a Stable Peace: Opportunities and Limits to Security Cooperation in Third World Regional Conflicts', *International Journal*, 45:2 (1990), pp. 476–85.

19 S. Chubin, 'Post-War Gulf Security', *Survival*, 33:2 (1991), p. 143.

20 F. al-Mazidi, *The Future*, p. 5.

21 Ibid., p. 6.

22 *BBC Summary of World Broadcasts*, ME/2186, 23 December 1994.

23 Ibid., ME/1602, 2 February 1993.

24 Ibid., ME/1604, 4 February 1993.

25 Quoted in A. Hashim, *The Crisis*, p. 44.

26 *BBC Summary of World Broadcasts*, ME/2117, 4 October 1994.
27 Ibid., ME/1603, 3 February 1993.
28 'Iran's Winning Ways', *Gulf States Newsletter*, 21:543 (1996), p. 10.
29 *Tehran Times*, Tehran, 28 December 1995.
30 *The Economist Intelligence Unit (EIU), Country Report Iran*, London, 2nd quarter 1995, p. 12.
31 K.L. Afrasiabi, *After Khomeini*, p. 101.
32 *EIU, Country Report Saudi Arabia*, London, 3rd quarter 1996, p. 12.
33 *BBC Summary of World Broadcasts*, ME/2630, 5 June 1996.
34 T.M. Basheer, 'Structural Challenges to Security in the Gulf', *Mediterranean Quarterly*, 2:4 (1991), p. 27.
35 For more details see A. Plascov, 'Modernization, Political Development and Stability' in S. Chubin (ed.), *Security in the Persian Gulf* (3 vols., Aldershot, Gower, 1982) vol. 3, pp. 10–12.
36 J.A. Kechichian, 'Iraq and the Arab World', *Conflict*, 11:1 (1991), p. 12.
37 W.T. Tow, *Subregional Cooperation*, p. 18
38 S. Chubin, Post-War Gulf Security, p 140.
39 *Adelphi Papers*, 264 (1991/92), p. 81.
40 J. Calabrese, *Revolutionary Horizons*, pp. 130–1.
41 *Kabul Times*, Kabul, 19 April 1979.
42 H. Emadi, 'Exporting Iran's Revolution: The Radicalization of the Shiite Movement in Afghanistan', *Middle Eastern Studies*, 31:1 (1995), p. 3.
43 Ibid., p. 5.
44 J. Calabrese, *Revolutionary Horizons*, p. 132.
45 H. Emadi, Exporting, pp. 5–8.
46 A. Ehteshami, 'Wheels within wheels: Iran's foreign policy towards the Arab World' in H. Amirahmadi and N. Entessar (eds.), *Reconstruction and Regional Diplomacy in the Persian Gulf* (London and New York: Routledge, 1992), p. 181.
47 H. Amirahmadi, Iranian–Saudi Arabian Relations, p. 147.
48 J. Calabrese, *Revolutionary Horizons*, p. 135.
49 Ibid., p. 136.
50 *Jumhuriye Islami*, Tehran, 24 February 1993.
51 F. Halliday, 'Introduction' in A. Ehteshami and M. Varasteh (eds.), *Iran and the International Community* (London, New York: Routledge, 1991), p. 3.
52 A. Ahady, 'Iran's Frustration in Afghanistan', *US–Iran Review*, 2:4 (1994), p. 6.
53 R.F. Oxenstierna, *Saudi Arabia in the Post-Gulf War: The Search for Stability and Security in the Gulf* (London: Gulf Centre for Strategic Studies, 1992), p. 26.
54 A. Hashim, *The Crisis*, p. 25.
55 *Tehran Times*, Tehran, 6 July 1992.
56 A. Ahady, Iran's, pp. 6–7.
57 A. Rashid, *The Resurgence of Central Asia. Islam or Nationalism?* (London: Zed Books, 1994), p. 213.
58 J. Calabrese, *Revolutionary Horizons*, p. 140.
59 *Al-Bilad*, Riyadh, 4 October 1994.
60 J. Reissner, Der Iran, pp. 36–7.
61 A. Hashim, *The Crisis*, p. 40.
62 Ibid.

63 N.R. Keddie, *Iran and the Muslim World: Resistance and Revolution* (Houndmills: Macmillan, 1995), p. 120.
64 *BBC Summary of World Broadcasts*, ME/2165, 29 November 1994.
65 J. Calabrese, *Revolutionary Horizons*, pp. 155–6.
66 H Amirahmadi, Iranian–Saudi Arabian Relations, p. 147.
67 J. Calabrese, *Revolutionary Horizons*, p. 156.
68 G.E. Fuller and I.O. Lesser, *A Sense of Siege: The Geopolitics of Islam and the West* (Boulder: Westview Press, 1995), p. 129.
69 J. Calabrese, *Revolutionary Horizons*, p. 156.
70 A.S. Sidahmed, 'Tehran–Khartoum; a New Axis or a Warning Shot?', *Middle East International*, London, 7 February 1992, p. 18.
71 M. Mohaddessin, *Islamic Fundamentalism: The new Global Threat* (Washington DC: Seven Locks Press, 1993), p. 95.
72 G.E. Fuller and I.O. Lesser, *A Sense*, p. 129.
73 *Washington Post*, Washington DC, 12 March 1992.
74 J. Calabrese, *Revolutionary Horizons*, p. 157.
75 *Washington Post*, Washington DC, 12 March 1992.
76 A.S. Sidahmed, Tehran–Khartoum, p. 18.
77 J. Calabrese, *Revolutionary Horizons*, p. 157.
78 *Financial Times*, London, 17 December 1991.
79 J. Calabrese, *Revolutionary Horizons*, pp. 157–9.
80 Ibid., p. 158.
81 *Resalat*, Tehran, 2 February 1993.
82 J. Calabrese, *Revolutionary Horizons*, p. 158.
83 Ibid.
84 M. Abir, *Saudi Arabia*, p. 213.
85 *Foreign Report*, London, 11 May 1995, p. 1.
86 *Washington Post*, Washington DC, 12 March 1992.
87 Ibid.
88 Ibid.
89 J. Calabrese, *Revolutionary Horizons*, p. 65.
90 A.S. Sidahmed, Tehran–Khartoum, p. 18.
91 *Al-Jazira*, Riyadh, 15 December 1994.
92 A. Ehteshami, Wheels, p. 205.
93 M. Pohly, *Political Extremist Organizations: The Islamic Network* (Washington DC, Jewish Institute for National Security Affairs, 1996), pp. 24–5.
94 A. Ehteshami, Wheels, p. 205.
95 *Echo of Iran (EOI)*, 42:81 (1994), p. 4.
96 *Salam*, Tehran, 21 November 1993.
97 A. Ehteshami, Wheels, p. 204.

5

Central Asia

When Iran made overtures to the states on the Arabian Peninsula after the Second Gulf War, it encountered insurmountable obstacles hindering any further cooperation. Any Iranian attempt to establish mutual safety agreements was blocked by the opposite side. When the GCC would not tolerate even Egypt or Syria stationing military forces permanently on its soil, the Iranians realized that no GCC state would ever offer them a say in its security matters.[1] The Deputy Foreign Minister, Abbas Maleki, made it very clear that, even in the immediate future, Iran would only play a marginal role in the Arab-dominated politics of the Near and Middle East, thus forcing it to look in other directions to create some relief.[2] The overall political situation in the area was not conducive to the achievement of Iran's ambitions.

Insecurity at Iran's northern borders

Between the First and the Second Gulf Wars the Soviet Union collapsed. Given that there was 2,500 kilometres of common border between Iran and the Soviet Union – the longest border Iran had with any country – the disintegration of the Soviet Empire must have had serious consequences for Iran. The leadership in Tehran regretfully remembered the supportive attitude of the Soviet Union during the Iraq–Iran war, and the subsequent blossoming of ties between the two states, accompanied by the improvement in personal relations between the two presidents, Gorbachev and Rafsanjani. It was one of the very few points of agreement between the Iranian government and the West that both were keen to see the return of Gorbachev after the August 1991 coup and were fully supportive of his efforts to restore order to the Soviet Union. Tehran had no interest in a disorderly break-up of the USSR at that juncture.[3] To maintain the territorial integrity of the Soviet Union, Iran was prepared to offer generous compromises. When Soviet troops forcibly suppressed the Shia rebellion in Azerbaijan in January 1990, the Iranian President merely voiced his 'deep regret' and remained neutral, behaviour inconceivable during Khomeini's lifetime.[4]

But as we know now, history decided otherwise. The Soviet Union finally collapsed in December 1991, causing a political vacuum in Iran's Central Asian neighbourhood that both existing states and new countries born from the bankrupt estate of the USSR tried to fill. The emergence of new republics in the southern regions of the former Soviet Union replaced a single stable actor on Iran's northern border with several unstable and conflicting powers. All these new republics had to cope with the many problems attendant on establishing independent statehood in a remarkably limited period of time.

Many problems and conflicts from the past, covered over during seven decades of Soviet Union domination, re-emerged, with a danger of spilling over into neighbouring countries like Iran. Disputes immediately arose over access to and resources in the Caspian Sea, which has a coastline shared by Iran as well as Caucasian and Central Asian states.[5] Domestic political unrest and bitter power struggles became endemic in most of the new republics. A war flared up on the borders of Armenia and Azerbaijan, accompanied by civil war in Tajikistan. Clearly, Iran had to take great care that its internal unity was not threatened by any possible unravelling of neighbouring states.[6]

It should not be forgotten that Iran is a multi-ethnic state – non-Persian peoples make up half the total Iranian population, which numbers some 60 million.[7] Its ethnic minorities differ from each other not only in terms of historical development but also in the strength of their commitment to their quest for autonomy. But they share certain characteristics that have constituted a serious security risk: they live at the periphery of the central Iranian plateau, that is, they are transborder minorities (Iranian Kurds live across the border from Iraqi Kurds, Azeris live both in Iran and in the now independent Azerbaijan, and so on). The leadership in Tehran was worried that transborder populations could be used to destabilize Iran.

The Islamic Republic had thus to secure its national integrity against potential secessionist movements in Azerbaijan and Kurdistan, and incursions from bordering states – especially those in the process of disintegration such as Iraq and Afghanistan or those engaged in conflicts such as Azerbaijan and nearby Tajikistan.[8] In addition, Iran feared an influx of refugees fleeing the armed conflicts that had broken out in nearly all the regions on its borders, worsening a situation already complicated by millions of Afghans and Iraqi Shia who had sought shelter in the Islamic Republic. Sometimes it seemed to Tehran that every newly independent republic on its northern borders was another Trojan horse.[9]

It was either a delusion or mere propaganda when Deputy Foreign Minister Maleki blandly maintained: 'A glance at the surrounding environment of the Islamic Republic of Iran, from Central Asia to the Middle East proper, attests to the multitude of problems relating to the legitimacy of governments and ethnic conflicts. Iran, on the other hand, sits calmly in the midst of all this trouble, preserving its territorial integrity, enjoying security and allowing for easy ethnic interaction.'[10]

On the contrary, due to the many challenges arising out of the unsettled situation in the north and out of Iran's own uncertainties about its ethnic minorities, Rafsanjani decided in the beginning of the 1990s that it was best to keep a low profile.[11] He was only too well aware that active Iranian intervention in Central Asia could provoke Iran's ethnic minorities, already rebellious and intolerant of any form of centralized, authoritarian power that limited their traditions.[12] Despite 14 million Azeris living in Iran (compared with only 7.1 million in Azerbaijan) Iran was very hesitant to become involved in the Nagorno-Karabakh dispute between Armenia and Azerbaijan. Indeed so fearful was it of any degree of engagement that in the spring of 1993 the Iranian Azeri population living in the province of Eastern Azerbaijan was split up and forcibly settled in the provinces of Tabriz and Ardebil.[13]

Nevertheless, the picture of Iranian ethnic problems is not complete if it is only limited to its transborder aspects. Notwithstanding Ayatollah Khomeini's declaration that 'no difference exists in our revolution', the spectre of domestic sectarianism has haunted the Islamic Republic from the very beginning.[14] Immediately after the revolution, the Tehran government had to fight centrifugal ethnic tendencies with military force.

Only when Iran felt its national identity challenged by Iraq during the First Gulf War did the minorities forget their grievances and defend the common homeland. But during peace time the government has to take care to keep this multinational state united. This is the reason for the constant affirmation of the Iranian nation state and the vehement rejection of the partition of Iraq or the establishment of a state for the Kurds.

Iran's ethnic problem is further aggravated by its religious aspects. In the Islamic Republic, where Twelver Shiism is the official state religion, some 10 per cent of the population are Sunni, constituting the largest religious minority. Ayatollah Khomeini and his disciples have maintained that Islam is one, and this unity is irreconcilable with international and national divisions among Muslims. Non-Muslim minorities are 'protected' second-class citizens in the Islamic Republic, with political representation in the Majlis. But Sunni Iranians do not have such representation. For the Islamic Republic the Sunni above all – Baluchis, Arabs in the Bandar Lengeh area, Turkomen and Kurds – constitute a threat because they were engaged in insurgency in remote border regions during the early days of the Republic. 'Their existence as Sunnis in a Shi'i state poses a religious, political and security dilemma for a state that has yet to integrate them actively into the body politic.'[15] Some aspects of the situation have changed, however, in the course of time, though not entirely in favour of the government. Cities in the peripheral regions such as Sanandaj, Mahabad, Kermanshah, Zahedan, Zabol and Iranshahr have grown quickly during recent years. Furthermore, many Sunni have migrated to the big cities of the Iranian plateau, in particular Tehran. In this respect the Sunni are no longer in the same sociogeographical position as they were immediately before the revolution. Since many cities now have more than 300,000 inhabitants and are now far too large to be solely dominated by tribal affiliations, their political relationship with central government has changed, too. Therefore, with decreasing regard to tribal obligations, local Sunni officials, religious leaders and intellectuals widened their political horizons and have no qualms about intervening in politics at central government level. They try to do so as Iranians with full rights, and as Kurds, as Baluchis, as Arabs, as Turkomen, but also as Sunni. They are a challenge to the Shia government on its own turf. The Sunni now form a political force that the Iranian leadership, faced with a fait accompli, can no longer ignore as merely peripheral, archaic or tribal.[16]

The province of Khorasan, for example, has become Sunni by default because of the combination of its Turkoman minority and the large, and destabilizing, Afghan refugee population. Fortunately for the Tehran government, the majority of its indigenous Sunni population cannot imagine forming political alliances with neighbouring states, for they have a strong sense of Iranian national identity. In spite of that however, they do not refuse outside help, for example in Baluchistan, where most children attend private Sunni schools financed by Pakistan.[17] Only very few of them really do more. The large bomb which exploded at the Shia shrine of Imam Reza in Mashdad in June 1994 was almost certainly placed there by Sunni extremists based in Peshawar. In the same year riots also erupted in Zahedan, the capital of Baluchistan, when Shia replaced Sunni teachers.[18] The only large and relatively homogeneous Sunni group that is not ready to tolerate Shia dominance in Iran are the Kurds, who revolt from time to time despite the loss of many important leaders.

Summing up this consideration of the many ethnic and confessional problems the Iranian government has to deal with, one can conclude that the initial hesitation of the Islamic Republic about involvement in Central Asian and Caucasian conflicts was understandable. But after a few months of careful reflection on future policy towards Central Asia, new considerations emerged.

From wait-and-see to active politics

Even though Iran originally may not have had the inclination or resources to be drawn into Central Asia, it found it difficult to hold back because its government was sure that the existing power vacuum on its northern flank would be filled, be it by Turkey, Russia again, or – however extraordinary it might seem – by Saudi Arabia and the United States. Therefore, for Rafsanjani and his followers there was no other choice but for Iran to become a major player in the new Great Game. After that decision was reached, it was only natural for the Iranian government to make every effort to be accepted as this major player when casting the new roles.[19]

By 25 December 1991 Iran had formally recognized all seven Caucasian and Central Asian Republics (CCARs) – Armenia, Azerbaijan, Tajikistan, Turkmenistan, Kyrgyzstan, Uzbekistan and Kazakhstan. As of January 1992, Iranian embassies were opened in the respective CCARs, and Ali Velayati was one of the first foreign ministers to visit the seven. In May 1992, President Rafsanjani followed suit touring the region, visiting Kyrgyzstan, Uzbekistan and participating in a summit, held in the Turkmen capital, of the presidents of the Central Asian republics, Turkey and Iran. Moreover, Iran was the first Muslim country outside the CIS to recognize Armenia and to invite its foreign minister on a visit.[20]

In general, Iran's low-profile approach to Central Asia, as pursued during the Gorbachev era, has been replaced since the end of 1991 by a major drive to spread Iranian influence in the Muslim republics. Looking back to the time when the new Iranian approach towards Central Asia started, which was also when Rafsanjani's policics of pragmatism and the economic reconstruction of Iran were at their first height, it is not surprising that Iran's activities there should be dominated by domestic economic and political pressures. Establishing economic links with the new states of Central Asia and the Transcaucasus became an integral component of Iran's reconstruction and development plans.

Since then almost all major visits to the CCARs by senior Iranian officials have focused on economic cooperation, commerce and trade. The collapse of the Soviet Union and greater access to Central Asia and the Transcaucasus presented Iran with fresh economic opportunities. Since both regions are geographically isolated from the West but contiguous with or near Iran, Tehran was interested in presenting itself as a stable commercial throughfare, joining East and West.[21] After all, Iran could offer access to Gulf ports for its landlocked neighbours in the north, thus providing the governments of these states with an alternative to Russia.[22]

But the main attraction of Iran's northern neighbours lay in their potential wealth, in their natural resources, especially their vast deposits of oil and natural gas. Iran was thus eager to foster cooperation in the field of energy. It had to persuade the CCARs of the value of developing their common commercial interests. Tehran offered economic assistance and some technical advice and signed a string of bilateral economic cooperation agreements with the new republics. In February 1992 it also created an opportunity for Azerbaijan, Turkmenistan, Uzbekistan, Tajikistan and Kyrgyzstan to join the Economic Cooperation Organization (ECO),[23] promising membership in a future Muslim Common Market as well.

Knowing the limits of its economic capacity, the Iranian leadership looked for other means to cement its foothold in Central Asia. The transmission of Persian culture became an important aspect of Iranian diplomacy in the CCARs. 'Persian influence in Central Asia should not be underestimated. Geographical proximity, historical relations, linguistic and ethnic ties, . . . all help to promote and sustain Iran's interests in Central Asia.'[24] Therefore a special emphasis on revitalizing the Persian language and Persian culture became a noticeable element in the aid which Iran offered to the CCARs. It should not be forgotten that Persian was once widely understood from Mesopotamia to western China and throughout the Indo–Pakistan sub-continent. Today Tajikistan is the only Central Asian republic where Persian is the predominant language, but Iran has nevertheless exhibited an interest in promoting it in all the CCARs.

The Islamic Republic founded new cultural institutes and libraries, and organized cultural weeks, exhibitions and festivals in Central Asia. Central Asian students were admitted to Iranian teacher training colleges, and the Islamic Republic donated school textbooks and other books in Persian, as well as initiating exchange of lecturers. The broadcasting of news and other radio and TV programmes to Central Asia became an integral part of Iran's efforts to foster cultural ties with its northern neighbours.[25]

Last but not least, Islam was to become a major link between Iran and Central Asia. A state like the Islamic Republic of Iran, based on Islamic precepts, is obliged to revise the form as well as the content of its overall relationship with other countries. Islam has always been an important element of Persian culture, but with the Islamic revolution it emerged as the dominant factor. Thus, to speak of the variety of Iran's diplomatic relations with its northern neighbours means to speak of ties grounded mainly, though not exclusively, in Islam. Deputy Foreign Minister Abbas Maleki stated: 'What does it mean to say that we insist on our Muslim identity as a foreign policy objective? It simply means that we are concerned about the plight of our Muslim brethren throughout the world and consider relations with them as a foreign policy priority. It does not mean that we are the source of all troubles throughout the Muslim world or seek an adventurist foreign policy.'[26]

Iran's establishment of cultural, economic and political relations with the CCARs nearly always included the propagation of Islam, not as simply an interest in encouraging worship, but in supporting the Islamic Republic's vision of a politicized Islam. Iran's religio-cultural activities in the former Soviet republics were at the same time political activities. This was demonstrated, above all, by the fact that such activities were conducted through official Iranian channels. They were, then, not separate from Iranian diplomacy, but a vital part of it.

Moreover, inasmuch as none of the former Soviet republics instituted an Islamic government, the utilization of diplomatic missions to encourage them to do so gives such activities a transnational character. But Iranian officials did not deny that their religio-cultural activity has an underlying political purpose. Instead, they insisted that such activities aimed to foster cooperation and denied that they served as a vehicle for interference in the internal affairs of the Soviet successor states.[27]

One may believe Rafsanjani and those of his diplomats who maintained that the Islamic element in Iran's politics was naturally inherent in every single activity abroad and did not require foolish or tactless propaganda. Their Iran First policy had a wide range of objectives and was intended above all to strengthen the Islamic Republic, setting an example of a successful Islamic state for the outside world to emulate rather than exporting its more unpolished features to nervous neighbours. But as in other cases, Rafsanjani had to struggle with influential Islamic revolutionaries in his own country who preferred exactly the opposite: Islam first, regardless of international laws and norms of behaviour. Their powerful organizations spent about US$ 4,500 million on Islamic propaganda in the CCARs, whereas the government allocated only US$ 130 million.[28] Iranian radicals sent out 1,300 preachers to proselytize in the CCARs. In addition, they established four centres in Qum, Mashhad, Tabriz and Tehran for training Central Asian clerics.[29]

By establishing additional radio transmitters and directing them at its northern neighbours, Tehran was able to introduce special Islamic programming that dealt with the decadence and the cultural onslaught of the West, broadcast in 18 different languages.[30] There were two advantages for Iran in directing Islamic propaganda at its northern neighbours. After the break-up of the former Soviet Union, the Muslims of Central Asia discovered their independence along with an opportunity to practise Islam without any fear of repression by the state – both had eluded them for a long time. Within the framework of emerging political pluralism they were also able to view Islam as a political alternative. Neighbouring Iran presented itself as a proponent of Islamic government. Having implemented this kind of a government in the aftermath of revolution, the Iranians were viewed as a source of emulation and inspiration by Central Asian Muslims. Thus, emphasizing the pan-Islamic aspects of its foreign policy throughout Central Asia gave Iran the means to attract a considerable amount of sympathy, and even generate euphoria, in Muslim Central Asia – at least at the popular level.[31]

But even disregarding Islamic propaganda by others competing for influence in Central Asia, there were disadvantages for Iran's Islamic foreign policy inherent in Iranian Islam itself as well as in the state of Islam in the CCARs. Except for Azerbaijan, whose inhabitants are predominantly

Shia, all the CCARs have Sunni populations, even if they are to some degree Persian speaking. Thus, it should be mentioned from the outset that profound differences between Iranian culture and Shiism on one hand and Central Asian culture with its Sunni tradition on the other hand do not offer many convincing opportunities for realizing the vision of Iranization or of Shia Islamization in Central Asia.[32]

In addition, one should bear in mind that Muslim Central Asia had been cut off from the debates within the Islamic world for seventy years. Soviet communism, and before that years of Russian imperialism, created a largely secularized Muslim population.[33] Certainly, a vast number of ordinary Muslims in the CCARs have a very outdated, selective, poor and even naive understanding of the principles of Islam. Even after independence, folkloristic Islam, mysticism and isolated sectarianism were more widespread than any sense of pan-Islamic solidarity.[34] In such a situation it became extremely difficult for Iranian preachers to successfully propagate a single, coherent version of Islam in all of the Central Asian republics.

These and other difficulties provided sufficient argument for Rafsanjani and his government not to depend unilaterally on Islam when shaping foreign policy towards the CCARs. The Iranian President was convinced that the Islamic Republic first needed to create the conditions for its economic recovery and thus required stable and predictable relations with all of its neighbours. He was aware of continuing Russian interests in Central Asia. Weighing the pros and cons of fruitful relations with Russia or the elusive prospect of successfully islamizing Central Asia the Iranian way, he chose the first option. According to Rafsanjani, Russia, despite its weakness, was the only accountable global political power able to help Iran overcome international isolation and resist the containment policies of the United States and its Western allies. He therefore sought to convince the Russian leadership that his government rejected adventurist, destabilizing policies in Central Asia, not giving Russia any cause for believing Iran would promote Islamic radicalism and thus, he hoped, providing a favourable position for continuing and even increasing cooperation with Moscow.

The connections made with the Soviet Union during the First Gulf War were now continued with the Russian Federation. In 1991, in a series of articles the semi-official daily paper *Tehran Times* supported the idea of creating a regional security arrangement 'without ethnic considerations'.[35] Contrary to many Western expectations, official Iranian policy towards Central Asia continued to show a considerable level of restraint, which was clearly demonstrated in a number of cases.

Iran's neutrality during Soviet suppression of rebel Shia in Azerbaijan in January 1990 has already been mentioned, but this approach was not only displayed in matters concerning the Soviet Union. When war broke out between Armenia and Azerbaijan over the possession of Nagorno-Karabakh, Iran – along with Russia – supported Christian Armenia and not the Shia Azeris. Both Iran and Russia were motivated by a desire to contain the increasing influence of Turkey in Central Asia, which was assisting Azerbaijan. This cooperation is significant proof that during Rafsanjani's rule the national interests of Iran prevailed over pan-Islamism. Only when Armenia became victorious in late 1994, seizing considerable areas of Azeri territory, did Iran become alarmed.

Tehran was afraid that destabilization might follow after this type of nationalist military success and started to pressurize Armenia to withdraw its forces from Azeri territory. But there was a second reason for putting pressure on Armenia. Iran's government feared that millions of frustrated Azeris in Iran, impelled by disastrous defeats at the hands of the Iranian-backed Armenians, might demand unification with former Soviet Azerbaijan. Refugees were sent home immediately, but Tehran also provided financial aid for the upkeep and maintenance of refugee camps within former Soviet Azerbaijan. Nevertheless, these measures were not sufficient to allow any relaxation or complacency.

Azerbaijan's second President, Abolfazl Elchibey, who was profoundly pro-Turkish and pro-Western, constantly attacked Iran for its pro-Russian politics and called the Islamic Republic 'an empire ripe for dissolution.'[36] On occasion he was even quoted as having said that his country had the duty to 'liberate the Azeri population in Iran'.[37] Even when he was replaced in 1993 by Gaidar Aliev, a former Soviet politician, an anti-Iranian and pro-Turkish mood prevailed in Azerbaijan. Many Azeri Shia complained that a notorious triangle formed of Iran, Russia and pro-Russian elements of the former Soviet Azeri nomenclature was suppressing their real independence and that this conspiracy proved the hypocrisy of the Iranian regime.[38]

But there are more illustrations of the Iranian desire not to antagonize Russia. Tehran kept a remarkably low profile during the war between former communists and a coalition of Islamists and nationalists in Tajikistan. Initially Iran had supported the Islamic forces, but active Russian support for the communists quickly prompted Tehran to change that policy. As a face-saving measure Tehran pushed hard for a compromise settlement between the warring factions. The gathering of all concerned elements in Tehran in 1994 (the Tajik government, the opposition, the United Nations and Russia) was sold by the Iranian government as one of the major successes of its skilful foreign policy.[39]

A similar attitude was adopted to the Chechen conflict. Russia's violent suppression of Chechen attempts to gain independence led Iran merely to issue statements regretting both the bloodshed in Chechnya and Moscow's inability to solve the conflict peacefully. In this case also, Iran tried to avoid any possible provocation of Russia, still seen by them as a superpower. It may have been facing serious trouble but it was much more important for Iranian strategic objectives than the sectarian Islamic groupings of Central Asia.

A factor which may have contributed to this approach is that the Chechen Muslims are predominantly Sufi and thus somewhat disapproved of by official Iranian Shia doctrine. 'Iran's position on the Chechen crisis showed an obvious desire to maintain good relations with Russia despite its onslaught against Iran's Chechen Muslim brethren. Iran's national interest in stability and security on its northern borders and its need to maintain access to Russian arms and trade, as well as the prospects of new Trans-Caucasian oil pipelines, have all weighed against a destabilizing Iranian role in the former Soviet Islamic republics or even a clear condemnation of Russian "anti-Muslim" actions.'[40]

As usual, Rafsanjani was constantly under attack from Iranian radicals for his policy of appeasement in Central Asia. Their media criticized the pro-Russian 'puppet regimes' in Central Asia and asked the Iranian government to stop supporting the 'communist nomenclature governments' in that region because it might initiate a 'second Afghanistan'.[41] But unlike his efforts in the other surrounding regions, Rafsanjani's strategy in Central Asia was rather successful and as a result he could withstand the pressure from his domestic adversaries.

There is no doubt that his position was strengthened in this particular case by the political vacuum in Central Asia which followed the dissolution of the USSR. Whereas the balance of power in the Gulf region seemed to be fixed, including the influential position of the United States and its Western allies, the question of who would gain dominance in Central Asia was still open. Even the most notorious grumblers among the Iranian radicals seemed to accept that it would be more prudent, and in the interests of the Islamic revolution, to support Iran as a potential player in the new Great Game rather than risk minimizing its prospects in Central Asia by weakening the government's authority – all the more so when they suspected that the Great Satan, America, would try to deny Iran its rightful role in Central Asia as well.

Anti-Iranian countermeasures

In fact, the Iranian leadership had good reason to be suspicious of US intentions for the region. Washington was concerned to prevent the Iranians achieving major foreign policy successes in Central Asia thus increasing the vitality and attractiveness of the Islamic revolution. Nevertheless, the Americans preferred indirect tactics. They particularly encouraged Turkey and Saudi Arabia, and to a lesser degree Egypt and Israel, to sabotage Iranian activity in the region and to create alternative partnership opportunities for the CCARs. All these countries responded positively to Washington's encouragement.

Pan-Turkism, accompanied by secularism and a pro-Western attitude, given financial support by Saudi Arabia and military and technological support by the United States, was to outmanoeuvre Iranian sponsored pan-Islamism in Central Asia. Channels for interaction and cooperation, similar to those opened between Iran and the CCARs, were also initiated by Iran's other rivals. This strategy sharpened the competitive features of Iran's relations with other regional players.[42]

Sometimes, however, the heterogeneity of interests in the anti-Iranian camp backfired. The Al Saud, for example, were not keen to spread secularism among the peoples of Central Asia and were not prepared to accept Israel as a major player in the game, whereas Washington was sure that extensive Israeli penetration of Central Asia's economies would help to establish a Western, rather than an Islamic, orientation within the political systems of the CCARs. From time to time, Saudi Arabia even actively countered the expansion of Israel's influence in the region. When a delegation from Uzbekistan visited Riyadh in April 1992, the guests were urged to sign a joint communique that called for a 'just solution to the Palestinian issue, including the implementation of the all-encompassing national rights of the people of Palestine'.[43]

But in general, the cooperation within the anti-Iranian camp worked well because all the participants had strong individual interests in gaining influence in Central Asia and denying the Islamic Republic a dominant role. This was especially true for Turkey. Ankara openly competed with Tehran for the best opportunities in order to benefit from strategic promises and economic development in the future. As Piacentini stated, the power vacuum in Central Asia created perfect conditions for competition between the medium-sized powers of the region, such as Iran and Turkey: 'these, probably, only with the aim of avoiding developments which would run contrary to their own national interests, interests which run counter to each other should the area be polarized in support of a particular regime or of various groups fighting for power. In this case it is possible that Turkey would move in support of a "Turkophone" republic and Iran in a "Persophone" direction.'[44]

Indeed, similar to Iran's efforts to increase ties with the Persian speaking peoples of the region and to foster common cultural traditions, Turkey has revived its pan-Turanian aspirations of the early twentieth century, which were based on having an origin, language and culture in common with several Central Asian peoples. The government in Ankara was certain that Turkey's image as the Islamic world's most secular state, with its relative modernism and special relations with the West, would be more appealing to Central Asia than the radical Islamism of 'war-ravished and relatively backward Iran'.[45] The Turkish government's optimism was well founded. The CCARs governed by former members of the Soviet nomenclature, highly suspicious of revolutionary Islam, were more likely to turn to Turkey and to the West for alternative cultural, social, economic and political models.[46] So Turkey tried to attract the majority by creating the Black Sea Economic Organization of the CCARs.

Thus the Iranian government had every reason to take the Turkish challenge seriously. On the economic front it tried to counter Turkish efforts by sponsoring the Caspian Sea Organization comprising Iran, Russia, Turkmenistan, Azerbaijan and Kazakhstan. But that was not enough to dispel its anxieties. Tehran suspected Turkey of territorial ambitions in northern Iraq and feared its role as a front line of defence for the Western alliance, exemplified by its membership of the North Atlantic Treaty Organization.[47] But there were additional reasons to fear Ankara's pan-Turkism. As previously mentioned, several ethnic Turk groups, related to the Turkophone groups within Central Asia by kindred language and historical bonds, live inside Iranian borders. Including the great confederations of the Qashqa'i, the Hamza and the Esfandyari, they are concentrated largely in Iranian Azerbaijan, along the Zagros range and along the eastern borders in Sistan and Baluchistan.[48] What if these various peoples became tools in the hands of Ankara?

But faced with this threat Tehran did not despair and sought to utilize ethnic disputes to minimize the Turkish advantage. According to Iran's thinking, the Kurds might provide the much-needed solution. Kurdish guerrillas in Turkey had long before begun to use Iran as a base from which to launch attacks against Turkish government troops; thus Iran had something to offer. After several meetings with high-ranking Turkish officials between 1991 and 1994, Tehran promised to shut down the bases if Turkey adopted a less aggressive policy towards the Islamic Republic. That the Turkish officials agreed may be due to other aspects of the Kurdish problem. There was much anxiety in both Iran and Turkey over the establishment of the Kurdish enclave in Iraq. This could become the base for an independent Kurdish entity 'that could act as a magnet for restive Kurdish minorities in both Turkey and Iran.'[49]

At present, Turkish–Iranian competition for influence in Central Asia has eased. Both continue to pursue their own interests in the region, but they have abandoned a course of open confrontation. Turkey realized that it was very costly to meddle in an area separated from its own territory by the Caucasus mountains, an increasingly turbulent region where its relations, not only with the Kurds but above all with the Armenians, are marked by tension.[50] It became more valuable to cultivate Iran as a major trading partner and a cooperative co-member of the ECO. Relations between both countries improved even further when Erbakan's Islamist Refah (Welfare) party won the Turkish elections and formed a government. Although Erbakan's government collapsed within a few months, the Islamic political movement in Turkey remained strong. The Iranian government saw no reason to antagonize it by enforcing an anti-Turkish policy.

Thus for Iran, on the issue of rivalry in Central Asia, Saudi Arabia mattered more than Turkey. The emergence of independent Central Asian Muslim states definitely widened the geographic area of strategic competition between the two giants of the Persian Gulf. Saudi Arabia felt itself strong enough to challenge its main Gulf adversary even in such a remote area as Central Asia and both states were eagerly looking for opportunities to enhance their political influence there. Although Saudi Arabia played an important *partita* in the American Concert for Central Asia, the Al Saud had their own, Muslim, interests in the region and thus challenged the Islamic Republic of Iran at its very root. The Islamic variable therefore became one of the most important means of exercising influence for both of them. The Al Saud saw their activities as a measure designed to counter Iranian claims to be recognized as the focus of inspiration for the world's Muslims.

Riyadh therefore gave strong support to the Sunni re-Islamization of Central Asia by encouraging the spread of an integralist current which, although known locally as Wahhabism, is not strictly affiliated to the original movement based in the Arabian Peninsula. The Mufti of Central Asia and Kazakhstan, Mamaiusupov, had maintained a purely personal religious content for Central Asian Wahhabism. Thus it became difficult for Saudi Wahhabism to be imposed on the Central Asian Muslims as a religious doctrine. Turning again to Valeria Piacentini's analysis:

> The greatest obstacle to the diffusion of Saudi Arabian Wahhabism is, in effect, Central Asian Islam itself, which is incompatible with the rigorous Wahhabite doctrine. One example of this incompatibility can be found in the Central Asian reformist tradition which finds its main expression in Jadidism, that particular cult of saints which is so widespread and so deeply rooted in the local culture. One has only to think of Ahmad Yasavi, Yusuf Hamadani, Najm od-Din Kubrah and Baha od-Din Naqshband himself, the founder of the Naqshbandiyyah (whose teachings spread from Central Asia to large parts of the Islamic world and whose name is still venerated in many "external" regions of the area) to realise this. And then there is popular Islam . . ., rich in legends and superstitions of a far from Islamic nature but so closely interwoven in the popular consciousness as to constitute today perhaps its most lively element.[51]

Saudi Wahhabism is thus not very attractive to Central Asian traditions of Islam. In addition to that, Central Asian Muslims are aware that Wahhabism, although it has its roots in the Hanbali school, has distanced itself from the other three mainstream Sunni schools (Hanafi, Maliki, Shafii), and is thus opposed by other major Islamic centres in the Arab world, including Cairo and Damascus. Saudi Wahhabism is justified and established in the area only because of the money it can and has spent in order to acquire influence for the Saudi state.[52] Riyadh is wise enough not to insist on strict acceptance of its national confession when promoting the general spread of Sunni Islam. The Saudi message became a socio-cultural instrument in the service of groups opposed to the current regimes of the CCARs, representing a force for both domestic and international instability.[53] There is a remarkable irony in the fact that the Islamic Republic of Iran, the self-proclaimed home of the world's Islamic revolutionaries, has, more or less, supported the post-communist regimes in Central Asia, whilst Saudi Arabia, a stronghold of conservatism in the Middle East, has been assisting the radical Islamic opposition of the region.

But Saudi Arabia cannot depend on that image. Until now, many Muslim activists in Central Asia fear that Saudi support is only due to its political and geo-strategic ambitions. They know that Saudi Islam is conservative by nature and thus attracted to stability and the status quo, while Iranian Islam has proved to be highly politicized, proactive and anti-status quo. Therefore it may be wise to tolerate a temporary Iranian appeasement of Russia and its local satraps because it is likely to underpin Iran's general aim to create a new balance of power in an area stretching from the Persian Gulf to Central Asia.[54] These considerations have produced a stalemate between Saudi Arabia and Iran in their attempts to influence Central Asian Muslims. This stalemate could have led some specialists, including K.L. Afrasiabi, to believe that the Saudis' missionary drive in Central Asia and the Caucasus does not necessarily represent a permanent challenge to Iran's strategy for the region. In fact these efforts could well complement Iran's own attempt to increase the Islamic consciousness of the peoples of the region in order to counteract their ethnic and, more particularly, Turkish consciousness. Saudi Arabia and Iran are thus indirectly cooperating in fighting the growth of pan-Turkism.[55]

But it would seem that such a point of view underestimates the depth of the rivalry between Iran and Saudi Arabia. However in other respects Afrasiabi is right: 'a more likely scenario [is] that Iran could make a significant inroad in the internal politics of the Muslim republics, in which case the Saudis . . . would participate in a coalition of political and religious forces in the region to reverse Iran's fortunes. This means that Iranians had to worry about the consequences of too much success via their Islamicist strategy, whereas a more moderate success lowered the risks of paranoid backlashes and gave the Iranian diplomacy in its second orbit a margin of safety.'[56]

Be that as it may, at present it is almost impossible to ascertain whether the Saudi initiatives in so distant an area as Central Asia really are aimed at religious revival and an overwhelming victory of the Wahhabi branch of Sunni Islam over Iranian Twelver Shiism or whether they are politically motivated. Both possibilities are credible. Saudi Arabia's efforts to reinforce an orthodox Sunni Islamization of Central Asia has cut into Iran's influence at precisely the point where Tehran is most at its ease in international politics, that is, the propagation and reinforcement of Islam.

Because of the established Sunni majority in Central Asia, the Saudis have been given a well-prepared ground on which Shia Iran can be nothing but inferior. But there are also indications that, by forcing Iran into competition in Central Asia, which is much more important for it than for Saudi Arabia, the Al Saud are deliberately distracting Iran from the Gulf: 'In other words, Saudi actions would seem to be aimed at limiting the Iranian presence in the Gulf by means of greater involvement in Central Asia.'[57] But Saudi Arabia has other trumps apart from Islam with which to challenge the Iranian role in Central Asia.

First of all its tremendous wealth should not be forgotten. The Saudi monarchy has been quite active in furnishing the cost of hajj for pilgrims from various Central Asian countries, in supplying millions of copies of the Qur'an and other religious texts in the local languages and scripts, and in funding thousands of new religious schools and mosques. Moreover, it finances schools teaching missionary tactics and the training of Imams and, above all, movements that carry forward programmes aimed at re-founding the state on a strictly Islamic basis.[58] When it comes to funding Tehran has no choice but to take second place. The slowness of the Iranian economic recovery, due among other factors to low world oil prices as well as the high cost of extraction and transport (US\$ 9 per barrel compared to US\$ 3 for Saudi Arabia), has left Iran at the mercy of a Saudi-dominated OPEC,[59] thus decisively limiting Iran's financial competitiveness.

Furthermore, as

> a country whose economy has experienced devastations stemming from the revolutionary turmoil since 1978, and from the war against

Iraq between 1980 and 1988, Iran's economic capabilities are quite limited . . . While its oil income is down, its expenditures are skyrocketed. It is spending enormous amounts of money rebuilding its economy. In addition, Iran has also adopted an ambitious program of military build-up. Given these major outlets for huge capital expenditures, Tehran can offer few monetary enticements for the Central Asian states, whose economies are badly in need of capital investments. What Iran can do – and it has been active along these lines – is to supply in-kind assistance, such as establishing air and railway linkages, signing joint exploration and production ventures, etc. It cannot, however, offer these countries generous cash subsidies to start a number of economic projects.[60]

In this instance Riyadh has a remarkable advantage.

Up to now Saudi Arabian financial assistance for Central Asia has been four times greater than the aid furnished by Iran.[61] When Saud al-Faisal visited Uzbekistan, Tajikistan, Turkmenistan and Azerbaijan in February 1992 he offered US$ 3 billion in financial aid.[62] This gesture was clearly aimed not only at underscoring the high degree of Saudi interest in Central Asia, but also at expressing annoyance over the formation of the ECO from which it felt it had been deliberately excluded. But apart from grumbling, Riyadh has also been channelling large sums of money through joint ventures in a large number of Central Asian countries. The Al-Baraka–Kazakhstan Bank is one such example.[63]

Pan-Islamic organizations under Saudi control, such as the OIC, should also be mentioned. Riyadh invited the Central Asian states to attend the OIC, which led to full membership of the organization for Azerbaijan, Kyrgyzstan, Tajikistan, and Turkmenistan. Kazakhstan, however, preferred observer status. Members are entitled to obtain funds from the Islamic Development Bank[64] which has itself initiated a number of projects in Central Asia, including advice on the transition to a market economy.[65]

Finally, as the birthplace of Islam, Saudi Arabia also gained a special position among Central Asian Muslims. Central Asians respect the status of the Al Saud as the guardians of Islam's Holy places, which gives them much authority in religious matters.

But all these advantages cannot extinguish the simple fact that Iran is situated next to Central Asia while Saudi Arabia is far away. In all basic matters of economic and political survival the CCARs will always look first to Iran.

In the past, Saudi Arabia tried to change this balance in its favour by instrumentalizing the GCC. Indeed, some GCC members also became very active in Central Asia. Representatives of the Kuwait-based Organising Committee for Muslims in Asia toured the capitals of the CCARs, offering financial support for developmental and educational projects. The Kuwaiti government gave aid to Uzbekistan in form of food processing technologies and oil supplies which were paid for with fruit, vegetables and cotton. Furthermore, it signed an oil deal with Kazakhstan, including the building of oil extraction and refining facilities. Oman also became involved, negotiating cooperation, notably with Azerbaijan, in the oil industry. Masqat invested US$ 200 million in Azerbaijan's oil fields and offered university exchanges. It also started negotiations with Uzbekistan on the development of Uzbek resources and the provision of investment and technological requirements. The same procedure was followed with Kazakhstan, resulting in Omani aid for agriculture and industry, and the provision of credit and development of the oil-refining industry. Even Qatar opened talks with different CCARs, particularly with Turkmenistan.[66]

Nevertheless, the outcome of the Iranian–Saudi Arabian competition in Central Asia can be better evaluated by looking at each individual Caucasian or Central Asian republic.

Armenia and Azerbaijan

Saudi Arabia has less influence in Armenia than in the other CCARs, whereas Iran has gained by supporting Erevan in its war against Azerbaijan. Given the involvement of Russia as well as the Turkish charm offensive in Azerbaijan, Rafsanjani considered it vital for Iran to develop and maintain good relations with Armenia.[67] The centrepiece of a more lasting partnership between Iran and Armenia was an agreement envisaging the almost total supply of Armenian gas requirements by Iran, perforating Azerbaijan's economic blockade of Armenia in the early 1990s. A number of informal agreements allowed Iran to recruit top Armenian scientists, including highly qualified military experts.[68]

Despite the many difficulties – some of which have already been mentioned – that Iran faced in its relations with Azerbaijan, this Caspian littoral state has always been of importance to the Islamic Republic due to their common border, their transborder population and a Shia majority of some eighty per cent in Azerbaijan. Given the confessional Shia, but ethnic Turk, nature of the population, Iran had to compete with Turkey for influence rather than with Saudi Arabia. The various governments of independent Azerbaijan always tried to balance between the poles of Tehran and Ankara.

It was no accident that the first President of independent Azerbaijan, Mutalibov, paid his very first official state visit to Iran. Even before the establishment of formal diplomatic relations he signed bilateral economic cooperation agreements on matters including the establishment of air and rail links with Tehran in August 1991. It is also telling in this context that the Azerbaijani delegation which attended the sixth summit of the OIC in Senegal that December was attached to the Iranian delegation.[69] In early 1992, an agreement was reached which provided for Iran refining Azeri oil, as well as an agreement to expand the telecommunication link. The government in Tehran encouraged Iranian businessmen to seek opportunities for joint ventures in Azerbaijan. Altogether, economic and trade cooperation between Iran and Azerbaijan mainly occurred in such fields as oil technology, textile industries, automotive industries, the manufacturing of household appliances and garments.[70] Iran became the main trading partner of Azerbaijan after the CIS.[71] The first government of independent Azerbaijan sincerely tried to establish a 'special relationship' with Tehran.

In 1992, the largest of all the 57 delegations which came from all over the world to participate in the celebrations marking the thirteenth anniversary of the Iranian revolution was the one from Baku. One of the delegates deliberately tried to disperse Iranian fears of a probable pan-Azeri drive in Baku when he stated: 'Separation of East and West Azerbaijan from Iran and the creation of a united Azerbaijani state is impossible considering the complete freedom of Azerbaijanis in Iran and the outstanding role which they play in the state and private sector.'[72]

But as already stated, the honeymoon between Iran and Azerbaijan inevitably came to an end. During the presidency of Elchibey relations soured remarkably. Moreover, Iran proved unable to fulfil the astronomical expectations of the Azerbaijani government regarding Iranian economic aid. The United States tried to take advantage of the mutual disillusionment that had arisen. During the embryonic phase of bilateral relations between Iran and Azerbaijan both governments had started making plans not only to exploit the huge oil and gas resources of Azerbaijan and the

Caspian Sea together but also to transport them to Europe. The inaugural phase of the plan even included the Tengis oil field in Kazakhstan in a design for a gigantic transport network of pipelines which would pass through Iranian territory. The Clinton administration vehemently urged Western oil companies to offer alternatives to Azerbaijan, with the object of preventing Iran's inclusion in a promising restructuring of Middle Eastern and Central Asian oil production and transport.

Baku gave in to American pressure, turning to Russia, Georgia and Turkey for transport routes, even if it made no economic sense whatsoever. Elchibey's successor, Aliev, did not harbour the anti-Iranian feelings his predecessor had done, but pragmatically weighed up the pros and cons of angering either the United States or Iran. The results of this deliberation constituted an unpleasant reminder for Iran of the power of the United States, even in an area that Iran had come to consider its own. Nevertheless, Aliev tried to sweeten the decision by offering Iran cooperation in other fields and suggesting swap deals. 'Swap arrangements have much potential, as Iran has access to large ports in the Persian Gulf. This is another advantage Iran possesses over Russia as a transport route.'[73]

The ups and downs of post-Soviet Iranian–Azerbaijanian relations were also decisively influenced by cultural and especially religious matters. Aware of the Shia majority in Azerbaijan, the Islamic Republic had already tried to gain a foothold there during the early days of Gorbachev's glasnost policies. Iranian envoys particularly fostered the Islamic Party of Azerbaijan, which was established as an underground movement in 1975, aiming to boost its political fortunes. In the late 1980s, Iran gave the party help in the publication of its daily newspaper and in strengthening its organizational structure. These measures were designed to improve the party's electoral prospects.[74] And indeed, during the decisive months preceding Azerbaijan's independence, millions of Azeris could be seen marching through the streets of Baku and other major cities carrying pictures of Ayatollah Khomeini and shouting Islamic and pro-Iranian slogans.[75] But, as we know now, this naive and unquestioning pro-Iranian attitude could not be carried into the 1990s.

The Iranian leadership might have felt more comfortable with the pragmatic President Aliev, rather than the pro-Turkish Elchibey, especially in economic terms, but he – as a former communist – had no desire to move his country in the direction of Islamization. Always suspicious of

Iran's revolutionary Islamic character, he preferred a secular state. When Aliev tried to stipulate the separation of state and religion in Azerbaijan's Constitution, he provoked an outcry, particularly among Iranian radicals. For example, Ayatollah Jannati, the Speaker of the Council of Guardians and Friday's Imam of Tehran, condemned this move in harsh words. It was a

> sickening incident in Azerbaijan, which was totally unthinkable and unexpected, especially considering that Azerbaijan is a country which has recently been emancipated from a power which was against God, religion and Islam, and a country which for 70 years experienced the bitter taste of secular and anti-religion measures. It was God's will that the dominating power was destroyed and these people gained freedom and were able to live freely. But now suddenly a constitution is proposed there which talks about the separation of religion from politics, and the establishment of a secular state. It also speaks of banning the teaching of religious sciences at schools. One is really amazed about the way some people allow themselves to move against the will of the Muslim people of the region and against Islam in such a way. Everyone knows that the honourable people of Azerbaijan are Muslims and Shi'is. How can a nation such as them suddenly be deprived of its Islam? How, for instance, can one remove the instruction that the president must swear on the Koran? How can one say that political affairs should not be confined to religious boundaries and the statesmen are free to do what they want, whether these comply with religion or not? In sum, the proposal is very much against the spirit of Islam . . . However, we see that in a country with such a history of suffering under the communists, the same communist elements come forward and write a constitution which repeats the same things as the old days. We want to take the opportunity here to express our condemnation of the move.[76]

Given the long, deep-rooted Islamic and specifically Shia traditions in Azerbaijan, no one should exclude the possibility that the rule of people such as Aliev might be merely transitional, and that a future government in Baku might be more sympathetic towards the Islamic Republic of Iran. But it is not likely that Azerbaijan will ever become the exclusive property of Tehran.

Kazakhstan and Kyrgyzstan

Although Kazakhstan is the second largest Muslim republic in Central Asia, religion is not a major factor in its politics. Given the unique ethnic composition of Kazakhstan, Islam will inevitably be of less importance than in other CCARs, for the foreseeable future at least. This is partially due to the presence of a non-Muslim (atheist, Russian-Orthodox and others) population which almost equals its Muslim population. The ethnic composition has changed slightly in recent years because many Russians and other non-Muslims have left the country and the birth rate of the Kazakh population has increased, but the rate of change is not fast enough to alter the present ethnic and confessional balance fundamentally. Muslims in Kazakhstan as in other CCARs became more active and self-confident around 1990, when they gained independence from the decaying Soviet Union, but no single Muslim personality or organization was able to attract all the believers and unite them around one consistent programme.

In April 1990, to give one example, an Islamic party called Alash demanding independence for Kazakhstan was established. Under the leadership of Aron Atabek and Rashid Yutoshev the party campaigned for the creation of an Islamic state in Kazakhstan, but it was too weak to enforce its demands. In Almaty, the capital of Kazakhstan, there was a total of only 85 Alash members. This was not the only reason for Iran's lack of interest in the party. Its leaders were consistently pan-Turk, calling for the consolidation of the Turkic peoples of the former USSR in a 'peace-loving republic of Great Turkistan'.[77] Instead smaller, pro-Iranian groups were fostered by Tehran. One of them was attached to the Iranian delegation attending the OIC summit in Senegal in 1991,[78] but none of them were strong enough to bring real Iranian influence to bear in Almaty. On the contrary, Kazakhstan emerged as the most loyal supporter of the CIS among the CCARs, promising, and to a large extent providing, equal treatment for its Russian population.[79]

Nevertheless, the particular limits on Islamic influence in Kazakhstan did not prevent fruitful economic cooperation between Iran and this Central Asian republic. To avoid complete dependence on Russia when exporting its oil, the Kazakh government signed several agreements with Tehran confirming the supply of a certain amount of Kazakh oil to Iran via the Caspian Sea and Iran would then export the same amount of oil via the Persian Gulf (swap deals).[80] As mentioned before, Kazakhstan also became a member of the ECO at the historic meeting of the organization held in Tehran in February 1992, though it initially only sought observer status. Apart from the creation of air and sea links between the two countries, Kazakhstan's proximity to China was of real importance to Iran. According to Tehran, Kazakhstan could act as a conduit between Iran and China in the ostentatiously labelled Silk Route Project.[81]

There is an additional fact that makes Kazakhstan very interesting to the Iranian government – its possession of a nuclear arsenal. According to MOSSAD sources, Kazakhstan has already supplied 2 nuclear warheads of 40 kilotons each to Iran, as well as a nuclear bomb of between 50 and 500 kilotons designed for the MiG 27 aircraft.[82] Both Tehran and Almaty have flatly denied this, but according to some experts the mere possibility that such trade could take place gives Iran the vital stimulus to develop stronger ties with Kazakhstan. Although Almaty has promised to turn Kazakhstan into a non-nuclear state within a decade, this declaration has, up to now, only led to well-intentioned support for the country by the West without any guarantees in return that its present or future leaders will not depart from the de-nuclearization plan.[83]

Compared to Kazakhstan, Kyrgyzstan is less important or attractive to Iran and hence matters less for Iranian–Saudi Arabian competition. As in Kazakhstan, there is a sizeable Slavic population, making the success of radical Islamic forces less likely.[84] By and large Kyrgyzstan is more interested in improving relations with Turkey as a viable regional ally and – beyond this – partner of the West. Kyrgyzstan does not share a border with either Iran or Saudi Arabia, and its lack of access to the Caspian Sea does not encourage Iran to act as a conduit for Kyrgyz relations with the Middle East. Although the Iranian Foreign Minister, Ali Velayati, received a warm welcome when visiting Bishkek in December 1991, and the Kyrgyz President responded by heading a large economic and political delegation to Tehran in June 1993, Tehran did not show much vigour in cultivating relations with Kyrgyzstan. 'Kyrgyzstan's overtly pro-Russian stance in regional matters, and its apparent warmth toward Israel, have helped to keep relations cool between [Tehran] and Bishkek.'[85]

Tajikistan

Matters are quite different in Tajikistan. Here the ratio of non-Muslim to Muslim in the population is substantially smaller than in Kazakhstan.

Given the large number of Muslims, the extent of government repression and the relative weakness of democratic forces, the environment is much more conducive to the growth of radical Islam than that in some of the afore-mentioned republics. Tajikistan contains the ingredients for political turmoil with a religious dimension.[86] The daily presence of Islam in the life of the Tajiks makes them attractive to the Islamic Republic of Iran. But in addition there is the ethnic and linguistic commonality between Iran and Tajikistan creating a useful basis for cooperation, 'as the Tajiks are culturally Iranian rather than Turk and speak an eastern dialect of Farsi [Persian]'.[87] When Velayati paid a first official visit to Tajikistan in November 1991, he tried to make the best use of this common ground.

Right from the beginning Iran wanted to make it clear that Tajikistan belonged to its sphere of influence and not to that of Turkey, Saudi Arabia, Uzbekistan or indeed any other country, and sought to protect that influence with a net of economic and cultural ties. In addition to the creation of air and rail links and plans for joint investment, Iran was eagerly looking for arms deals below the nuclear level.[88] To make the Tajik government interested in this special treatment, Tehran extended credit of US$ 50 million to its neighbour in July 1992.[89]

But even when Velayati insisted that the Islamic Republic had no interest in supporting Islamic groups or in becoming involved in Tajikistan's domestic affairs, it very soon became obvious that the Iranian leadership would not hesitate to take advantage of the common bonds between Iran and Tajikistan. As of 1990, Tehran was supporting a variety of Islamic groupings in Tajikistan, such as the Islamic Revival Party (IRP) which held its founding congress in Astrakhan on 10 June 1990. It was originally designed to function as a supranational party and for this reason about 150 delegates from several CCARs took part in the congress, among them 24 from Tajikistan. The party's declared goals were based around a 'revival of the ideals of Islam', but it was quite obvious that its objectives were political. The party called for the establishment of Sharia courts and the teaching of Islam in secular schools. Due to the favourable conditions in these states, the IRP developed its most advanced organizational reach and mobilization capacities in Tajikistan and – to a lesser degree – in Uzbekistan.[90]

Besides supporting Islamic groups, the Iranian leadership undertook other official initiatives. It built mosques as well as Islamic schools and opened branches of various Iranian universities in Dushanbeh. By July 1992 Iran had furnished Tajikistan with equipment to enable it to receive radio and television transmissions from Tehran and to further extend Tehran's field of transmission as far as Bukhara and Samarkand in Uzbekistan, as well as to parts of Afghanistan and the Indian sub-continent.[91] By broadcasting Persian programmes on Tajik radio and television under the pretext of familiarizing the Tajiks with their mother tongue, by promoting Tajikistan's Persian heritage and asserting its common identity with Iran, the Iranian leadership was undeniably trying to plant the ideals and visions of the Islamic revolution in Tajik society. The Iranian presence in Dushanbeh became decisive. For instance, in October 1992, although the entire diplomatic corps of 6 countries numbered around 20 diplomats in Tajikistan's capital, the Iranian mission alone comprised 21 official diplomats and some 50 staff members.[92]

The Iranian representatives did their utmost to outmatch the growing funding and support for Tajikistan from Saudi Arabia, Pakistan and the Afghan mujaheddin. Saud al-Faisal's visit to Dushanbeh in February 1992 signalled a high degree of Saudi interest in the country and a strong desire on the part of the Al Saud not to be left out. Endowed with greater funds, Saudi Arabia has taken on a fundamentalist missionary role in Tajikistan with the utmost zeal, sometimes even surpassing the vigour of the Iranians – Tajiks are, after all, Sunnis, and therefore, despite all differences, are more inclined to Wahhabism than to Shiism. Pro-Saudi Tajik religious leaders started underscoring the significant differences between Iran's Shiism and their own Sunni Islam. But the powerful spiritual leader, Qazi Akbar Toradzhou Zoda, head of his own militia of some 8,000 men, did not prevent the Iranians from funding the building of a new madrasa for Dushanbeh's central mosque, declaring that he wanted help only from Allah, 'but if some of our neighbours are really Muslim and they help us for Allah's sake, then that is fine'.[93]

On the other hand, the Qazi opposed Iranian missionary activity several times as well as the economic aid linked to it.[94] Besides suffering from the weak Tajik response to Shiism, the Iranians also made their own mistakes. They often annoyed even sympathetic Tajik Muslims by behaving arrogantly. They conceded that the Tajiks possessed a Persian culture but then criticized it for being imperfect. Only they, the Iranians, could guide the Tajiks on their way to perfection. They made other mistakes as well. Most of the school textbooks, Islamic literature and propaganda brochures were printed in Arabic script and therefore useless to readers educated in Cyrillic and/or Latin script.[95]

But the most serious disadvantage Iran suffered in the quest for decisive political influence in Tajikistan was the scattered political landscape of the country. A variety of Islamic or pro-Russian political factions, each of them with a different tribal background, fought for power in Dushanbeh. Of course, the civil war gave outside powers such as Iran the opportunity to divide and rule the warring parties, and Iran did its best to support as many of them as it could, supplying money, food and military aid. But none of these parties had either the mandate or the military clout needed to assert itself throughout the country. However, it sometimes seemed as if the Iranians would be successful in the end, for instance when they encouraged the opposition to topple the pro-Russian President, Nabiev, in September 1992.

Nabiev had angered them by cultivating ties with the United States as part of a policy of neutrality. He knew that such a policy would expose him to domestic Islamic as well as Iranian criticism, but he recognized the urgent need to gain access to the West in order to secure the influx of significant amounts of capital and expertise.[96]

Nevertheless, for a long time the Iranians could not celebrate their victory. Unrest continued and after some weeks Ali Rakhmanov, a former Soviet functionary from the Kuljab region, was elected President. Meddling in Tajikistan's affairs was increasingly costly for Tehran, and the Iranian government began to express disquiet at the turmoil in the neighbouring country. Rafsanjani stated in a press conference: 'Regarding Tajikistan, we are truly sorry about the events that are taking place in that country. Instead of reconstructing their country, the popular forces have become divided and are destroying their country; events are taking place contrary to the interests of the people. We, however, will not intervene. Our policy is not intervention, but we do express our opinion.'[97] Iran did however intervene, and it made the best out of the situation by directing its energies towards mediation between the warring factions. As mentioned above, in 1994 they proclaimed their organization of a peace conference for Tajikistan in Tehran a great success.

In the long run Iran was not interested in offending the Russians for some minor gain in Tajikistan, nor was it in favour of continued political polarization in that country. Without doubt, its long-term economic policy towards Tajikistan depended on the establishment of political stability there. The threat posed by an ongoing civil war to Iran's growing economic interests could not be overlooked by the Iranian government.[98]

Turkmenistan and Uzbekistan

In general, Iran had more success in its attempts to improve its relations with Turkmenistan, a state which some very outspoken experts had labelled the weakest of the Central Asian democracies: '. . . the combination of a small intelligentsia and a politically apathetic public has severely retarded the growth of democratic principles and institutions, denying the republic a powerful instrument to combat the possible advances of radical Islam.'[99] What is surprising to some observers is that up to now Iran had not seriously utilized these probable advantages. However when, for instance, the Turkmen Minister of Culture, on a visit to Tehran, asked his Iranian counterpart for help to restore cultural sites in his country,[100] he received a positive reply. Like the other CCARs, Turkmenistan also received its share of Iranian cultural and religious support, including money, textbooks and teachers.

But Tehran also wanted to prevent Turkmenistan from becoming another Tajikistan, politically unstable and so a source of grave concern for the Iranian government. Iranian officials therefore carefully relied on geographic proximity and ancient political ties between the two countries to provide the bond. Underlining their immediate neighbourhood, the Iranian government tried to present Iran as Turkmenistan's most convenient route to the sea, comparing favourably with transport routes through the Caucasian powderkeg or to conflict-prone Pakistan via Afghanistan. Instead, Iran could supply an excellent link between Turkmenistan and the south-eastern Iranian port of Chah Bahar.[101] Turkmenistan is rich in oil, gas and minerals which are best exported via the sea, and until Iran made that possible, Turkmenistan was forced to export these products through neighbouring republics.

Iran had, therefore, cause to expect a positive reply to its offer of wide-ranging economic cooperation in 1991. In October of that year Velayati signed a deal in Ashkabad paying for a road and rail link from the Turkmen capital to the northern Iranian city of Mashhad. When completed, these links would facilitate a high volume of trade between the two countries and also between Iran and Uzbekistan via Turkmenistan. At the same time Velayati promised that Iran would purchase up to three billion cubic metres of gas and 150,000 tons of diesel fuel from Turkmenistan for sale abroad. In exchange Iran would provide 6.5 million tons of refined petroleum products for Ashkabad, set up a refinery to produce lubricants and help in further exploration for oil and gas.

Altogether four trade protocols between Iran and Turkmenistan, worth over US$ 130 million, were signed when the Turkmen President, Niyazov, heading a 60 strong delegation, visited Tehran later that month.[102] The agreements, for instance, included joint ventures to build dams over border rivers and the establishment of (Caspian) sea and air links.[103] In November, for the first time since the Iranian revolution, the border was opened. Although Turkmen citizens are not allowed to travel more than 40 miles inside Iran, a flourishing barter trade was initiated between northern Iran and Turkmenistan. In cooperation with the Ukraine, both countries are planning to establish a free trade zone in the border area.[104] By the end of 1991, Tehran had given Ashkabad US$ 50 million in credit to buy Iranian goods.[105]

The economic cooperation between Iran and Turkmenistan was able to maintain its drive in the following years. There were hints of arms deals, too,[106] but in the main economic cooperation between the two countries was confined to the civilian sphere. The two countries agreed to build a 1,500 mile pipeline to transport natural gas from Turkmenistan through Iran to Europe. The pipeline will require more than US$5 billion before it is completed. Iran will have to provide eighty per cent of the initial investment and in return will receive natural gas from Turkmenistan. 'The pipeline would connect Europe to one-fourth of the world's natural gas reserves. Iran is by far the most economically feasible route for transporting Central Asian gas.'[107]

The prospect of economic cooperation with Turkmenistan was too inviting to expect Saudi Arabia to keep away. Saud al-Faisal visited Ashkabad during his Central Asian tour in February 1992. Riyadh invested US$ 10 billion credit in Turkmenistan's oil industry.[108] Nevertheless, Ashkabad remained pro-Iranian. The government continued to increase its economic ties with Iran. The Turkmen President was clearly trying to please the Iranians when stating: 'I have always said, and I continue to believe, that no problem in the region can be solved without the presence of the Islamic Republic of Iran.'[109]

Unlike Turkmenistan, Uzbekistan is similar to Tajikistan in that its non-Muslim population is far smaller than its Muslim population.

Hence, given also the unstable economic and political situation in the country after the downfall of the USSR, radical Islam had a fair chance there. By the end of the 1980s a number of Muslim political parties such as the Islamic Revival Party (IRP) and the Islamic Democratic Party (IDP) had become active. The latter openly advocated the creation of a theocracy modelled on the Islamic Republic of Iran. One of the party's leaders, Dadkhan Hassan, praised the leader of the Iranian revolution, maintaining that 'Khomeini was very good for us.' The IDP called for the veiling of women and the imposition of Islamic law on Uzbek society. Skilfully following pragmatic tactics, Hassan nevertheless pointed out that 'we will not attempt to seize power by force . . . our strategy first is to unite all our Muslims . . . and then to educate the new generation in the spirit of Islam.'[110]

In the light of this development as well as of the strong historical bonds that exist between Iran and Uzbekistan, the forging of ties received primary attention from Tehran. Even before the official independence of Uzbekistan, Velayati visited the country, initiating the creation of an Iran–Uzbekistan Cultural Society. Since then, the Iranian government has devoted considerable time and attention to the sensitive issue of cultural–religious ties with Uzbekistan.[111] The matter was sensitive because of the politics of the Uzbek President, Karimov, a former communist, and his cabinet. The secular government in Tashkent felt threatened by the expectations of its former Russian mentors and by its own population's hopes for a better standard of living, as well as by Iranian designs to radicalize Uzbek Muslims. Moreover, the Uzbek President considered Iran to be at the root of the Tajik civil war and to have exacerbated political instability in the region in the name of the Islamic revolution.

On the other hand, Karimov could not deny the importance of Iran as the only direct route to the high seas nor the need to forge better transportation and communication ties with Iran.[112] Knowing the nature of the Islamic Republic, Karimov could be sure that he had a choice either to live with both economic *and* cultural–religious ties, or with nothing at all. But he tried to keep the religious relationship at a low profile. He signed both economic and cultural agreements whilst visiting Tehran, but the bilateral relations continued to be marred by suspicion. For example, the Iranian cultural week in Uzbekistan opened two days late because Uzbek security agents were carefully inspecting all the books presented by Iran. According to Iranian sources, displaying the Qur'an and religious books was not allowed.[113] There were numerous other occasions where Iran was vilified by Uzbek institutions.

Nevertheless, the Iranian government tried to stay calm and not overreact, since strategically Uzbekistan was important to Iran, not only, that is, the country itself, but its role in Central Asia as a whole, especially in Iran's neighbour Afghanistan where the Uzbek leader, General Dostam, held a powerful position.[114]

In addition to this, Iran did not want to give way to Saudi Arabian efforts to gain a foothold in Uzbekistan. Tehran knew about the high percentage of Muslims in Uzbek society, but it also had to consider that most of them are Sunni. Sunni concentration is extremely dense in the Ferghana valley where seven million people, one-third of the total population of Uzbekistan, live. The Ferghana valley has a long tradition of active Central Asian Wahhabism. But the valley is overpopulated and there is an acute land shortage. Unemployment has increased to almost 35 per cent of the total workforce. This economic crisis has given radical Wahhabis an effective political base for campaigning for the overthrow of the secular government. Their most active organization, the Ahle Sunna movement, is funded by Saudi Arabia. The equivalent of an estimated 500 million roubles, an astronomical sum in Central Asia, has been spent by Riyadh on building mosques and madrasas and on educating some 15,000 students. The leaders of the Ahle Sunna admitted that their aim was to overthrow what they termed the 'communist government of Karimov' and to spearhead an Islamic revolution throughout Central Asia. A massive propaganda campaign is under way to unite the population under the slogan: 'First Ferghana, then Uzbekistan and then the whole of Central Asia will become an Islamic state.'[115]

The government has no immediate answers. A source in the Interior Ministry admitted that the situation in the Ferghana valley could explode at any time, and if that happened, nobody could do anything to stop it. Uzbek officials furthermore claim that Ahle Sunna militants have formed a secret army, that religious students are undergoing weapons and martial arts training and that, even in cities outside the Ferghana valley, hit squads have been set up, designed to attack government officials and create disturbances at any, appropriate, moment.[116]

But Saudi Arabia is pursuing a double strategy in Uzbekistan in order to strengthen its grip on the country. Although it supports Sunni radicals, it offers a helping hand to the government in order to counter official Iranian influence. Two months after Saud al-Faisal's visit to Uzbekistan in February 1992, one of Saudi Arabia's biggest companies agreed to a deal with Uzbekistan under which it would export electricity cables in exchange for copper products and cotton. Riyadh also initiated educational exchanges with Uzbekistan on an official level.[117] It proposed to finance the construction of additional mosques and religious schools under the condition that Saudi Imams be appointed after they were built. Knowing the other, unofficial, aspects of the Saudi programme, the Uzbekistan government declined the offer, pointing out that they already had enough mosques and that they preferred their own Imams. They had a reasonable case since in Bukhara alone there are 365 mosques, one for each day of the year.[118]

Thus, in Uzbekistan, there is a balance in Saudi–Iranian competition for influence, though with certain, minor, advantages for Saudi Arabia.

Closing the circle

Taking a general look at the race for influence in Central Asia, it becomes clear that for Tehran the Persian Gulf area still has priority over Central Asia. There were too many problems preventing Iran making the former Soviet republics a real counterweight to its lost influence in the Gulf: working lines of communication including roads, railways and airports have still to be established, Tehran lacks the financial and technological resources necessary for an effective economic penetration of the region, and the reactions of Russia, Turkey and the West have clearly indicated their rejection of a decisive Iranian role in the region, an attitude that Iran could not ignore.[119]

Therefore, perhaps contrary to certain expectations, the cornerstone of Iran's policy towards the CCARs has been trade and economic agreements, rather than a campaign of political Islamization. Iran also demonstrated this in its eagerness to develop cooperative ties with non-Muslim former Soviet republics, such as Armenia, Ukraine and Georgia.[120]

> Indeed, Iran has much to fear, from instability on its northern borders, from ethnic upheavals that could influence its own multitude of minorities and from economic isolation if the CCARs become monopolized by a trade orientation towards the West.

Moreover, Iran has a history of competition with Turkey (the Ottoman empire) and, in the Persian Gulf, Saudi Arabia. If this competition is to be played out in Central Asia and the Transcaucasus . . . then Iran needs stronger links with both the CCARs and extra-regional players than mere political alliances which at the moment are inevitably fragile and in a state of flux . . . Geographical proximity, traditional relations, linguistic, religious and other ethnic ties, all help to promote and sustain Iran's profile in this region.[121]

Iran scored most of its winning points in Central Asia by exploiting to the full, and with great ability, its own geographic position as an ideal transit route between Central Asia and the outside world, thus helping the CCARs overcome their geographical isolation.

NOTES

1 J. Reissner, 'Zwischen Persischem Golf und Zentralasien: Neuorientierung der regionalen Aussenpolitik Irans' in A. Zunker (ed.), *Weltordnung oder Chaos? Beiträge zur internationalen Politik* (Baden Baden, Nomos-Verlag, 1993), p. 370.

2 Ibid., p. 366.

3 A. Ehteshami, 'New Frontiers: Iran, the GCC and the CCARs' in A. Ehteshami (ed.), *From the Gulf to Central Asia: Players in the New Great Game* (Exeter: University of Exeter Press, 1994), p. 98.

4 J. Hart, 'Iran as a "Good Neighbor"', *Defense & Diplomacy*, August/September 1991, p. 27.

5 F. al-Mazidi, *The Future of the Gulf: The Legacy of the War and the Challenge of the 1990s* (London and New York: IB Tauris, 1993), p. 5.

6 S. Sharabi and F. Farhi, 'Security Considerations and Iranian Foreign Policy', *Paper presented to the International Seminar on Security, Trade and Advanced Technologies in South Asia: Opportunities and Strategies for Regional Cooperation*, Karachi, 1995.

7 L. Lamote, 'Iran's Foreign Policy and Internal Crisis' in P. Clawson (ed.), *Iran's Strategic Intentions and Capabilities* (Washington DC: Institute for National Strategic Studies, 1994), p. 21.

8 S. Chubin, 'Iran's Strategic Intentions and Constraints' in ibid., p. 69.

9 L. Lamote, Iran's Foreign Policy, p. 21.

10 A. Maleki, 'The Islamic Republic of Iran's Foreign Policy: The View from Iran', *The Iranian Journal of International Affairs*, 7:4 (1996), p. 746.

11 H.Y. Freij, 'State Interests vs. the Umma: Iranian Policy in Central Asia', *Middle East Journal*, 50:1 (1996), pp. 80–1.

12 V. Piacentini, 'Islam: Iranian and Saudi Arabian Religious and Geopolitical Competition in Central Asia' in A. Ehteshami (ed.), *From the Gulf*, p. 38.

13 J. Reissner, Zwischen Persischem Golf, p. 367.
14 A. Hashim, *The Crisis of the Iranian State* (Oxford: Oxford University Press, 1995), p. 26.
15 Ibid.
16 L. Lamote, Iran's Foreign Policy, p. 16.
17 Ibid.
18 A. Hashim, *The Crisis*, p. 27.
19 R. Montazami, 'Naqsh-e Iran dar nezam-e jadid-e asiyayi markazi va janub garbi (Iran's position in the emerging system of Southwest and Central Asia)', *Ettela'at siyasi-eqtesadi*, 8:3/4 (1994), pp. 40–3.
20 A. Ehteshami, New Frontiers, pp. 98–9.
21 J. Calabrese, *Revolutionary Horizons: Regional Foreign Policy in Post-Revolutionary Iran* (New York, St. Martin's Press, 1994), p. 79.
22 A. Hashim, *The Crisis*, p. 42.
23 R.F. Oxenstierna, *Saudi Arabia in the Post-Gulf War: The Search for Stability and Security in the Gulf* (London, Gulf Centre for Strategic Studies, 1992), p. 25.
24 A. Ehteshami, *After Khomeini: The Iranian Second Republic* (London and New York: Routledge, 1995), p. 159.
25 J. Calabrese, *Revolutionary Horizons*, pp. 83–4.
26 A. Maleki, The Islamic Republic, pp. 748–9.
27 J. Calabrese, *Revolutionary Horizons*, p. 85.
28 H.Y. Freij, State Interests, p. 81.
29 R.F. Oxenstierna, *Saudi Arabia*, p. 25.
30 H.Y. Freij, State Interests, p. 81.
31 M.E. Ahrari, *The New Great Game in Muslim Central Asia* (Washington DC, Institute for National Strategic Studies, 1996), pp. 47–9.
32 V. Piacentini, Islam, p. 37.
33 R.N. El-Rayyes, 'An Arab Perspective on the Central Asian Republics in the Context of the New World Order' in A. Ehteshami (ed.), *From the Gulf*, p. 226.
34 A. Rashid, *The Resurgence of Central Asia. Islam or Nationalism?* (London: Zed Books, 1994), p. 101.
35 *Tehran Times*, Tehran, 24, 25 and 26 June 1991.
36 Quoted in A. Hashim, *The Crisis*, p. 43.
37 Quoted in W.S. Harrop, 'The Caucasus Charybdis; Iran's Stand on Azerbaijani–Armenian Nightmares', *US–Iran Review*, 1:6 (1993), p. 7.
38 F. Sarabi, 'Iran's Policy Toward Azerbaijan and Russia', *US–Iran Review*, 2:4 (1994), pp. 8–15.
39 *Echo of Iran (EOI)*, 42:81 (1994), p. 3.
40 H.J. Agha and A.S. Khalidi, *Syria and Iran: Rivalry and Cooperation* (London: Pinter, 1995), p. 39.
41 *Salam*, Tehran, 8 February 1993.
42 J. Calabrese, *Revolutionary Horizons*, pp. 78–9.
43 Quoted in A. Ehteshami, New Frontiers, pp. 96–7.
44 V. Piacentini, Islam, pp. 34–5.
45 M. Abir, *Saudi Arabia: Government, Society and the Gulf Crisis* (London and New York: Routledge, 1993), p. 212.
46 H.Y. Freij, State Interests, p. 82.
47 A. Hashim, *The Crisis*, p. 39.

48 V. Piacentini, Islam, p. 38.
49 A. Hashim, *The Crisis*, pp. 39–40.
50 V. Piacentini, Islam, p. 40.
51 Ibid., p. 42.
52 R.N. El-Rayyes, An Arab Perspective, pp. 226–7.
53 V. Piacentini, Islam, pp. 41–2.
54 M.E. Ahrari, *The New Great Game*, p. 50.
55 K.L. Afrasiabi, *After Khomeini: New Directions in Iran's Foreign Policy* (Boulder: Westview Press, 1994), p. 134.
56 Ibid., p. 135.
57 V. Piacentini, Islam, p. 43.
58 Ibid., p. 42.
59 Ibid., p. 38.
60 M.E. Ahrari, *The New Great Game*, p. 48.
61 J. Calabrese, *Revolutionary Horizons*, p. 85.
62 A. Ehteshami, New Frontiers, p. 97.
63 M.E. Ahrari, *The New Great Game*, pp. 49–50.
64 Ibid., p. 50.
65 A. Ehteshami, New Frontiers, p. 97.
66 Ibid., pp. 97–8.
67 Ibid., p. 99.
68 K.L. Afrasiabi, *After Khomeini*, p. 126.
69 A. Ehteshami, New Frontiers, pp. 158–9.
70 K.L. Afrasiabi, *After Khomeini*, pp. 125–6.
71 F. Sarabi, Iran's Policy, p. 9.
72 Quoted in A. Ehteshami, New Frontiers, p. 99.
73 H. Amirahmadi, 'Persian Gulf Stability Hinges on US–Iran Dialogue', *The Washington Report on Middle East Affairs*, 14:8 (1996), p. 96. See also G. Joffe, 'Iran: Tearing itself apart?', *Jane's Intelligence Review*, 7:10 (1995), p. 453.
74 J. Calabrese, *Revolutionary Horizons*, p. 85.
75 N.R. Keddie, *Iran and the Muslim World: Resistance and Revolution* (Houndmills: Macmillan, 1995), p. 122.
76 *BBC Summary of World Broadcasts*, ME/2465, 20 November 1995.
77 M. Haghayeghi, *Islam and Politics in Central Asia* (New York, St. Martin's Press, 1995), pp. 86, 210.
78 A. Ehteshami, *After Khomeini*, p. 159.
79 J. Calabrese, *Revolutionary Horizons*, p. 82.
80 J. Reissner, Zwischen Persischem Golf, p. 36; M.E. Ahrari, *The New Great Game*, p. 49.
81 K.L. Afrasiabi, *After Khomeini*, p. 126.
82 *Arab–Asian Affairs*, 17:9 (1994), p. 3.
83 K.L. Afrasiabi, *After Khomeini*, pp. 126–7.
84 M. Haghayeghi, *Islam*, p. 210.
85 A. Ehteshami, New Frontiers, p. 108.
86 M. Haghayeghi, *Islam*, pp. 210–11.
87 M.E. Ahrari, *The New Great Game*, p. 47.
88 *Arab–Asian Affairs*, 17:9 (1994), p. 3.
89 K.L. Afrasiabi, *After Khomeini*, p. 127.

 90 M. Haghayeghi, *Islam*, p. 87.
 91 J. Calabrese, *Revolutionary Horizons*, p. 84.
 92 A. Rashid, *The Resurgence*, p. 180.
 93 Quoted in ibid., p. 180.
 94 H.Y. Freij, State Interests, p. 81.
 95 M. Atkin, 'Iran's Relations with Tajikistan', *US-Iran Review*, 1:6 (1993), p. 3.
 96 J. Calabrese, *Revolutionary Horizons*, p. 82.
 97 *BBC Summary of World Broadcasts*, ME/1603, 3 February 1993.
 98 K.L. Afrasiabi, *After Khomeini*, p. 127.
 99 M. Haghayeghi, *Islam*, p. 210.
100 H.Y. Freij, State Interests, p. 81.
101 V. Piacentini, Islam, pp. 37–8, 41.
102 *Kayhan Hava'i*, Tehran, 25 October 1991.
103 K.L. Afrasiabi, *After Khomeini*, p. 126.
104 J. Reissner, Zwischen Persischem Golf, p. 36.
105 A. Rashid, *The Resurgence*, p. 203.
106 *Arab–Asian Affairs*, 17:9 (1994), p. 3.
107 H. Amirahmadi, Iranian–Saudi Arabian Relations, pp. 90, 96.
108 A. Ehteshami, New, p. 97; M.E. Ahrari, *The New Great Game*, p. 49.
109 *BBC Summary of World Broadcasts*, SU/1537, 13 November 1992.
110 Quoted in M. Haghayeghi, *Islam*, pp. 85–6.
111 K.L. Afrasiabi, *After Khomeini*, p. 127.
112 Ibid.
113 H.Y. Freij, State Interests, pp. 81–2.
114 J. Reissner, Zwischen Persischem Golf, p. 36.
115 Quoted in A. Rashid, *The Resurgence*, p. 100.
116 Ibid.
117 A. Ehteshami, New Frontiers, p. 97
118 R.N. El-Rayyes, An Arab Perspective, p. 226.
119 V. Piacentini, Islam, p. 39.
120 A. Ehteshami, New Frontiers, p. 109.
121 Ibid.

6

The Struggle for Religious and Economic Leadership

Religious contradictions belong to the permanent, long-term causes of conflict in the Near and Middle East. They have been, to a certain extent, concentrated in relations between Saudi Arabia and Iran but are by no means restricted to these countries. The variety of denominations, however, under no circumstances implies permanent, violent conflict between the believers. Centuries of relatively peaceful juxtaposition speak for the success of this plurality. As in the cases of Ethnos and Nation, religious differences are rather an arsenal for the parties in the regional conflicts, to be utilized at almost any time.

When the Wahhabi Al Saud conquered the Hijaz in 1924–6, and the holiest places in Islam, Mecca and Medina, came under their control, the Muslim world was very wary of their future behaviour. Wahhabism was seen in the light of raids by Ikhwan militias, their fanaticism and iconoclasm, and the insistence of the Wahhabi clergy that they represented the only true Islam.

After the foundation of the Kingdom of Saudi Arabia in 1932, King Abd al-Aziz ibn Saud and his successors made tremendous efforts to dispel these suspicions and to present themselves as worthy custodians of the Holy shrines. Only if they succeeded in establishing their image as devout Muslims, and not merely sectarian Wahhabis, could they expect the recognition of the Muslim community. As elaborated particularly in Chapter 1, acceptance within the umma as the custodians of Mecca and Medina also created the basis of their legitimacy within Saudi Arabia.

Nobody would dare challenge the rule of a family seen by all the world's Muslims as responsible for protecting the Kaaba. Thus, Saudi Arabia created, more or less successfully, an image of itself as *the* pre-eminent Islamic state in the world, enabling the Al Saud to pose as unbiased arbitrators and intermediaries in Islamic affairs, even beyond the borders of Saudi Arabia.[1] As long as they maintained an Islamic credibility, domestically and internationally, the Al Saud could claim legitimacy. Apart from the constraints of the Sharia, Islam even confers absolute power on them, because the King is simultaneously the leading sheikh, chief Imam, head of his family and head of state.

Challenging the Saudi quest for Islamic leadership

With that constellation of roles in mind, one can imagine what an earthquake the Islamic revolution and the creation of an Islamic republic next to their borders meant for the Al Saud. Even if Ayatollah Khomeini had not rejected monarchy as an acceptable form of government in Islam or had not criticized Saudi Arabia for its strong links with the West, the mere fact of the emergence of a state proclaiming itself not only as an alternative, but as the only true Islamic government must have been regarded by the Al Saud as a fundamental challenge.

Consider also Khomeini's perpetual calls for Islamic unity. In his view, the source of the Muslim world's problems was its estrangement from the divine path of Islam, its adoption of the corrupt ways of either Eastern communism or Western imperialism and its fragmentation, which was partly due to the intrigues of the oppressors. Salvation would have meant a return to Islam, the establishment of a truly Islamic government and the overcoming of divisions to achieve unity: 'There is no difference between Muslims who speak different languages, for instance the Arabs and the Persians. It is very probable that such problems have been created by those who do not wish the Muslim countries to be united . . . They create the issues of nationalism, of pan-Iranism, pan-Turkism, and such isms, which are contrary to Islamic doctrines. Their plan is to destroy Islam and Islamic philosophy.'[2]

It is no surprise then that Khomeini secured the inclusion of a paragraph in the Iranian Constitution making the achievement of Islamic unity a duty for the Islamic Republic. Article 10 reads: 'All Moslems form a single nation, and the government of the Islamic Republic of Iran has the duty of formulating its general policies with a view to the merging and union of all Moslem peoples, and it must constantly strive to bring about the political, economic and cultural unity of the Islamic world.'[3] The revolution's leader often said that 'nobody could defeat one billion Muslims if they were united.' Thus, the Muslims and other oppressed groups and nations should cooperate in order to change the global balance of power and to put an end to their subjugation and exploitation.[4]

No one needs reminding that in the early days of the revolution the entire Iranian leadership spoke with one voice on this issue. Even Rafsanjani declared at Friday prayers in 1982: 'If the Islamic world had acted on the basis of Islam and the words of the Prophet, it would be the most powerful force in the world. I don't exaggerate when I say "the most powerful force" . . . Some of you may ask: "Bigger than America? More powerful than the Soviet Union? Stronger than China?" I say "Yes!" Right now, we would have been stronger than China, stronger than the Soviet Union, stronger than America and all their satellites if only we had been able to establish a global and united Islamic government.'[5]

Mere calls for Islamic unity could have been tolerated by the Al Saud, but right from the early days of the revolution, Iran presented itself as the centre of that aspiring, world-wide drive for Islamic unity, as a model all Muslims should follow, as an alternative to the existing Arab Muslim regimes. Mohammad Javad Larijani went so far as even to advocate the acceptance of the principle of Velayat-e Faqih by other Muslims: '. . . we have and have had the velayat, both during the Imam's (Khomeini's) time and during Ayatollah Khamenei's. This velayat is a righteous jurist ruling the entire Islamic nation. Muslims may not even realize that we have such a jurist ruling here, but this does not undermine the reality of this guardianship. Of course, it affects the ruling jurist's effectiveness, but not the principle. As long as this guardianship exists, the velayat is responsible for the Islamic world, and it is the duty of the Islamic world to protect the ruling jurist . . . As long as our country is the seat of the true ruling jurist, we are responsible for the whole Islamic nation, and the Islamic nation is duty-bound to safeguard the Umm al-Qura.'[6]

In addition to this, the Islamic revolution had to make it clear to Muslims that nationalism, socialism, communism and capitalism, all Western imports, had been tried and found wanting. Political Islam, indigenous, comprehensible to the Muslim masses, both literate and illiterate, was shown by Khomeini and his disciples to be a viable belief system, even when opposed by a militarily formidable monarch supported by a superpower[7] – the parallels with Saudi Arabia were obvious. In this regard, A.N. Memon wrote enthusiastically: '. . . Iran, as an Islamic republic, has inspired numerous Muslims to advocate changes in their own governments. The Iranian Revolution has become a symbol of defiance against the West. Iran has superseded Saudi Arabia as the leading voice among many Muslims seeking an alternative to Western culture.'[8]

Ali Velayati even used the word 'Mecca' in connection with Iran's revolution to show that the centre of gravity in the Islamic world had shifted to Iran. 'Iran's friends and foes alike perceive Iran as the country that is the centre and Mecca of the aspirations of all Muslims . . . Iran is a model for the fifty Islamic countries. This is because the domineering powers have not had very pleasant experiences regarding Iran.'[9]

Becoming a source of inspiration and emulation for all Muslims, not an unattainable goal in the Middle East and the Gulf region where Islam is dominant, would result in increased political strength and diplomatic manoeuvrability for Iran. The radical Iranian leadership could point to the suffering within the Islamic world if it wanted to gain respect and sympathy for the revolution. The majority of Muslims around the world, including those in the oil-rich Middle East, live under conditions of economic hardship and/or political oppression. Regardless of the real influence of Iran among Muslims, the revolution had a great impact on them simply because it opposed the status quo and supported the deprived Muslim majority. Thus its popularity was also the outcome of inept economic policies pursued by the existing governments of the region.[10]

However, apart from this and Iran's assertion that it is the only country in the world where Islam has officially become the foundation of society and government, thus implying that it is the duty of all Muslims to support it, there were other reasons for Muslims to admire the Iranian revolution. Among them were Iran's uncompromising stand on the Palestinian issue and the question of Jerusalem and its strict adherence to an independent and non-aligned foreign policy, both of which have great appeal for many Muslims.

Its growing influence among Muslims and Islamic movements led to visions among Iranian leaders of using these movements as some sort of Fifth Column.[11] But contrary to many allegations and/or expectations there was never an institution such as an Islamic Comintern, with headquarters in the holy city of Qom instructing Muslims and directing their activities according to a grand strategy worked out by the Iranian leadership. Iran's record of influencing Muslims has rather been characterized – like many other aspects of its post-revolutionary life

– 'by a great deal of parallel, and often contradictory, actions by a host of official and semi-official organizations and groups. Similarly, Iranian activities in regard to the export of revolution rather than following a strategic blueprint have been marked by what could be called tactical opportunism. Thus, Iran seems to have concentrated its efforts in areas where local conditions have created opportunities for it to expand its influence.'[12]

The Sunni–Shia question

Itself consisting of a considerable Shia population, Saudi Arabia had many reasons to confront the Iranian posture. As mentioned above, in the early days of the Iranian revolution the Al Saud became increasingly fearful of the effect of Iranian radicalism on its own Shia population in the province of al-Hasa, the centre of the Saudi oil industry; Riyadh later recognized however that it was exactly these Shia aspects of the Iranian revolution that could be best used as a tool against the Iranian challenge.

First of all, Iran's attempt to present itself as the centre of a worldwide Muslim awakening, overriding denominational differences, and as defender of the oppressed creating a fresh basis for agreement not only between Shia Iranians and non-Iranian Sunnis, but between the Muslim East and the non-Muslim Third World,[13] had to be challenged. Saudi propaganda started by condemning the Iranian revolution for being exclusively Shia, underlining the point that Shiism was always antithetical not only to Wahhabism but also to other schools of Sunnism, and that for these reasons Khomeini's interpretation of Islam had to be considered blasphemous.[14] Furthermore, to reduce its appeal to Sunni Muslims and Arabs, the revolution was characterized as an upheaval of heretic Iranians who were trying to continue the previous policies of Iranian expansionism, but this time painted in Islamic colours.

There is no doubt that Wahhabism, as a puritan form of Sunnism, is anathema to Shiism. One of the basic tenets of Wahhabi doctrine is the duty of the believers to fight polytheists. Due to their strong belief that only Iman Ali and his successors had the legitimacy to lead the Muslim umma, the Shia were put next to unbelievers, therefore liable to severe sanctions, including jihad. This enmity remained latent over the centuries. The more quietist rather than activist Shiism during Safavi, Zand and Qajsar rule avoided any permanent state of confrontation between Persia and the first Wahhabi states in the eighteenth and nineteenth centuries.

Only when Khomeini developed his concept of Velayat-e Faqih, rule by an Islamic jurist as necessary to protect society from corruption, and began to realize it through the Islamic revolution, did the enmity come truly alive. According to this concept, the legitimacy of any other political system, whether headed by Muslims or not, can be brought into question, including the Muslim governments in the Gulf states and particularly Wahhabi rule in Saudi Arabia.

In contrast to the Shia concept of a government only being truly legitimate when it is the rule of the Twelfth Imam, the Sunni have managed to accommodate temporal authority by legitimizing the governments of Muslim states as long as they uphold Islamic law. Nevertheless, throughout Sunni history, there have been periodic efforts to purify religion by returning to the fundamentals of the Sharia. Exactly that happened in the centre of the Arabian Peninsula more than 200 years ago.

Taking up Ibn Taymiya's rejection of innovative practices and his call for a return to the original doctrines of Islam, Mohammad ibn Abd al-Wahhab set in motion a revival of Hanbalism in the first Saudi Arabian state. Thus, for the Saudis, not only is the Iranian brand of Muslim revival exclusively Shia, but it comes more than 200 years after their own revival. Proud of this head start, the Al Saud were pleased to observe that the doctrinal impact of the Iranian revolution on the Sunni population of Saudi Arabia and the Gulf was virtually nil. When fundamentalist ideas were aired, they were more influenced by the writings of Ibn Taymiya, Mawdudi and Qutb than by those of Khomeini.[15]

Nevertheless, the Al Saud knew that it would not be politically wise under the prevailing circumstances to overemphasize the Wahhabi/Shia dichotomy. Trying to contain the Iranian revolution by referring to its Shia nature had proved useful in several ways, but there was also the other side of the coin. Relying exclusively on Wahhabi concepts might remind fellow Sunni believers all over the world of their former suspicions of Wahhabism. Leading Iranian clerics such as Tehran's Imam Jom'e, Ayatollah Jannati, constantly rubbed salt in the wound by accusing the Saudi government of attempting to force its Wahhabi brand of Islam on the rest of the world.[16] Furthermore, this could alienate the Shia, not only in al-Hasa but also in other countries. Insulting Shiism would only provoke the Iranian Twelver Shia as well as other branches of Shiism

liberation movements in the manner done by the communists or should it engage in plotting coups d'état as was practised by the US or other Western powers? The answer to both options is clearly and forthrightly negative . . . our understanding of the Islamic renaissance values its generative potential *within* various countries.'[35]

Compared to Khomeini's ideal, which envisaged a complete merging of all Muslims into one organic umma, this new approach suggested that the Iranian government would handle the issue flexibly and be more sensitive to the possible adverse impact of their objective. The post-Khomeini foreign policymakers – at least within the government – no longer subscribed to the utopia of a Muslim world without national frontiers. They advocated instead increasing Muslim solidarity. 'Theoretically, this reflects a shift from a monist concept of Umma to a more complex and pluralistic concept in which the principle of ethnic and national difference . . . is respected.'[36]

But one should not conclude from these changes that the government's commitment to sustain and spread Islam was less firm than that of the previous leadership.[37] It simply revised and refined the methods employed to fulfil the mission. Three major factors in this tactical adjustment should be borne in mind.

First of all, continued attempts to subvert governments in the name of true Islam, particularly when applied to the Gulf region, were incompatible with efforts to forge economic ties with those same governments, which latter issue was much more important for the survival of the Islamic Republic. Secondly, emphasis on spreading Iran's brand of Islam can be too easily exploited by Iran's detractors who tend to accentuate the differences between Shiism and Sunnism. And thirdly, experience has shown – especially in the Gulf region – that Iran's revolutionary call to topple existing governments has had limited appeal.

Nevertheless, the post-Khomeini leadership continued to insist that Iran's Islamic responsibility transcended national borders, although it appeared to have accepted – tactically, pragmatically and perhaps temporarily – international boundaries. However, this has neither implied nor required abrogation of Iran's belief in its responsibility to assist Islamic communities within other states in their struggle for true Islam. Iran's 1990 budget reportedly allocated US$ 120 million to support Islamic groups and movements. This amount was increased by 20 per cent the following year.[38]

Rivalry within the OIC

But accepting realities also meant Iran had to re-evaluate its attitudes to international organizations and institutions, especially Islamic ones. Instead of criticizing Saudi Arabia for monopolizing the OIC for instance, Iran now tried to increase its own influence in that organization by actively creating support for its views. When the OIC met in Senegal in October 1990, Tehran was quick to argue that the organization should seek to resolve the Kuwait crisis itself, avoiding Western meddling and providing an Islamic solution to a dispute between two Islamic states. Disappointingly for the Iranian government, the OIC did not become significantly involved in the crisis, either before or during the Second Gulf War.

The Iranian media echoed the government's sharp criticism of this attitude, accusing the OIC of having been an instrument of Saudi, that is to say American, politics. Deputy Foreign Minister Larijani even doubted whether the OIC was a suitable institution for Islamic countries at all: 'Some member states are constituting problems for the OIC itself. Either we change that organization or we found a new institution!'[39] But that was only rhetoric. Iran was much more interested in utilizing the existing structures of the OIC on two vital issues. First, the OIC would enable it to voice support for Islamic movements abroad, be they Indian Muslims, Kashmiri irredentists, Afghan mujaheddin or Lebanese Hizballah.[40] Secondly, Iran wanted to convince the member states by careful degrees that they should limit Saudi Arabia's say in the organization.

For instance, during the 1991 Dakar summit, Rafsanjani tangled with the Saudis on the subject of the Madrid Peace talks. The Iranian President lobbied for the continuation of jihad aimed at establishing true Islam all over the world and linked this to opposition to the United States. The policies of Iran and Saudi Arabia diverged most sharply on issues directly related to American policy in the Middle East. Furthermore, Iran used the OIC to mobilize support for the Bosnian Muslims. The organization served as a forum in which Iran could criticize the West's inadequate response to the conflict. Similarly, Saudi Arabia was pressured into demonstrating its leadership by responding to the Bosnian crisis.[41] It was Iran that called for an extraordinary session of the OIC to consider a collective response to the Bosnian crisis, thus spreading doubts about Saudi Arabian commitment to the faith.[42]

Iran was also eager to demonstrate its value to the CCARs by initiating a campaign for their membership of the OIC. Saudi Arabia, supporting their membership in principle, tried in vain to prevent Iran from collecting the credit for this initiative. These challenges raise an interesting question about future Iranian–Saudi Arabian competition for influence within the OIC. It is an open question if or when some stability is achieved in the CCARs, Sudan or other states politically indebted to Iran, whether then the balance of influence within the OIC will swing in Iran's favour or remain with the Saudis.[43]

Once again – the hajj issue

Returning to the fundamental point that bilateral relations between Iran and Saudi Arabia were influenced by religion, it should be mentioned – last but not least – that the hajj issue retained its potential for conflict despite the improvements of the early 1990s. Besides some minor exceptions, the Saudi authorities continued to prohibit the rallies denouncing infidels, which were top of the list of Iranian official activities during the pilgrimage.

In 1993, Saudi irritation was displayed when Agence France Presse (AFP) reported an agreement had been reached between Iran and Saudi Arabia on permission to hold a rally calling for deliverance from paganism in front of the office of the Iranian hajj mission in Mecca. When the first few hundred pilgrims tried to gather in front of the building, the Saudi authorities forcibly hindered them from entering the area, which led to some clashes. The incident caused the Iranian Foreign Ministry to make an official statement: 'The recent Saudi action raises serious questions to which the Saudis are urged to provide reasonable and acceptable answers. We must note that some people believe that the domestic political crisis in Saudi Arabia has played a part in the adoption of the recent Saudi attitude to the hajjis visiting God's inviolate house . . . Because of their political difficulties, the Saudi authorities feel that any occurrence or action that is hostile to the United States or Israel might further undermine the country.'[44]

The Saudi Press Agency was instructed by the government not to reply in the same polemical tone but simply to declare that Mohammad Reyshahri, the head of the Iranian pilgrims, had been informed in advance through official channels that Saudi Arabia continued to forbid any congregations, demonstrations or processions in Mecca, in the sacred shrines and in Medina during the pilgrimage season.[45]

Thus, a solution to the whole issue was deferred until 1994. Ahmad Purnejati, then deputy head of the Iranian hajj delegation, once again referred to Saudi permission to hold rallies during the pilgrimage, supposedly agreed upon after intensive talks between the Foreign Ministers of the two countries: 'The ceremony was held in an acceptable manner in 1991 and 1992. However, we wonder why Saudi officials banned the ceremony last year despite the agreement. The Saudis should know once and for all that the antipathy towards disbelievers is considered by the Iranian pilgrims as a religious duty rather than a "temporary political tactic".'[46]

The Saudi press flatly denied the existence of any such agreement:

> The rulers of Tehran are spreading lies against the Kingdom of Saudi Arabia which go as far as to say that the Kingdom has agreed to allow the Iranian pilgrims to stage demonstrations and cause disorder in Mecca . . . With these claims, the rulers of Tehran are aiming to deceive the Muslim world and slander the Kingdom in order to fool the Iranian people and distract them with a new lie. They will then try to hold the Kingdom responsible for not allowing more pilgrims from Iran to perform this religious duty.[47]

The Saudi daily's mention of the number of Iranian pilgrims points to another continuing disagreement between Iran and Saudi Arabia concerning the hajj. Efforts by the Saudi authorities to cut the number of Iranian pilgrims in 1994 to 55,000 were harshly rejected by Tehran. Iran cited an agreement between both sides signed in 1991 that set the quota of Iranians permitted to perform the hajj at 115,000.[48] Eventually, the Saudi Ministry for Hajj and Awqal was induced to issue a statement asking the Iranian officials to observe some basic points. First, to:

> respect the fact that the number of pilgrims coming from the Islamic republic of Iran should be in harmony with the quota that was allocated to the rest of the Islamic states as defined by the resolution of the OIC foreign ministers' meeting held in Amman . . . second, not to allow at all any form of gathering, marches, chanting of slogans, holding banners or distributing leaflets before, during and after the pilgrimage season . . . and third, to unite the Iranian pilgrimage delegation in one single official delegation.[49]

Saudi Interior Minister, Prince Nayif Ibn Abd al-Aziz, further stressed that

> we do not see any excuse for the Iranian campaign since the matter had already been discussed between the two countries and Iran was informed about everything that is required. An agreement was also reached on matters regarding the number of Iranian pilgrims and the condition for the presence of the hajj delegation from Iran . . . security measures exist to protect the safety of the pilgrims and to protect the country's security and also to enable the pilgrims to perform the rites as prescribed in God's book and the teachings of His Prophet and as Muslims have been performing them for hundreds of years or for over 1,400 years. Anything which departs from this for a worldly objective or with the aim of adding something has nothing to do with hajj and is totally unacceptable . . .[50]

Nayif's remarks presented a most welcome excuse to the Iranian leadership to resurrect the old accusation that the Al Saud were forcing the entire Muslim world into abiding by Wahhabi rites. Ayatollah Meshkini, Friday Imam of Qom, stressed that it could not to be tolerated that all Muslim nations and sects who come to Mecca, be they Shafii, Hanbali, Maleki, Hanafi, Jafari, Ismaili, Zayidi or any other sect, should have to behave according to the conclusions that the Saudi ulama had drawn from the Koran.[51]

Ayatollah Jannati added:

> a group of Najd clerics (representing the Wahhabi sect), who are in fact the most reactionary clerics Islam has seen, seek to impose their ideas, with the support of the Saudi leaders, on about 1.2 billion Muslims and deprive them of freedom of action. They want everyone to follow what they consider as Islam and refrain from what they term non-Islamic. This does not follow any logic, given what Islam says about the two holy shrines. According to Islam's point of view, these shrines are international Islamic centres. Instead of belonging to one single group, these shrines belong to all Muslims.[52]

Ayatollah Javadi Amoli, a member of the Assembly of Experts, put it more poetically:

> And the Saudi officials should not make a mistake. The pyramids might be under the control of the ruling class in Egypt and the wall

of China might be under the control of the Chinese government but the Holy sanctuaries are neither the Egyptian pyramids nor the wall of China. The God of the sanctuaries named the Kaaba the house of the ancient. This house was no one's property nor domain in ancient times and will not be so in the future. No owner or king will have the Kaaba . . . The Wahhabi ulama must understand this. The Saudi officials must understand this.[53]

Virulent differences between Iran and Saudi Arabia over the hajj remained despite attempts on both sides to ease the tension. In November 1995, Mohammad Husain Reza'i, Deputy Culture Minister and head of Iran's Hajj and Endowments (vaqf) Organization, arrived in Jiddah to discuss with his counterpart, the Saudi Minister of Pilgrimage Affairs, Mahmud Safar, a whole bundle of problems that had built up over the previous years. Commenting on the talks, Reza'i concluded that both sides had made great efforts to improve the quality of services to enable Iranian pilgrims to perform hajj 'in peace and comfort.'[54] Nevertheless, the religious differences between revolutionary Iran and Saudi Arabia are too deeply rooted to lead us to expect more than cosmetic retouching through negotiations such as these.

Economy

The competition between Iran and Saudi Arabia for influence in the Middle East clearly has some important economic aspects. Iran, with a much larger population and greater economic needs than Saudi Arabia, also wants to establish itself as a dominant economic power in the Gulf region. Since the modern sector of the Iranian economy depends 65 per cent to 75 per cent on the world market, for everything from raw material to technology, these imports must be paid for with oil revenues which constitute more than ninety per cent of the country's foreign exchange earnings. Oil is, in short, the Iranian economy's lifeline. Yet, Iran has only limited control over the production, export and price of oil, as these are largely determined by changes in the world oil market and by OPEC.[55] In general, the country's oil reserves, though large, are not great enough to dominate the market and thus provide predictable, stable, and long-term revenue for its people.

Saudi Arabia's advantages within OPEC

Throughout recent decades, Saudi Arabia has been the main impediment to an improvement of Iran's position on the world oil market. Saudi policies relating to oil production and pricing usually run contrary to Iranian interests. Ultimately, any cutbacks have depended on Saudi Arabia, and Saudi policies and objectives have conflicted with those of Iran because of superior Saudi reserves of oil and money. Only by destabilizing Saudi Arabia and ending its subjugation of Iranian ambitions can Iran in the long run hope to realize its economic objectives.[56] A brief look at the history of their bilateral relations will show whether such a scenario is probable or not.

In order for the Islamic Republic to dominate the Middle East and to win the contest for power with Saudi Arabia through economic rather than military means, it would have to take the lead in OPEC. Such a development is rather unlikely. Since its founding, OPEC has tried to promote an image of itself as a cartel. But in reality, it has stopped short of becoming one, because a real cartel would set the oil prices to serve the interests of all of its members. In fact, the Saudi Arabian government has increasingly set OPEC prices to serve its own interests and those of its allies.[57]

Following the 1973 oil-price hike, there was an open and unpredictable power struggle between Iran and Saudi Arabia for leadership of OPEC, although Riyadh gained some decisive advantages. As a result of this competition, OPEC became increasingly politicized. This trend gained considerable importance shortly before and during the Iranian revolution. In late 1978, ARAMCO produced some 2.5 to 3 million bpd, more than its production earlier that year. Although the Saudis' overproduction policy had already begun by the mid-1970s, it became a well-established practice during the revolution. By immediately meeting ever consumer demand, Saudi Arabia became the absolute 'swing producer' of OPEC after the downfall of the Shah, a position that helped it aquire a dominant role within the organization in the following years. Riyadh used its new-found power to make economic as well as political gains and friends. Among the latter, the United States and their Western allies in particular profited. After the Iranian revolution, traditional friendly relations between Saudi Arabia and the West developed to a real symbiosis, serving the interests of both.

First of all, by regulating oil prices according to the requirements of the West, Saudi Arabia proved its usefulness to its Western allies while simultaneously outmanoeuvring all potential competitors within OPEC.

Secondly, both partners were extremely interested in weakening, containing, and even overthrowing the Islamic revolution in Iran. Irrespective of the cost, by 1981 Saudi Arabia had succeeded in imposing its will on the other OPEC members, forcing them to realign at the lower Saudi rate.[58]

With the beginning of the Iraq–Iran war in 1980, the Saudi oil policy was not only concerned with weakening the Iranians, but with improving the chances of Iraq. As mentioned previously, Saudi Arabia's oil policy was designed to harm Iran while simultaneously earning enough money to finance the Iraqi war effort. After the oil slump of 1983–6, the Saudi government concluded that the only way to get out of the slump was for oil prices to plummet, thus boosting global demand. Anxious to bring some discipline to OPEC and to make the producers accept a quota system, Riyadh increased its own production which resulted in an even sharper decrease in the oil price.

The Saudi policy was devastating for Iran, whose exports had dropped tremendously during the revolution and the war with Iraq. In the last year of the Shah's rule, Iran had exported approximately 5.28 million bpd, whereas by late 1987 that figure was averaging 1.7 million bpd. In 1978, Iran's oil exports were worth US$ 21.7 billion per year, in 1987 the government received only US$ 2.2 billion.[59] Therefore, Tehran felt that a tighter control on supply was needed in order to maximize revenues for each barrel sold.[60]

But the oil market of the mid-1980s was not ready to give in to Iranian suggestions. By 1986, OPEC had lost some twenty million barrels per day of its potential production, of which approximately 15 million bpd had been taken away by non-OPEC producers, including those in the North Sea. Iran was hard hit by this development. Its share of OPEC production and exports of crude oil declined from 19.1 per cent in 1976 to 14.1 per cent in 1985 and its share of crude oil exports from 18.2 per cent to 13.4 per cent in the same period. In the meantime, the world oil market was flooded by Saudi Arabian oil resulting in a major oversupply by 1985.

The 'Saudi factor' finally caused the 1986 crash in the oil market. Whereas in January of 1986 oil prices were set at about US$ 28 per barrel, in April the market was only ready to accept US$ 10 per barrel.[61]

By the summer of 1986, the price fell to US$ 8 per barrel with US$ 5 looming on the horizon.[62] While all OPEC members suffered from the declining oil market and Saudi policies, it was Iran that suffered most. Although it is doubtful whether Saudi Arabia had really risked the crash in order to hurt Iran economically, it is undeniable that the crash occurred when Iranian troops captured the Iraqi port of al-Fao, increasing Saudi anxieties about Iraq's fate. Whatever the Saudi motives were, the Iranian leadership believed the policy was aimed principally at weakening the revolution[63] and constraining Iran's capacity to continue the war by limiting its access to funds.

The Saudi policy was termed 'the oil conspiracy' by the Iranian media. Regarding this 'conspiracy,' Ayatollah Montazeri declared in 1986: 'They sell oil which belongs to the Muslims and the oppressed, God-given wealth, at bargain prices. They pour it down the pockets of the superpowers at cheap prices in order to defeat revolutionary Iran.'[64] Rafsanjani also referred to the 'conspiracies of Iran's enemies to reduce the price of oil,' whilst President Khamenei warned that 'the price war is no less important to us than the military war.'[65]

In the end, it was helpful for Iran that the Saudis also came under increasing pressure from other OPEC and non-OPEC producers suffering as a result of lower oil prices and loss of revenue. At an OPEC meeting in August 1986, Iran and Saudi Arabia thus agreed to stabilize oil prices at about US$ 18 per barrel.[66] But the price war between Iran and Saudi Arabia was not over yet.

Immediately after the ceasefire between Iran and Iraq took effect, on 20 August 1988, Saudi Arabia stepped up its oil production again. By early October 1988, Saudi production had reached 5.7 million bpd, well above its OPEC quota of 4.3 million bpd.[67] In order to finance its economic reconstruction plans, Iran, in contrast, continued to be primarily interested in high prices for its faltering oil production, a larger OPEC share of exports and a frozen, or an even lower, level of OPEC output. The chances that Iran could achieve these three interrelated goals remained poor after the ceasefire with Iraq.

But suddenly, some hope emerged with the jump in oil prices following the Kuwait crisis in 1990–1 which netted Iran an income of US$ 18 billion.[68] However it was Saudi Arabia, as the dominant OPEC producer, that picked up most of the profits resulting from the international boycott of Iraqi oil. Tehran reacted furiously:

> In line with its illogical attitudes in OPEC, Saudi Arabia has once again threatened to produce an additional two million barrels per day to meet the shortfall caused by the UN-led embargo against Iraq and Kuwait . . . Saudi Arabia's intention to raise output is against the wish of the majority of OPEC members and indicates that the Riyadh government is still sticking to its past irrational attitudes . . . The Saudi claim that OPEC members should necessarily compensate for the shortfall of four million barrels caused as a result of the . . . embargo . . . is meaningless and unreasonable. Existing statistics show that there are now 180 million barrels of floating stock that can be offered to the oil consumers on the spot regardless of the strategic amount stockpiled by major industrial countries that can meet their needs for three months . . . The Saudis' new position indicates they are bent on safeguarding the interests of the oil consumers mostly in the West . . . Political analysts believe that Saudi Arabia by increasing its output and pushing down the price of oil intends to raise its own oil revenue in a bid to finance Washington's military expedition in the Persian Gulf.[69]

In general, Iran's hope that, in the absence of a major oil exporter such as Iraq, there would be a dramatic rise in OPEC prices, did not materialize.[70] The price increase in 1990 remained an isolated episode.

Aware that it did not have the upper hand, the Iranian government sought negotiations with Riyadh. When the Saudi Foreign Minister visited Iran in June 1991, the Iranians proposed a conference in Isfahan, intending to bring the two countries' viewpoints on the issue of oil production and prices closer together.[71] Still hoping to keep oil prices as high as possible and to maintain some form of price stability in an OPEC capable of influencing if not dictating prices, Iran relied on OPEC's internal solidarity and on the goodwill of its most important member, Saudi-Arabia. Iran wanted to convince the Saudis to grant it as large a quota as possible, anxiously supporting cutbacks based on historical quotas rather than production capacity which was low after the revolution and two wars. The Kingdom, with its production capacity of some nine million bpd can easily dictate prices both inside and outside OPEC, making its policies critically important for Iran's economic well-being.[72] But the Iranian initiative did not have the expected results.

Iran's economic shortcomings

On the contrary, the drop in oil prices after 1991 had a catastrophic effect on Iran's economic reconstruction programmes. Iran's petrodollar income fell to almost one-third of what it was just before the revolution. In terms of purchasing power, oil prices in the early 1990s were lower than they were twenty years before, whereas Iran's population had doubled to approximately 60 million, so that the country had more mouths to feed with a lower oil income.[73]

In addition to that, Iran's oil industry, which had not been modernized for almost two decades, badly needed an overhaul. Poor maintenance of equipment and lack of sufficient technical and managerial expertise in the oil production industry hindered the country from reaching its maximum production capacity of 4.2 bpd. Delaying that overhaul would lead – according to many analyses produced by independent oil experts – to Iran becoming a net oil importer within the next two decades, with devastating consequences for the Islamic Republic.[74] Aware of that danger, Tehran directed some US$ 5 billion into investment in the dilapidated oil sector in 1991, to maximize production and revenues with the knowledge that these investments would reduce profits in the short run. In 1992 and in 1993, the government invested US$ 2 billion to update its equipment and considered these investments an unavoidable burden.[75]

Proud of having recognized the problem in time, Iran temporarily raised its oil production to 4 million bpd in mid-October 1992 to illustrate the country's improved capacity and thereby buttress its claims for a larger share of OPEC's market. But Iran did not achieve an increased quota allocation at the OPEC conference in Vienna in the autumn of 1992, nor was it successful in reducing the output of other OPEC members, especially that of Saudi Arabia.[76] In 1992–3 Iran earned US$ 16 billion in revenue from oil exports, whereas in 1994 it barely made US$ 12 billion.[77] The floating oil price added to Iran's problems. The budget of 1993–4 was based on a price of US$ 17–18 per barrel, but Iranian crude oil was sold for US$ 13.5–14 per barrel, resulting in a deficit of about 20 per cent.[78] The deficit led the Majlis Economic and Finance Committee to propose revising the oil revenue forecast for 1994–5 to US$ 9.4 billion, as compared to the US$ 18 billion in 1990–1.[79]

But it was not the uncertainty of the oil market nor the obstructive policy of Saudi Arabia only that hampered the Iranian economy. By the mid-1990s, Iran was heavily in debt as well. Initially, foreign borrowing proved to be controversial in the Islamic Republic. Iran emerged from the war with Iraq with virtually no debts, unlike Iraq. Tehran's policy of prompt payment and efficient management of its external finances ensured an impressive credit rating. Being debt-free was an ideological stand. Iran's Islamic leaders wanted the country to avoid ties to the Western-dominated international financial markets.

One of the revolution's proudest accomplishments, as Tehran often boasted, was paying off the Shah's US$ 8.4 billion debt and freeing Iran from its Western creditors. Nevertheless, after the ceasefire with Iraq, it became clear that Iran's economic reconstruction and recovery programme required access to Western capital. The government simply did not have a significant budget surplus, and private investors in Iran were reluctant to invest in production, preferring to put their money into dormant savings or property.

The sudden surge in oil prices following Iraq's invasion in Kuwait had tempted the Iranian government, now certain of a steady rise in oil prices, into a spending spree. Tehran went on an uncontrolled post-war shopping binge spending billions of dollars on foreign consumer goods to placate a war-weary society. Furthermore, The Iranian Central Bank lost control of the number of letters of credit issued by the commercial banks.

As early as 1992, letters of credit payments on short-term debts fell behind schedule for the first time since the revolution, severely damaging Iran's credit rating. By 1993 the government's inability to control spending had produced a severe debt crisis, with Tehran acknowledging short-term debts of US$ 30 billion. By early 1994, the country was US$ 10 billion in arrears to its Western creditors. Between 1992 and 1994, Iran had been forced to cut imports by 50 per cent, depriving the country's industries of raw materials and spare parts and forcing many companies to freeze wages or to close down completely.[80] Even highly profitable projects like the US$ 1.7 billion deal to develop the South Pars gas and oil field had to be cancelled.[81] Iranian officials did their best to dispel anxieties over the extent of the country's debt.

Hasan Rohani, Khamenei's representative in the country's Supreme Security Council insisted in an interview that Iran's financial obligations were below US$ 30 billion in 1994 and completely within the expectations of the first Five Year Plan.

For a country like ours around 30 billion dollars in debt is not a big number. It is natural for a country with twenty to twenty-five billion dollars income to have debts around the same number. This is within international norms . . . Our next problem was the reduction of oil prices. This reduction brought about the same complications in payments of our debts. Today, the price of oil is unfavourable and is well below OPEC's minimum pricing. The next problem is dollar's exchange rate. The instability in the exchange rate has cost us US$ 6 billion because we sell in dollars but buy in German Mark or Japanese yen.[82]

Despite serious efforts to cut spending, Iran's debt ran to a record high of US$ 33 billion in 1996.[83]

Probable reasons for a compromise

Saudi Arabia's upper hand in the economic aspects of its struggle with Iran should not lead to an underestimation of the Kingdom's own problems with oil production and export. As in Iran, so in Saudi Arabia oil also dominates economic life. The revenues from the sale of oil have made it possible for Riyadh to construct a modern state with a highly advanced infrastructure as well as comprehensive public and welfare services. They have also provided the basic underpinning for the Kingdom's foreign policy, making Saudi Arabia a state to be reckoned with in trade, finance and diplomacy. Saudi Arabia's proven oil reserves are approximately twenty per cent of the world's total, larger than any other country, both in quantity and in percentage. Saudi oil is expected to last over a hundred years. Principally, this has provided Saudi Arabia with the ability to dictate terms within OPEC and to harm Iran, even when, as happens from time to time, such a policy might be unprofitable for the Saudi economy. The Saudi-generated oil crisis of 1986 illustrated to what extent the Saudis were ready to exploit their dominance of the international oil market for political reasons.

However, 1986 marked a turning point in the seemingly unlimited capability of the country to use its oil as a political weapon. As elaborated in detail in Chapter 3, the Kingdom has become practised in handling its economic affairs as well as those of the region as a whole, and has had to struggle with an increasingly severe financial crisis as well. If this financial crisis cannot be managed by the present government, then social and political crisis may engulf Saudi Arabia in the not too distant future.[84]

Thus, mounting economic problems in both Iran and Saudi Arabia, coupled with a stagnant global oil market, continue to provide the incentive for the two countries to compete within OPEC. Geological and demographic asymmetries have perpetuated both the differences between Iran and Saudi Arabia and the leverage that the Kingdom has enjoyed over Iran in controlling OPEC policy.[85] But there are no guarantees to ensure that precise balance of power in the future. In the 1990s Iran also continued to be the second largest OPEC producer after Saudi Arabia, holding the fifth largest proven OPEC reserves.[86] Nobody can ultimately exclude the possibility of an Iranian economic recovery, nor a simultaneous worsening of Saudi Arabia's economic situation.

What about Iran convincing the other OPEC members, tired of constant Saudi dictates on quotas and prices, to establish new policies which would benefit all the members? Perhaps forced more and more to consider the growing Islamic movements in their own countries, OPEC members might consider it counter-productive to obey Saudi Arabia's overall oil policy which serves the interests of the West rather than that of the Muslim peoples. In such a case, they would surely try to avoid conflict with a revolutionary Iran.[87]

Undoubtedly, the political economics of oil will continue to be central to the Persian Gulf. As major producers, Iran and Saudi Arabia are bound to remain vulnerable to global oil politics and their own clashing strategic ambitions will still be played out within OPEC. Thus, the prospect for continuing Saudi–Iranian conflict is very real for some time to come. The fortuitous removal of Iraq from the market enabled Iran and Saudi Arabia, for the most part, to avoid direct confrontation, and thereby created a breathing spell in the 1990s.[88] As long as Iraq does not export any significant amounts of oil, Iran can at least afford to tolerate the Saudi refusal to lower their production rates. The tension will definitely rise however when Iraq enters the oil market again. Then, a triangle of conflict over oil policy could develop between Iran, Iraq and Saudi Arabia.[89]

NOTES

1 S. al-Mani, 'Of Security and Threat: Saudi Arabia's Perception', *Journal of South Asian and Middle Eastern Studies*, 20:1 (1996), p. 77.

2 Quoted in H. Amirahmadi and N. Entessar, 'Iranian–Arab Relations in Transition' in H. Amirahmadi and N. Entessar (eds.), *Iran and the Arab World* (Basingstoke: Macmillan, 1993), p. 3.

3 Quoted in J. Calabrese, *Revolutionary Horizons: Regional Foreign Policy in Post-Revolutionary Iran* (New York: St. Martin's Press, 1994), p. 27.

4 S.T. Hunter, *Iran and the World: Continuity in a Revolutionary Decade* (Bloomington: Indiana University Press, 1990), p. 40.

5 *Hotba-ye namaz-e jom'e-ye Tehran* (4 vols., Tehran, Vezarat-e Ettela'at va Ershad-e Islami, 1989), vol. 4, p. 185.

6 Quoted in M. Mohaddessin, *Islamic Fundamentalism: The New Global Threat* (Washington DC: Seven Locks Press, 1993), p. 38.

7 G. Linabury, 'Ayatollah Khomeini's Islamic legacy' in H. Amirahmadi and N. Entessar (eds.), *Reconstruction and Regional Diplomacy in the Persian Gulf* (London, New York, Routledge, 1992), p. 33.

8 A.N. Memon, *The Islamic Nation: Status & Future of Muslims in the New World Order* (Beltsville MD: Writers' Inc. International, 1995), p. 150.

9 *Resalat*, Tehran, 15 February 1993.

10 H. Amirahmadi, 'Iran and the Persian Gulf: Strategic Issues and Outlook' in H. Zanganeh (ed.), *Islam, Iran, & World Stability* (New York: St. Martin's Press, 1994), pp. 116–8.

11 Ibid., pp. 117–8.

12 S.T. Hunter, 'Iran and the Spread of Revolutionary Islam', *Third World Quarterly*, 10:2 (1988), p. 740.

13 K.L. Afrasiabi, *After Khomeini: New Directions in Iran's Foreign Policy* (Boulder: Westview Press, 1994), p. 204.

14 S. Holly, *Conflict in the Gulf: Economic and Maritime Implications of the Iran–Iraq War* (Colchester, 1988), p. 15.

15 D.E. Long, 'The Impact of the Iranian Revolution on the Arabian Peninsula and the Gulf States' in J.L. Esposito (ed.), *The Iranian Revolution: Its Global Impact* (Miami, Florida International University Press, 1990), pp. 102–4, 114.

16 *EIU Country Report Iran*, London, 3rd Quarter 1996, p. 11.

17 W. Ende, 'Die iranische Revolution; Ursachen, Intentionen und Auswirkungen auf die Arabische Halbinsel' in F. Scholz (ed.), *Die Golfstaaten: Wirtschaftsmacht im Krisenherd* (Braunschweig, Westermann-Verlag, 1985), p. 153.

18 'Sunni vs. Shi'ah; a pitiful outcry', *Voice of the World's Islamic Movements*, February 1984, p. 17.

19 S.M. Badeeb, *Saudi–Iranian Relations 1932–1982* (London: Echoes, 1993), p. 86.

20 W. Buchta, 'Die inneriranische Diskussion über die islamische Einheit', *Orient*, 35:4 (1994), pp. 565–6.

21 See for instance: *Payam-e rahbar-e enqelab va vali-ye amr muslimin-e jahan Hezrat-e Ayatollah Khamenei beh hojjaj beyt Allah al-haram* (Tehran, Vezarat-e Ettela'at va Ershad-e Islami, 1993), p. 10.

22 Ibid., pp. 20–2.

23 D.E. Long, The Impact, p. 109.

IRAN'S RIVALRY WITH SAUDI ARABIA BETWEEN THE GULF WARS

24 *BBC Summary of World Broadcasts*, ME/2188, 29 December 1994.
25 C. Bina, 'Towards a New World Order: US Hegemony, Client-States and Islamic Alternative' in H. Mutalib (ed.), *Islam, Muslims and the Modern State* (New York: St. Martin's Press, 1994), p. 19.
26 E. Sciolino, *The Outlaw State* (New York: St. Martin's Press, 1991), p. 124.
27 *BBC Summary of World Broadcasts*, ME/2020, 13 June 1994.
28 Speeches held at the occasion of the beginning of the Hajj season of 1991. In: *Saudi Arabia*, Washington DC, August 1991, p. 2.
29 F.M. Dickman, 'A Post-Gulf-War Policy for the Middle East', *Asian Affairs: An American Review*, 17:1 (1991), p. 7.
30 *Saudi Arabian Bulletin*, London, April 1991, p. 6.
31 *Ettela'at*, Tehran, 6 June 1990.
32 Ibid., 9 June 1990.
33 Ibid., 28 June 1990.
34 S. Chubin, *Iran's National Security Policy: Capabilities, Intentions & Impact* (Washington DC, Carnegie Endowment for International Peace, 1994), p. 12.
35 M.J. Larijani, 'Iran's Foreign Policy: Principles and Objectives', *The Iranian Journal of International Affairs*, 7:4 (1996), p. 756.
36 K.L. Afrasiabi, *After Khomeini*, p. 203.
37 M.H. Fayazi, 'Barrasiye awamil mowatir dar dastiyabi wa 'adam dastiyabi beh ahdaf enqelab-e Islami (An analysis of the factors which improve the possibilities for the success of the objectives of the Islamic revolution)', *Faslnameh huquq wa 'ulum-e siyasi*, 2:2 (1992), pp. 47–60.
38 J. Calabrese, *Revolutionary Horizons*, p. 145.
39 *Resalat*, Tehran, 4 February 1993.
40 D.C. Barr, *Rafsanjani's Iran* (3 vols., London, Gulf Centre for Strategic Studies, 1991), vol. 2, p. 32.
41 J. Calabrese, *Revolutionary Horizons*, pp. 62–4.
42 Ibid., p. 161.
43 Ibid., p. 64.
44 *BBC Summary of World Broadcasts*, ME/1702, 31 May 1993.
45 Ibid., ME/1706, 4 June 1993.
46 Ibid., ME/1999, 16 May 1994.
47 *Al-Nadwah*, Riyadh, 17 April 1994.
48 *BBC Summary of World Broadcasts*, ME/1948, 17 March 1994.
49 Ibid., ME/1974, 18 April 1994.
50 Ibid., ME/1996, 13 May 1994.
51 Ibid., ME/2010, 31 May 1994.
52 Ibid., ME/2020, 13 June 1994.
53 Ibid., ME/2016, 7 June 1994.
54 Ibid., ME/2459, 13 November 1995.
55 H. Amirahmadi, 'Iranian–Saudi Arabian Relations since the Revolution' in H. Amirahmadi and N. Entessar (eds.), *Iran and the Arab World* (Basingstoke: Macmillan, 1993), p. 140.
56 S.R. Ali, *Oil, Turmoil, and Islam in the Middle East* (New York, Westport and London: Praeger, 1986), pp. 64–5.
57 A.D. Johanny, *The Myth of OPEC Cartel: The Role of Saudi Arabia* (New York, Brisbane and Toronto: Centron, 1980), p. 49.

58 H. Amirahmadi, Iranian–Saudi, pp. 141–3.
59 S. Holly, *Conflict in the Gulf: Economic and Maritime Implications of the Iran–Iraq War* (Colchester, 1988, p. 37.
60 S.T. Hunter, *Iran and the World: Continuity in a Revolutionary Decade* (Bloomington: Indiana University Press, 1990), p. 119.
61 H. Amirahmadi, Iranian–Saudi Arabian Relations, p. 141.
62 S.T. Hunter, *Iran*, p. 119.
63 Ibid.
64 *BBC Summary of World Broadcasts*, ME/8205, 12 March 1986.
65 *Pasdar-e Islam*, Tehran, 27 July 1986.
66 S.T. Hunter, *Iran*, p. 120.
67 H. Amirahmadi, Iranian–Saudi Arabian Relations, p. 144.
68 A. Hashim, *The Crisis of the Iranian State* (Oxford: Oxford University Press, 1995), p. 13.
69 *BBC Summary of World Broadcasts*, ME/0851, 24 August 1990.
70 K.L. Afrasiabi, *After Khomeini: New Directions in Iran's Foreign Policy* (Boulder: Westview Press, 1994), p. 39.
71 *BBC Summary of World Broadcasts*, ME/1093, 8 June 1991.
72 S. Chubin, *Iran's National Security Policy: Capabilities, Intentions & Impact* (Washington DC: Carnegie Endowment for International Peace, 1994), p. 10.
73 Ibid.
74 R. Wright, 'Dateline Tehran: A Revolution Implodes', *Foreign Policy*, 25:3 (1996), p. 16.
75 K. Ehsani, '"Tilt but don't spill". Iran's Development and Reconstruction Dilemma', *Middle East Report*, 24, November–December (1994), p. 19.
76 J. Calabrese, *Revolutionary Horizons: Regional Foreign Policy in Post-Revolutionary Iran* (New York: St. Martin's Press, 1994), p. 62.
77 A. Hashim, *The Crisis*, p. 13.
78 *Echo of Islam*, 41:68 (1993), p. 21.
79 *Resalat*, Tehran, 19 January 1994.
80 A. Hashim, *The Crisis*, pp. 14–15.
81 P. Clawson, 'Alternative Foreign Policy Views among the Iranian Policy Elite' in P. Clawson (ed.), *Iran's Strategic Intentions and Capabilities* (Washington DC: Institute for National Strategic Studies, 1994), p. 36.
82 *Echo of Islam*, 42:75 (1994), pp. 20–1.
83 R. Wright, Dateline, p. 17.
84 E.A. Nakhleh, 'Regime Stability and Change in the Gulf: The Case of Saudi Arabia' in R.B. Satloff (ed.), *The Politics of Change in the Middle East* (Boulder: Westview Press, 1993), pp. 128–9.
85 J. Calabrese, *Revolutionary Horizons*, p. 62.
86 F. al-Mazidi, *The Future of the Gulf: The Legacy of the War and the Challenge of the 1990s* (London and New York: Tauris, 1993), p. 2.
87 F.A. Khavari, *Oil and Islam: The Ticking Bomb* (Malibu, 1990), p. 107.
88 J. Calabrese, *Revolutionary Horizons*, p. 62.
89 H. Amirahmadi, 'Iran and the Persian Gulf: Strategic Issues and Outlook' in H. Zanganeh (ed.), *Islam, Iran & World Stability* (New York: St. Martin's Press, 1994), p. 128.

Conclusion

Stemming from a self-imposed obligation to spread the ideals of Islamic revolution, the leadership of Iran became the driving force behind an escalation of the traditional rivalry with Saudi Arabia which then developed into a contest for influence in the Islamic world. Most of the time, Riyadh merely reacted to Iranian political, ideological and economic offensives, but within these limits Saudi counter-measures also took the initiative from time to time, particularly in economics.

However, summarizing, or rather forecasting the future relationship between the two contenders, means primarily looking at the prospects of the Islamic Republic of Iran and, generally speaking, these prospects remain uncertain. Even after the election of the relatively moderate Hojjat al-Islam Mohammad Khatami as President in May 1997, the power struggle within Iran has continued, with all the uncertainties that brings for Iran's neighbours. The system of government created in Iran after the revolution of 1978–9 encourages the activity of several, parallel, power centres, constraining even the President from holding a balance between the different sources of power and influence. The pragmatic Rafsanjani began his presidency in 1989 with the same enthusiasm to modernize the country as Khatami has, only to become entangled in the tightly-knit network of mutual dependencies which controls the political elite of Iran, and as a result lost his vigour and his political fortune.

However, the future of Iran's political system will not depend entirely on domestic affairs. Not only the outcome of the Arab–Israeli conflict but also regional developments along Iran's northern and eastern borders as well as in the Persian Gulf will decisively influence Iranian behaviour. In addition, much will depend on the development of Islamic radical movements elsewhere. Although Iranian diplomats such as Kamal Kharrazi, previously Ambassador to the United Nations and now the new Foreign Minister, constantly insist that Islamic revivalism is limited to the respective countries and situations, and perhaps inspired, but not controlled by Iran,[1] the success of those movements might yet encourage the Iranian leadership to repeat its demand for hegemony in the Islamic world more frequently.

Iran's future behaviour will definitely be influenced by the actions of the West, particularly of the United States.[2] Western capitals might be right to criticize, for instance, Iran's human rights record, or to fight terrorism organized by Iranian radicals, but they will only strengthen the position of those same elements within the Iranian establishment in the long run if they continue an undifferentiating policy of containment.

As a result of the heterogeneity of its system of power with the continued influence of parallel power centres, Iran will, as in the past, seek both to normalize ties with its most important neighbours and to cultivate and maintain its options for subversion and agitation. Mohammad Khatami will probably try to start his presidency with a foreign policy that keeps Iran from deepening the rift with its neighbours and increasing its isolation. If this is so, he might also be interested in maintaining workable relations with Saudi Arabia.[3]

The Islamic Republic's economic potential and programmes in particular can help to further close the gap between itself and its Arab neighbours. In that case, and if its policy of moderation and cooperation will not simply continue but be improved under Khatami, the gap between Iran and the Gulf Arab states, particularly Saudi Arabia, could, gradually, be closed. Only months before Khatami's election, there were discussions in the Iranian media as to why the government so foolishly rejected every Saudi offer to improve the bilateral relationship.

According to *Ettela'at*, the Saudi Interior Minister, Nayif, had pledged to aim for a decisive improvement in the ties between the two countries. The newspaper speculated on the complete silence of Tehran regarding this offer, suspecting that there might be secret negotiations in hand, with Syria as an intermediary. In an attempt to defend the government's secrecy, *Ettela'at* pointed to the delicate situation within the Saud family, with its influential pro-American faction.[4]

Not only the antipathy of that faction, but the differences in religion, and culture related to nationalist aspirations, will remain a constantly divisive factor between the two states and will prevent a total closure of the gap. These differences, however, need not unavoidably interfere with diplomatic relations or prevent the two nations from expanding their cooperation and cultivating neighbourly relations in the political, economic, and cultural spheres.[5] But such an optimistic scenario also depends on the economic, and thus political, stability of Saudi Arabia. In the probable case of rapid economic deterioration in the Kingdom, accompanied by an increasing political awareness among its population, Iran might feel encouraged to capitalize on local discontent.[6]

As mentioned before, Iran is also faced with a variety of grave economic challenges. But whereas a reluctant and defensive Saudi Arabia might welcome foreign interference in a growing economic crisis, Iran could well reject it in the same situation. History has proved many times that governments tend to divert attention from severe domestic crises by initiating conflicts with foreign power. If forced to capitulate in the face of mounting economic problems, the Iranian leadership could be tempted to look for a way out of its dilemma by seeking confrontation with its neighbours. 'Iran's ambitions are vast, notwithstanding its serious internal problems.'[7] Nevertheless, these ambitions remain limited.

First of all, there is Iran's predominantly Persian nature. Despite the government's attempt to minimize Iranian nationalist sentiment, the Persianness of Iran has limited its ability to reach the Arab masses. On the contrary, ethnicity and nationalism have proved much stronger than an appeal to Islamic universalism.

Secondly, there is Iran's Shiism. This has also hindered Iran's ability to appeal to a wider group of Muslims beyond the Shia minorities in other states. Indeed, in some cases, Iranian activity has drawn Sunni fundamentalist opposition groups closer to their own governments. Iran has been forced to focus most of its attention and its efforts on those regions where the existence of Shia majorities or sizeable minorities creates an environment somewhat more receptive to its vision and influence. Thirdly, there are the financial and economic limitations on the state.[8]

The question remains, to what degree the Islamic revolution in Iran has influenced the Islamic world and to what degree it will continue to do so. Will there be repetitions elsewhere of what happened in Iran? In the first flush of victory, after the overthrow of the Shah, Iran was giddy with its own success and utterly confident that it could reshape the world in its own image. It rejected traditional diplomacy, traditional economics and even traditional theology in the pursuit of its own version of universal Islamic rule. The Islamic state supported terrorist groups, seized American hostages, rejected any dependency on either the Warsaw pact or Nato, turned up its nose at the United Nations and acquired a reputation as a maverick state in the Western hemisphere. This is the common experience of revolutionary societies. The toppling of the old regime, which had seemed impossibly powerful and well entrenched, is typically regarded as a miraculous event. It is no wonder that the revolutionaries expect their doctrines and ideas to spread everywhere. Most genuine revolutions carry the seed of new ideas that transcend mere locality or the parochial circumstances that first permitted it to take root and flourish.[9]

But returning to the original question, it is relatively easy to give a quick reply: the Iranian revolution has not spread and fundamentalism has been contained. However at best this is only half the answer, because it assumes too small a timescale. Revolutions and revolutionaries, whether Islamic or other, are impatient, and expect other peoples to imitate them immediately: in this regard they become disappointed just as quickly as their opponents become relieved.[10] When a transformation of the international system proves to be excessively difficult, dangerous or expensive, the proselytizing impulse usually wanes and becomes progressively subordinate to more traditional objectives. Thus, the activities of the revolutionary regime gradually come to resemble those of a conventional nation-state.[11]

In that sense, the Iran of 1998 was less of a threat to its neighbours, including Saudi Arabia, and to the international system, than the Iran of 1979–80. Much of the early ideological boisterousness of the revolution was eroded by the relentless pressure of economic realities and the unforgiving demands of governing a large country labouring under severe problems. At present, Iran is much less likely to embark on an adventurous and costly intervention in the affairs of its neighbours than it was in the early 1980s.[12] At least, this is the situation at present. Nobody can exclude radical and adventurous developments in Iranian foreign policy should the country be faced with a substantial economic crisis.

And there is the timescale to remember. The international impact of a revolution is not evaluated in a few years but over several decades. It was Chou En-lai who suggested that the effects of the French Revolution still continue to be felt two centuries after the event.[13] Thus, the impact of the Iranian revolution can only be thoroughly analysed by future generations. Even now the impact has been substantial, though no other state – except perhaps Sudan – has become an Islamic Republic quite in the manner of Iran. It is only necessary to look at the rise in Islamist political consciousness in a range of countries, or to recognize the increased popularity of Islamic dress, Islamic literature, and mosque attendance, for instance, to see how far Iran has influenced the behaviour of Muslims generally: 'Whether or not Islamist forces of the Iranian variety do come to power in the following years or decades, the impact of the revolution and of the broader trend with which it is associated is undeniable.'[14]

Closing the circle and returning to the Gulf region, it must be stated that Iran identifies itself at present primarily as a regional power, in an area including the Gulf and Central Asia. Thus, its regional foreign policy – especially after the East–West conflict – should not be seen exclusively as a source of trouble. With the ongoing involvement of the Islamic Republic in so wide a geographical area, Iran shares in the problems of all the region's countries: to be increasingly motivated and impelled politically by regional factors while remaining dependent economically and militarily on relations with the highly-industrialized countries.[15]

The Gulf, like most other regions, gained more independence after the Cold War. To be isolated from the West is a severe burden, given Western economic, financial, military and technological dominance. But escaping this dominance no longer inevitably leads to a country's complete isolation. Thus, the first step for Iran means securing the best possible standing within the region – confronting or cooperating with Saudi Arabia – before its official re-entry in global politics becomes a possibility.

NOTES

1 *US–Iran Review*, 1:2 (1993), p. 1.
2 F. al-Mazidi, *The Future of the Gulf: The Legacy of the War and the Challenge of the 1990s* (London and New York: IB Tauris, 1993), p. 3.
3 S. Chubin, *Iran's National Security Policy: Capabilities, Intentions & Impact* (Washington DC: Carnegie Endowment for International Peace, 1994), p. 11.
4 *Ettela'at*, Tehran, 8 January 1995.
5 H. Amirahmadi, 'Iranian–Saudi Arabian Relations since the Revolution' in H. Amirahmadi and N. Entessar (eds.), *Iran and the Arab World* (Basingstoke, Macmillan, 1993), pp. 157–8.
6 S. Chubin, *Iran's National Security Policy*, p. 11.
7 J.A. Kechichian, 'An Expansionist Iran is the Bitter Legacy of its Revolution', *Washington Report on Middle East Affairs*, 13:2 (1994), p. 18.

8 S.T. Hunter, *Iran and the World: Continuity in a Revolutionary Decade* (Bloomington: Indiana University Press, 1990), p. 180.

9 G. Sick, 'Iran: The Adolescent Revolution', *Journal of International Affairs*, 49:1 (1995), p. 147.

10 F. Halliday, 'The Politics of Islamic Fundamentalism: Iran, Tunisia and the Challenge to the Secular State' in A.S. Ahmed and H. Donnan (eds.), *Islam, Globalization and Postmodernity* (London and New York: Routledge, 1994), p. 96.

11 G. Sick, Iran, p. 147.

12 Ibid., p. 165.

13 Ibid., p. 147.

14 F. Halliday, The Politics, p. 97.

15 J. Reissner, 'Der Iran auf dem Weg zu einer Regionalmacht', *Aus Politik und Zeitgeschichte*, Bonn, 26 April 1996, p. 39.

Major Events in Iranian–Saudi Arabian Relations

1970

15 March

Introduction of a process of frequent consultations and conclusions between Iran and Saudi Arabia within the Organization of the Islamic Conference (OIC).

9–14 April

The Saudi Foreign Minister, Umar al-Saqqaf, negotiates in Iran about cooperation in defence of the Gulf region.

14–17 July

Iranian Foreign Minister Zahedi meets King Faisal in Riyadh for Gulf talks.

1971

16 May

King Faisal meets the Shah in Tehran.

12–17 October

Iran celebrates 2,500 years of monarchy at Persepolis.

30 November

Iranian forces occupy the islands of Tumb and Abu Musa.

1972

2 January

Signing of the first trade agreement between Iran and Saudi Arabia.

10 December

The Saudi Foreign Minister, Umar al-Saqqaf, declares after meeting the Shah in Tehran that both countries cooperate to 'defeat conspiracy in the Gulf'.

1973
23 December
The posted price of Persian Gulf crude oil reaches a record high of US$ 11.65 per barrel.

1974
20 June
The Saudi Foreign Minister, Umar al-Saqqaf, declares after talks with Shah Mohammad Reza Pahlavi that both countries harmonize all important matters of foreign policy.

1975
25 March
Assassination of King Faisal.

28–29 April
Shah Mohammad Reza Pahlavi travels to Riyadh for negotiations with the new Saudi king, Khalid.

1–3 July
Saudi Crown Prince Fahd visits Iran for talks on regional issues.

14 December
138 pilgrims die when a fire sweeps through a pilgrim camp at Mina.

1976
7 January
Protests against the use of the name Arabian Gulf rather than Persian Gulf. Iran recalls its ambassadors from seven Gulf states after they had formed the Arabian Gulf News Agency.

6–8 April
The Iranian Prime Minister, Amir Abbas Hoveida, talks with the Saudi Crown Prince Fahd in Riyadh.

24 May
King Khalid arrives in Tehran for negotiations with Shah Mohammad Reza Pahlavi.

1978
10 January
Shah Mohammad Reza Pahlavi meets with King Khalid and Crown

Prince Fahd in Riyadh on the Middle East situation and bilateral relations. They decide to harmonize their policies concerning the Horn of Africa to avoid destabilization there.

1979
16 January
Shah Mohammad Reza Pahlavi flees Iran.

1 February
Ayatollah Ruhollah Khomeini returns to Iran.

11 February
Victory of the Islamic revolution in Iran.

1 April
Proclamation of the Islamic Republic of Iran after a referendum.

Spring
The so-called Organization of the Islamic Revolution for the Liberation of the Arabian Peninsula (Munazamat al-Thawra al-Islamiya li tahrir al-Jazira al-Arabiya), popularly called 'the Islamic Revolution' (Al-Thawra al-Islamiya) begins to operate in the Saudi province of al-Hasa.

8 September
The Iranian Minister of National Guidance, Nasir Minachi, meets with Crown Prince Fahd in Ta'if.

24 September
A bomb explodes at the Saudi ambassador's residence in Tehran.

15 October
Ayatollah Khomeini is designated Supreme Leader.

November
Anti-Saudi riots in al-Hasa.

4 November
Occupation of the American embassy in Tehran.

20 November
Occupation of the Great Mosque in Mecca.

24 November
Ayatollah Khomeini declares that the US 'and its corrupt colony, Israel' are behind the occupation of the Great Mosque in Mecca.

1980

February
Fresh riots erupt at Qatif and other settlements in al-Hasa.

27 July
Shah Mohammad Reza Pahlavi dies in Egypt.

22 September
Iraqi troops invade Iran starting the eight-year First Gulf War.

10 December
The Saudi Defence Minister, Sultan ibn Abd al-Aziz, declares that a joint defence strategy has to be formulated between the Gulf monarchies, and Saudi Arabia begins to support Iraq financially.

1981

25–28 January
At the Islamic Foreign Ministers' meeting in Ta'if, Kuwait, Saudi Arabia, Bahrain, Qatar, the UAE and Oman all agree in principle to form a Cooperation Council.

May
New unrest in al-Hasa.

26 May
Foundation of the Gulf Cooperation Council (GCC) in Abu Dhabi.

20 September
Iranian pilgrims organize demonstrations during the hajj, attacking the United States and Israel, demanding the unity of all Muslims and a merciless revenge against the enemies of such unity.

23 September
Saudi authorities deport a total of 80 Iranian pilgrims from Medina, accusing them of having violated orders prohibiting political activity during the pilgrimage by distributing pictures of Khomeini and propaganda brochures.

24 September
About twenty Iranian pilgrims are injured in a clash with security forces in Mecca.

4 October
Saudi Arabia makes its Red Sea ports available for Iraqi civilian and military

imports. Influenced by Saudi Arabia, OPEC sets an export quota for Iran of 1.2 million barrels per day without the possibility of raising prices. This quota is intended to seriously reduce Iran's ability to earn foreign funds.

12 November
The Saudi Grand Mufti, Ibn Baz, issues a fatwa, rejecting the widespread tradition of celebrating the prophet's birthday, calling it a 'blasphemous and heretic custom'.

16 December
Saudi Arabia and Bahrain announce the arrest of 65 Arabs for planning to overthrow the governments in both countries. Although members of an Iraqi-based religious group al-Da'wa, the men confess to being trained in Iran.

1982

13 June
Death of King Khalid; he is immediately succeeded by his younger brother Fahd, hitherto Crown Prince.

10 September
Ayatollah Khomeini appoints Hojjat al-Islam Mohammad Musavi Kho'eniha, the head of the group of students who seized the US Embassy in Tehran three years earlier, as his personal representative and coordinator of the Iranian pilgrims.

9 October
Saudi authorities deport Iran's hajj supervisor Musavi Kho'eniha and 140 of his followers after several days of clashes between Iranian pilgrims and Saudi security forces.

4 November
Ayatollah Khomeini criticizes Gulf states supporting Iraq, calling them 'tools in the hands of America'.

11 November
The GCC secretly offers to pay Iran between US$ 25 and 30 billion in reparations in exchange for an Iranian guarantee to end the war with Iraq.

16 December
During an OPEC ministerial meeting, the Saudi delegation defeats an Iranian initiative to set production quotas determined by each member

country's need for foreign exchange, the size of its population, the capacity of its oil reserves and the quantity of its petroleum exports in the preceding decade; in addition it successfully organized opposition to the election of an Iranian Secretary General of OPEC when it was Iran's turn to fill that position.

1983
February
Saudi Arabia and Kuwait begin selling 330,000 barrels of oil per day to Iraqi customers, keeping the Iraqi war economy alive.

3 March
At a summit of non-aligned countries in New Delhi Iran rejects any mediation by the GCC to resolve the war with Iraq.

13 July
The Saudi Arabian government limits the number of Iranian pilgrims to 100,000.

24 July
Ayatollah Ali Montazeri harshly criticizes Saudi Arabia's treatment of Iranian pilgrims.

13 September
Clashes between Iranian pilgrims and Saudi security forces in Mecca.

19 September
Ayatollah Khomeini issues a warning to all countries supporting Iraq that Iran will block their access to the oil resources of the Gulf region.

1984
16 January
During the OIC summit in Casablanca secret negotiations are conducted between Iran and Saudi Arabia; the Saudi side tries to discover under what conditions Iran would accept a ceasefire.

26 April
Beginning of the tanker war which directly affected the economies of the Gulf Arab countries, most of all Saudi Arabia.

16 May
The Saudi tanker *Yanbu Pride* is hit by Iranian warplanes near Ras Tanura oil terminal.

24 May

The Iranian Speaker of Parliament, Hashemi Rafsanjani, promises to improve relations with Saudi Arabia if Riyadh would only 'condemn the Iraqi regime and put itself outside of the scene of action'.

5 June

Saudi aircraft ambush Iranian fighters as they prepare to attack two tankers leaving Saudi Arabian ports; later that day a second stand-off between eleven Iranian F-4s and eleven Saudi F-15s takes place, but the Iranians decide to withdraw. Soon after that incident the Saudi government establish the so called Fahd Line, an 'air defence interception zone' that extended beyond the commercial traffic control zone and the 12 mile zone of territorial waters.

12 June

King Fahd agrees to Iran's request to send 150,000 pilgrims to Mecca in September.

11 September

King Fahd invites the Speaker of the Iranian parliament, Hojjat al-Islam Rafsanjani, to take part in the hajj; Khomeini, however, blocks the invitation.

6 November

Iranian troops storm a Saudi jet hijacked to Tehran by two Yemenis; both hijackers get political asylum.

1985

18 May

The Saudi Foreign Minister, Saud al-Faisal, visits Iran on the first Saudi official visit after the revolution and offers to help end the war with Iraq; there are hints that he proposed that Riyadh shoulder the bulk of the Iranian reparation demands.

18 May

An Iranian-based 'Islamic Jihad Group' claims responsibility for the explosion of two bombs in Riyadh's Sulaimaniyah district, killing one person and injuring three others.

Spring

In a series of broadcasts on Radio Tehran, Ayatollah Montazeri, at the time considered Khomeini's successor, poses the rhetorical question whether the Saudi Wahhabis are true Muslims.

28 July
Saudi authorities turn back two flight-loads of Iranian pilgrims, despite a previous announcement to receive the same number of Iranian pilgrims as in 1984.

31 July
The Iranian Ministry of Islamic Guidance rejects a call by the World Muslim League that pilgrims to Mecca should refrain from political demonstrations.

11 August
Thousands of Iranian pilgrims demonstrate in Medina, calling for the overthrow of the US and Israel.

17 October
Official creation of the Rapid Deployment Force (RDF) of the GCC agreed upon in November 1982.

28 November
During their summit the GCC rulers decide to develop a more even-handed policy towards Iran and Iraq.

4–6 December
The Iranian Foreign Minister, Ali Akbar Velayati, makes a return visit to Riyadh primarily discussing the hajj problem; Iran removes Kho'eniha from the position of hajj coordinator as a friendly gesture towards the Saudis.

1986

Spring
The Saudi commitment to help Iraq causes a crash in the oil markets: Whereas in January oil prices were set at about US$ 28 per barrel, in April the market was only ready to accept US$ 10 per barrel; by the summer, the price had fallen to US$ 8 per barrel.

6 April
Iranian helicopters attack the Saudi tanker *Petrostar 16* setting it ablaze and wounding six sailors.

7 August
At an OPEC meeting, Iran and Saudi Arabia agree to stabilize oil prices at about US$ 18 per barrel.

10 August

Saudi authorities arrest 113 Iranian pilgrims upon their arrival in Jedda.

15 October

The Saudi government approves another US$ 4 billion 'loan' to Iraq and allows Iraqi planes to land and refuel in Saudi Arabia after sorties against Iranian oil facilities in the southern Gulf.

1987

24 March

The United States authorizes its navy to escort Kuwaiti tankers in the Gulf; by October, 40 American ships carrying 20,000 troops are patrolling Gulf waters.

19 May

The United States agrees to take eleven Kuwaiti tankers under its colours.

20 July

The UN Security Council adopts a ten point resolution (No. 598) urging an immediate ceasefire between Iraq and Iran.

31 July

About 402 people, 275 Iranians, 85 Saudis and 42 pilgrims of other nationalities die in Mecca after bloody clashes between pilgrims and the Saudi Arabian police; 649 people are injured.

2 August

The Speaker of the Iranian Majlis, Hashemi Rafsanjani, proclaims a 'day of hatred' (against Saudi Arabia) and promises vengeance.

18 August

During a meeting of the Arab League Foreign Ministers, Saudi Arabian Foreign Minister, Saud al-Faisal, calls the Iranian leadership 'terrorists', and urges sanctions against Iran.

18 October

The first American–Iranian clash occurs when a tanker under American colours is hit by an Iranian missile; in retaliation four destroyers of the US Navy damage two Iranian drilling platforms.

11 November

After active Saudi Arabian lobbying, the extraordinary meeting of the

Arab League in Amman condemns Iran for prolonging the war with Iraq, and urges it to accept Resolution No. 598.

26 December
A GCC meeting in Riyadh urges the UN Security Council to inflict an arms embargo against Iran enforcing Tehran to accept Resolution No. 598.

1988

16 January
Iran's government proposes a round of negotiations with the GCC to end all hostilities.

21–25 March
The OIC agrees a formula, whereby each Islamic nation would be permitted to send 1,000 pilgrims per million citizens, giving Iran a quota of 45,000; in protest, Ayatollah Khomeini decides not to let a single Iranian pilgrim leave for Saudi Arabia in 1988.

26 April
Saudi Arabia breaks off diplomatic relations with Iran.

28 April
King Fahd warns Iran that his country would not hesitate to use its newly acquired Chinese missiles to defend itself.

18 July
Iran officially accepts UNSC Resolution No. 598.

20 August
A ceasefire signed by Iran and Iraq ends the eight-year war between them.

4 September
The GCC Foreign Ministers' meeting expresses a desire for 'friendship between all the peoples of the Islamic nation'.

30 September
Four Saudi nationals are executed in al-Dammam for 'conspiring with Iran against the safety of their homeland'.

19 October
King Fahd instructs newspapers and radio stations to refrain from 'antagonizing Iran'.

19 November
Iran's Deputy Foreign Minister, Ali Besharati, explains that Iran is willing to talk with Saudi Arabia about overcoming the 'great misunderstanding'.

1989
1 April
The reconstructed refinery of Abadan begins to operate again.

Spring
With the approach of the hajj, Saudi Arabia insists on only admitting 45,000 Iranian pilgrims, whereas Iran makes clear that it is not prepared to send less than 150,000.

3 June
Death of Ayatollah Khomeini; Saudi Arabia neglects to send condolences, illustrating the deterioration in bilateral relations.

4 June
Election of Ayatollah Ali Khamenei as Khomeini's successor.

10 July
Two bomb explosions during the hajj kill a pilgrim from Pakistan and injure another 16.

28 July
Hashemi Rafsanjani is elected President of Iran by 94.5 per cent; a revised constitution is approved by referendum.

21 September
Saudi Arabia executes 16 Shia of Iranian and Arab origin found guilty of carrying out the bomb explosions on 10 July.

1990
15 April
The Saudi Ministry of Hajj and Awqaf declares that Saudi Arabia 'has renewed its categorical rejection of the method of one-upmanship, bargaining and pressures being practised by the Tehran government in attempts which reaffirm the latter's place outside Islamic unanimity'.

2 July
About 1,426 pilgrims die in the Mina (Mu'aysam) tunnel at Mecca when a crowd with an estimated total of more than 50,000 fill the tunnel, exceeding its capacity severalfold.

2 August
Iraqi troops invade Kuwait.

13 October
Ayatollah Khamenei calls for a jihad against Western troops at the Arabian Peninsula, despite official Iranian neutrality.

15 October
When the OIC meets in Rabat, Tehran is quick to argue that the organization should seek to resolve the Kuwait crisis itself, avoiding Western meddling and providing an Islamic solution to a dispute between two Islamic states.

22 December
The eleventh summit meeting of the GCC in Qatar acknowledges the necessity of new collaborative arrangements for security in the region between all the neighbouring countries including Iran.

1991

28 February
The Iraqi occupation of Kuwait ends after the victory of the allied forces.

26 March
Restoration of diplomatic relations between Iran and Saudi Arabia.

1 April
After the reopening of the Iranian embassy in Riyadh, the Saudi government allows 110,000 Iranians to participate in the hajj, plus 5,000 relatives of those pilgrims who had died in the hajj of 1987.

26 April
The Iranian Foreign Minister meets King Fahd in Jedda.

5–6 June
The Saudi Foreign Minister, Saud al-Faisal, returns the visit accompanied by the Oil Minister, Hisham Nazir; Iran and Saudi Arabia upgrade their diplomatic relations by appointing ambassadors.

18 June
Iranian pilgrims demonstrate in Mecca.

21 October
Iran's Deputy Foreign Minister for International Affairs, Manuchehr

Motaki, visits Riyadh to discuss the expansion of bilateral ties with his Saudi counterpart, Abd al-Rahman Mansuri.

17 December

The rapprochement between Iran and Saudi Arabia culminates in President Rafsanjani's visit to Riyadh; Rafsanjani tangles with the Saudis on the subject of the Madrid Peace talks.

1992

17 April

Iranian marines occupy those parts of the island of Abu Musa which had been left under Sharjah's control since 1971; all Arab residents – regardless of their citizenship – are deported.

28 September

Negotiations between Iran and the United Arab Emirates (UAE) on the occupation of the Gulf islands collapse.

22 October

Iran completes the instalment of eight missile launching pads on Abu Musa.

1993

20–25 May

The Iranian Foreign Minister, Ali Velayati, tours GCC member states.

25 May

The Saudi government prohibits the distribution of political leaflets, books, or tapes during the hajj.

27 May

The Iranian Deputy Foreign Minister, Ali Mohammad Besharati, protests against a Saudi ban on a 'deliverance from pagans' rally in front of the office of the Iranian hajj mission in Mecca, scheduled for that day.

13 June

Hashemi Rafsanjani is re-elected President of Iran with 63 per cent of the vote.

23 December

Iran rejects a GCC demand for negotiations with the UAE and reiterates its claims to sovereignty over the islands of Tumb and Abu Musa.

1994

12 January
When the Saudi Minister of Higher Education, Abd al-Aziz Khuwaithir, visits President Rafsanjani, the official 'Voice of the Islamic Republic of Iran' radio concludes: 'Though Iran–Saudi Arabian ties have undergone several ups and downs during recent years, the trend of events of recent months speaks for the fact that the two countries' officials have opened a new phase of bilateral ties with the intention of reinforcing unity among Islamic countries'.

18 May
Saudi security forces surround Iran's hajj headquarters in Mecca to prevent a deliverance from pagans rally.

1 September
At a speech to the UN Disarmament Conference the Iranian Foreign Minister proposes a Gulf defensive security pact.

27 October
Iran's Supreme Leader, Ayatollah Khamenei, warns the Arab states not to seek peace with Israel.

21 December
The Saudi Grand Mufti, Ibn Baz, delivers a fatwa legitimizing the conclusion of a peace treaty with Israel.

1995

7 May
Saudi security forces are deployed in and around Mecca in response to threats from Iranian pilgrims to stage anti-US rallies.

14 June
Shia residents from 'Awamiyah in eastern Saudi Arabia violently protest against the confiscation of their land.

11 November
Mohammad Husain Reza'i, Deputy Culture Minister and head of Iran's Hajj and Awqaf Organization, arrives in Jedda to discuss with his counterpart, the Saudi Minister of Pilgrimage Affairs, Mahmud Safar, a series of problems that had built up over previous years; commenting on the talks, Reza'i concludes that both sides have made great efforts to

improve the level of services in order to enable Iranian pilgrims to perform the hajj 'in peace and comfort'.

13 November

A car bomb explodes outside the offices of the Saudi National Guard in Riyadh killing seven foreign nationals (including five US citizens) and injuring a further 60 people.

Bibliography

Books

Abbas, H., *Fahd: al-watan wa'l-hadath* (Riyadh: Maktabat al-Wataniya, 1984).

Abir, M., *Saudi Arabia: Government, Society and the Gulf Crisis* (London and New York: Routledge, 1993).

Abu-Dawood, A.R.S., *International Boundaries of Saudi Arabia* (New Delhi: Galaxy Publications, 1990).

Afrasiabi, K.L., *After Khomeini: New Directions in Iran's Foreign Policy* (Boulder: Westview Press, 1994).

Agha, H. J. and A.S. Khalidi, *Syria and Iran: Rivalry and Cooperation* (London: Pinter, 1995).

Ahmed, A.S. and H. Donnan (eds.), *Islam, Globalization and Postmodernity* (London and New York: Routledge, 1994).

Ahrari, M.E., *The new Great Game in Muslim Central Asia* (Washington DC: Institute for National Strategic Studies, 1996).

Alaolmolki, N., *Struggle for Dominance in the Persian Gulf: Past, Present and Future Prospects* (New York: P. Lang, 1991).

Albers, H.H., *Saudi Arabia: Technocrats in a Traditional Society* (New York: P. Lang, 1989).

Ali, S.R., *Oil, Turmoil, and Islam in the Middle East* (New York, Westport and London: Praeger, 1986).

Amirahmadi, H. and M. Parvin (eds.), *Post-Revolutionary Iran* (Boulder: Westview Press, 1988).

Amirahmadi, H. and N. Entessar (eds.), *Reconstruction and Regional Diplomacy in the Persian Gulf* (London and New York: Routledge, 1992).

—*Iran and the Arab World* (Basingstoke: Macmillan, 1993).

Amirsadeghi, H. (ed.), *The Security of the Persian Gulf* (London: Croom Helm, 1981).

Anderson, S.K., *The Impact of Islamic Fundamentalist Politics within the Islamic Republic of Iran on Iranian State Sponsorship of Transnational Terrorism* (Ann Arbor: University Press, 1994).

Arab Report and Record (London,1974).

Ayoob, M. (ed.), *Regional Security in the Third World* (Boulder: Westview Press, 1986).

Azhary, M.S. (ed.), *The Iran–Iraq War* (London: Croom Helm, 1984).

Badeeb, S.M., *Saudi–Iranian Relations 1932–1982* (London: Echoes, 1993).

Bakhash, S., *The Politics of Oil and Revolution in Iran* (Washington DC: Brookings Institution, 1982).

Barr, D.C., *Rafsanjani's Iran* (2 vols., London: Gulf Centre for Strategic Studies, 1990–91).

Brinton, C., *The Anatomy of Revolution* (New York: Vintage Books, 1965).

Calabrese, J., *Revolutionary Horizons: Regional Foreign Policy in Post-Khomeini Iran* (New York: St. Martin's Press, 1994).

Chubin, S. (ed.), *Security in the Persian Gulf* (Aldershot: Gower, 1981), vol. 2.

—*Iran's National Security Policy: Capabilities, Intentions & Impact* (Washington DC: Carnegie Endowment for International Peace, 1994).

Chubin, S. and C. Tripp, *Iran–Saudi Arabia: Relations and Regional Order* (Oxford: Oxford University Press, 1996).

Chubin, S. and S. Zabih, *The Foreign Relations of Iran: A Developing State in a Zone of Great-Power Conflict* (Berkeley and Los Angeles: University of California Press, 1974).

Churchill, R. and J. Welch (eds.), *New Directions in the Law of Sea* (London: Croom Helm, 1973), vol. 3.

Clawson, P., *Iran's Challenge to the West: How, When and Why?* (Washington DC: The Washington Institute for Near East Policy, 1993).

—*Iran's Strategic Intentions and Capabilities* (Washington DC: Institute for National Strategic Studies, 1994).

Conant, M.A., and R. King, *Consequences of 'Peace': The Iranian Situation and Outlook* (Washington DC: Conant and Associates, 1988).

Constitution of the Islamic Republic of Iran (Tehran: Ministry of Information and Islamic Guidance, 1979).

Cordesman, A.H., *Western Strategic Interests in the Southern Gulf: Strategic Relations and Military Realities* (Boulder: Westview Press, 1987).

Cunningham, A.H., *Hostages of Fortune. The Future of the Western Interests in the Arabian Gulf* (London: Brassey's Defence, 1988).

Davies, C. (ed.), *After the War. Iran, Iraq and the Arab Gulf* (Chichester: Carden Publications, 1990).

Dawisha, A. (ed.), *Islam in Foreign Policy* (Cambridge: Cambridge University Press, 1983).

Dessouki, A.E.H. (ed.), *The Iraq–Iran War: Issues on Conflict and Prospects for Settlement* (Princeton: Princeton University Press, 1981).

Doran, C.F. and S.W. Buck (eds.), *The Gulf, Energy, & Global Security: Political & Economic Issues* (Boulder: Westview Press, 1991).

Ehteshami, A. and G. Nonneman (eds.), *War and Peace in the Gulf. Domestic Politics and Regional Relations into the 1990s* (Reading: Ithaca Press, 1991).

Ehteshami, A. and M. Varasteh (eds.), *Iran and the International Community* (London and New York: Routledge, 1991).

Ehteshami, A. (ed.), *From the Gulf to Central Asia: Players in the New Great Game* (Exeter: University of Exeter Press, 1994).

—*After Khomeini: The Iranian Second Republic* (London and New York: Routledge, 1995).

Esposito, J.L. (ed.), *The Iranian Revolution: Its Global Impact* (Miami: Florida International University Press, 1990).

Faris, A., *Al-Jumhuriya al-Islamiya* (Beirut: Sharikat al-matbu'at li't-tauzi' wa'l-nashr, 1987).

Farsoun, S.K. and M. Mashayeki (eds.), *Iran. Political Culture in the Islamic Republic* (London and New York: Routledge, 1992).

Foran, J. (ed.), *A Century of Revolution: Social Movements in Iran* (London: UCL Press, 1994).

Fuller, G.E. and I.O. Lesser, *A Sense of Siege: The Geopolitics of Islam and the West* (Boulder: Westview Press, 1995).

Fürtig, H., *Der irakisch–iranische Krieg 1980–1988: Ursachen, Verlauf, Folgen* (Berlin: Akademieverlag, 1992).

Gaury, G. de, *Faisal* (Paris: Edition l'Harmattan, 1963).

Grummon, S.R., *The Iran–Iraq War: Islam Embattled* (New York, Westport and London: Praeger, 1982).

Gurdon, H., *Iran – the continuing struggle for power* (Outwell: MENAS, 1984).

Haghayeghi, M., *Islam and Politics in Central Asia* (New York: St. Martin's Press, 1995).

Hameed, M.A., *Saudi Arabia, the West and the Security of the Gulf* (London: Croom Helm, 1986).

Harik, I. and D.J. Sullivan (eds.), *Privatization and Liberalization in the Middle East* (Bloomington: Indiana University Press, 1992).

Hasan, H. al-, *Al-Shi'a fi al-mamlaka al-arabiya al-Saudiya* (1938-1991), n.l.: (Mu'assasat al-baqi' li-ahya al-turath, 1993), vol. 2.

Hashim, A., *The Crisis of the Iranian State* (Oxford: Oxford University Press, 1995).

Heller, M.A., *The Iran–Iraq War: Implications for Third Parties* (Cambridge MA: Harvard University's Center for International Affairs, Paper no. 23, 1984).

Heller, M.A and N. Safran, *The New Middle Class and Regime Stability in Saudi Arabia* (Cambridge MA: Harvard University Press, 1985).

Holly, S., *Conflict in the Gulf: Economic and Maritime Implications of the Iran–Iraq War* (Colchester: Lloyds of London Press, 1988).

Hunter, S.T., *Iran and the World: Continuity in a Revolutionary Decade* (Bloomington: Indiana University Press, 1990).

—*Iran after Khomeini* (New York, Westport and London: Praeger, 1992).

Huyeth, S.S., *Political Adaptation in Saudi Arabia* (Boulder: Westview Press, 1985).

Al-Imam al-khumaini: al-fikr wa al-tawra (Beirut: Dar al-hadatha, 1990).

Iranian Links With Radical Organizations (London: Gulf Centre for Strategic Studies, 1994).

Issa, A., *Legitimität und Stabilität im Nahen Osten: Saudi Arabien* (Siegen: Verlag der Universität Siegen, 1988).

Jeandet, N., *Un Golfe pour trois rêves: le triangle de crise Iran, Irak, Arabie* (Paris: Edition l'Harmattan, 1993).

Johanny, A.D., *The Myth of OPEC Cartel: The Role of Saudi Arabia* (New York, Brisbane and Toronto: Centron, 1980).

Joyner, C.C. (ed.), *The Persian Gulf War: Lessons for Strategy, Law and Diplomacy* (New York, Watford and London: Greenwood Press, 1990).

Khadduri, M., *The Gulf War: The Origins and Implications of the Iraq–Iran Conflict* (Oxford: Oxford University Press, 1988).

Khamenei, A., *Chahar sal ba mardom* (Tehran: Sazeman-e Tablighat-e Islami, 1985).

Khavari, F.A., *Oil and Islam: The Ticking Bomb* (Malibu, 1990).

Keddie, N.R., *Iran and the Muslim World: Resistance and Revolution* (Houndmills: Macmillan, 1995).

Keddie, N.R. and E. Hooglund (eds.), *The Iranian Revolution and the Islamic Republic* (Syracuse NY: Syracuse University Press, 1982).

Kemp, G., *Forever Enemies? American Policy & the Islamic Republic of Iran* (Washington DC: Carnegie Endowment for International Peace, 1994).

Krämer, G. and P. Pawelka (eds.), *Die Golfregion in der Weltpolitik* (Stuttgart, Berlin and Cologne: Kohlhammer, 1991).

Krommer, A., *Entwicklungsstrategien der arabischen Golfstaaten* (New York: P. Lang, 1986).

Litvak, R., *Security in the Persian Gulf: Sources of Inter-State Conflict* (Aldershot: Gower, 1981).

Martin, L.G., *The Unstable Gulf. Threats from Within* (Aldershot: Gower, 1984).

Mashat, A.M. al-, *National Security in the Third World* (Boulder: Westview Press, 1985).

Massie, M., *Rafsanjani's Iran* (London: Gulf Centre for Strategic Studies, 1991), vol. 3.

Mazidi, F. al-, *The Future of the Gulf: The Legacy of the War and the Challenge of the 1990s* (London and New York: IB Tauris, 1993).

Memon, A.N., *The Islamic Nation: Status & Future of Muslims in the New World Order* (Beltsville MD: Writers' Inc. International, 1995).

Menashri, D. (ed.), *The Iranian Revolution and the Muslim World* (Boulder: Westview Press, 1990).

Migdal, J.S., *Strong Societies and Weak States: State–Society Relations and State Capabilities in the Third World* (Princeton: Princeton University Press, 1988).

Moaddel, M., *Class, Politics, and Ideology in the Iranian Revolution* (New York, 1993).

Mohabadian, B.A., *Fundamentalistische Bewegungen im Islam am Beispiel des Iran* (Marburg: Verlag der Universität Marburg, 1992).

Mohaddessin, M., *Islamic Fundamentalism: The New Global Threat* (Washington DC: Seven Locks Press, 1993).

Muhajeri, M., *Islamic Revolution. Future Path of the Nations* (Tehran: Jihad Sazandegih, 1983).

Mutalib, H. (ed.), *Islam, Muslims and the Modern State* (New York: St. Martin's Press, 1994).

Naqeeb, K.H. al-, *Society and State in the Gulf and the Arab Peninsula* (London: Routledge, 1990).

Netton, I.R. (ed.), *Arabia and the Gulf: From Traditional Society to Modern States* (London: Croom Helm, 1986).

Niblock, T. (ed.), *State, Society and Economy in Saudi Arabia* (London: Croom Helm, 1982).

Nowaiser, S.K. al-, *Saudi Arabia's and the United States' Strategic Partnership in an era of turmoil: A study of Saudi–American political, economic, and military relationship 1973–1983 – Dependence or Independence?* (Ann Arbor: University Press, 1988).

Noyes, J., *New Perspectives on the Persian Gulf. Hearings before the Subcommittee on the Near East and South Asia of the Committee on Foreign Affairs* (Washington DC: House of Representatives, 1973).

Odell, P.R., *Oil and World Power* (Harmondsworth: Penguin, 1986).

Oxenstierna, R. F., *Saudi Arabia in the Post-Gulf War: The Search for Stability and Security in the Gulf* (London: Gulf Centre for Strategic Studies, 1992).

Palmer, M., *Dilemmas of Political Development: An Introduction to the Politics of the Developing Areas* (Itasca ILL: F.E. Peacock Publishers, 1989).

Peyam-e rahbar-e mo'azem-e enqelab va valiye amr moslimin-e jahan hedrat Ayatollah Khamenei . . . (Message of Ayatollah Khamenei to Iranian Pilgrims, 18 May, 1993). Tehran.

Piscatori, J. (ed.), *Islamic Fundamentalism and the Gulf Crisis* (Chicago: American Academy of Arts and Sciences, 1991).

Pohly, M., *Political Extremist Organizations: The Islamic Network* (Washington DC: Jewish Institute for National Security Affairs, 1996).

Pridham, B.R. (ed.), *The Arab Gulf and the Arab World* (London: Croom Helm, 1988).

Rahnema, A. and F. Namani, *The Secular Miracle: Religion, Politics & Economic Policy in Iran* (London: Zed Books, 1990).

Rahnemudhaye Imam (Tehran: Vezarat-e Ershad-e Islami, 1979).

Rajab, S., *Hukma al-'umma wa'l-azma al-Halij* (Cairo: Dar al-fikr, 1992).

Rajaee, F., *Islamic Values and World View. Khomeyni on Man, the State and International Politics* (Lanham, New York and London: University Press of America, 1983).

Ramazani, R.K., *Revolutionary Iran: Challenge and Response in the Middle East* (Baltimore: Johns Hopkins University Press, 1986).

Rashid, A., *The Resurgence of Central Asia. Islam or Nationalism?* (London: Zed Books, 1994).

Rashid, N. I. and E. I. Shaheen, *Saudi Arabia and the Gulf War* (Joplin MO: International Institute of Technology, 1992).

Rezun, M. (ed.), *Iran at the Crossroads: Global Relations in a Turbulent Decade* (Boulder: Westview Press, 1990).

Robins, P., *The Future of the Gulf: Politics and Oil in the 1990s* (Aldershot: Gower, 1989).

Safran, N., *Saudi Arabia: The Ceaseless Quest for Security* (Cambridge MA: Harvard University Press, 1988).

Sariolghalam, M., *Arab–Iranian Rapprochement: The Regional and International Impediments.* Paper presented to the conference on Arab–Iranian Relations: Contemporary Trends and Prospects for the Future, Qatar, 11–14 September 1995.

Satloff, R.B. (ed.), *The Politics of Change in the Middle East* (Boulder: Westview Press, 1993).

Scholz, F. (ed.), *Die Golfstaaten: Wohlfahrtsmacht im Krisenherd* (Braunschweig: Westermann-Verlag, 1985).

Schönherr, S. and A.J. Halbach, *Der Golf nach dem Krieg: Wirtschaft, Politik, Rüstung* (Munich, Cologne and London: Weltforum-Verlag, 1991).

Schutz, B.M. and R.O. Slater (eds.), *Revolution and Political Change in the Third World* (Boulder: Westview Press, 1990).

Sciolino, E., *The Outlaw State* (New York: St. Martin's Press, 1991).

Selected Messages and Speeches of Imam Khomeini (Tehran: Ministry of Information and Islamic Guidance, 1980).

Sharabi, S. and F. Farhi, *Security Considerations and Iranian Foreign Policy.* Paper presented to the International Seminar on Security, Trade and Advanced Technologies in South Asia: Opportunities and Strategies for Regional Cooperation held in Karachi 1995.

Sindelar, H.R. and J.E. Peterson (eds.), *Crosscurrents in the Gulf* (London: Routledge, 1988).

Soun, T., *Between Qur'an and Crown: The Challenge of Political Legitimacy in the Arab World* (Boulder: Westview Press, 1990).

Stookey, R.W. (ed.), *The Arabian Peninsula* (Stanford: Stanford University Press, 1984).

Tahtinen, D.R., *National Security Challenge to Saudi Arabia* (Washington DC: Institute for National Strategic Studies, 1979).

Tow, W.T., *Subregional Security Cooperation in the Third World* (Boulder: Westview Press, 1990).

World Military Expenditures and Arms Transfers 1967–1978 (Washington DC: US Arms Control and Disarmament Agency, 1978).

Yearbook Iran 1989/90 (Bonn: Edition Ausland, 1990).

Zanganeh, H. (ed.), *Islam, Iran & World Stability* (New York: St. Martin's Press, 1994).

Zunker, A. (ed.), *Weltordnung oder Chaos? Beiträge zur internationalen Politik* (Baden Baden: Nomos-Verlag, 1993).

Periodicals

Adineh, Tehran
Ahbar al alam al-Islami, Tehran
American–Arab Affairs, Washington DC
Al-Arab, London
Arab–Asian Affairs, London
Arab Gulf Journal, London
Arab Month, London
Arab News, Jedda
Arab Studies Quarterly, Chattanoga
Arabia, The Islamic World Review, London
Asian Affairs: An American Review, Washington DC
asien, afrika, lateinamerika (aala), Berlin
Aus Politik und Zeitgeschichte, Bonn
Aussenpolitik, Bonn
Bamdad, Tehran
BBC Summary of World Broadcasts, Reading
Al-Bilad, Riyadh
Blätter für Deutsche und Internationale Politik, Bonn
British Journal of Middle Eastern Studies, Durham
Conflict, New York, Philadelphia, Washington DC
Conflict Studies, London
Current, Washington DC
Current History, Philadelphia
Daily Telegraph, London

Defense & Diplomacy, McLean
La Dernière Heure, Brussels
Echo of Iran (EOI), Tehran & London
Echo of Islam, Tehran
The Economist, London
The Economist Intelligence Unit (EIU), Country Report Iran, London
The Economist Intelligence Unit (EIU), Country Report Saudi Arabia, London
Enqelab-e Islami, Tehran
Ettela'at, Tehran
Ettela'at-e siyasi-eqtesadi, Tehran
Europaarchiv, Bonn
Far Eastern Economic Review, London
Faslnameh huquq va 'ulum-e siyasi, Tehran
Financial Times, London
Foreign Affairs, Washington DC
Foreign Broadcast Information Service–Near East Series (FBIS–NES), Washington DC
Foreign Policy, Washington DC
Foreign Report, London
Frankfurter Allgemeine Zeitung, Frankfurt (Main)
The Guardian, London
Gulf News, Cairo
Gulf States Newsletter, Crawley
Al-Hawadith, Beirut
Al-Hayat, London
International Herald Tribune, Paris
International Journal, Toronto
International Journal of Middle East Studies, Cambridge MA
Iranfocus, London
The Iranian Journal of International Affairs, Tehran
Jane's Intelligence Review, Coulsdon
Al-Jazira, Riyadh
Jerusalem Post, Jerusalem
Journal of Arab Affairs, Fresno
Journal of International Affairs, New York
Journal of South Asian and Middle Eastern Studies, Villanova
Jumhuriye Islami, Tehran

Kabul Times, Kabul
Kayhan, Tehran
Kayhan Hava'i, Tehran
Kayhan International, Tehran
Majallat-e Siyasat-e Khariji, Tehran
Mediterranean Quarterly, Durham NC
The Message of Revolution, Tehran
Mideast Mirror, London
The Middle East, London
Middle East Economic Digest (MEED), London
Middle East Insight, Washington DC
Middle East International, London
Middle East Journal, Washington DC
Middle East Newsletters – Gulf States, London
Middle East Policy, Washington DC
Middle East Report, Washington DC
Middle East Review, New York
Middle Eastern Studies, London
Monday Morning, Beirut
Al-Nadwah, Riyadh
New York Times, New York
Orient, Hamburg
Pasdar-e Islam, Tehran
Peyam-e Shahedan, Mashhad
Resalat, Tehran
Al-Riyadh, Riyadh
Al-Safir, Beirut
Salam, Tehran
Saudi Arabia, Washington DC
Saudi Arabian Bulletin, London
Sentinel. The Gulf States, Coulsdon
Al-Shahid, Tehran
Al-Sharq al-awsat, London
Soroush, Tehran
Süddeutsche Zeitung, Munich
Survival, Oxford
Tehran Journal, Tehran
Tehran Times, Tehran

Third World Quarterly, London
Ukaz, Riyadh
Umm al-Qura, Riyadh
US–Iran Review, Washington DC
Voice of World's Islamic Movements, Manchester
Washington Post, Washington DC
Washington Report on Middle East Affairs, Washington DC
World Politics. A Journal of International Relations, Baltimore

Index